PROJECT: READINESS

a guide to family
EMERGENCY PREPAREDNESS

PROJECT: READINESS

a guide to family
EMERGENCY PREPAREDNESS

LOUISE E. NELSON

Horizon Publishers

INTERNATIONAL STANDARD BOOK NUMBER
0-88290-036-6

LIBRARY OF CONGRESS CATALOG CARD NUMBER
80-82503

Second Printing, June 1980

Printed and Distributed in the
United States of America
by

**Horizon
Publishers &
Distributors**

P.O. Box 490
50 South 500 West
Bountiful, Utah 84010

TABLE OF CONTENTS

PART ONE
EMERGENCY AND DISASTER PLANNING

PART TWO
FOOD STORAGE

PART THREE
STORING NON-FOOD ITEMS

PART FOUR
OTHER ASPECTS OF EMERGENCY PREPARATION

LIST OF CHARTS AND TABLES

LIST OF ILLUSTRATIONS

PREFACE

The modern American family finds itself in a unique situation. Modern technology, prosperity and communications have created a sense of security. Most of today's young families have never known truly hard times. Life's necessities are almost taken for granted in most of this country today.

Yet, the social unrest of the 1960's and the economic problems of the 1970's have called up fading memories of the depression of the 1930's and the deprivations of World War II. They have jarred many people into realizing that this sense of security is false.

We live in an interdependent society. This makes us very vulnerable in hard times and in times of emergency or disaster.

Many families are seeking to become more independent. They are striving to become prepared so as not to be vulnerable to the effects of hard times, emergency or disaster. And most families are seeking ways to counter the effects of inflation.

Project: Readiness contains vital information needed to assist families in formulating a plan of action for emergency preparedness.

It is my hope that it will be a source of motivation, guidance, and strength for many who recognize the importance of personal and family readiness.

ACKNOWLEDGEMENTS

My greatest thanks go to my husband Ted for his encouragement and his patience during the writing of the book and also for many of the illustrations. And to my family for their love and understanding all the while the book was being written.

I would also like to thank all those who helped along the way with suggestions, recipes and most of all, encouragement.

One's editor and publisher cannot be overlooked. Many thanks go to Duane S. Crowther and Horizon Publishers for the suggestions for expansion and revision to improve the quality of the finished work.

A special word of thanks goes to my sister-in-law, Marjorie Nelson, for all the hours she spent at the typewriter helping to get the manuscript ready.

Louise E. Nelson

INTRODUCTION

Why PROJECT: READINESS?

There are several types of difficult situations that a family may face:

(1) **Short-term emergencies** lasting two weeks or less such as unexpected bills; temporary loss of income due to illness, strike or lay-off; temporary interruption in utility service, transportation or communication facilities due to bad weather.

(2) **Long-term emergencies** lasting more than two weeks such as prolonged unemployment; overwhelming medical expenses; extended strikes affecting transportation or other essential services or causing loss of income; or loss of the breadwinner.

(3) **Natural or man-caused disasters** such as fire, flood, tornado or war.

Since such situations do not always happen to the "other guy," family emergency preparation can save the affected families from much of the inconvenience and grief that result from these emergencies.

In every disaster or emergency many families discover that, even though local civil defense and public welfare officials have tried to prepare for the situation, their plans do not always provide the kind of help the families need at the very time that they need it. The plight of a family, however desperate, may still not qualify it for public assistance. Also, there is the ever-present possibility that supplies and shelter provided by these agencies may be inadequate to meet the needs of all those requiring it.

Our families deserve the best kind of preparation we can provide for them.

PART ONE

EMERGENCY AND DISASTER PLANNING

CHAPTER I

EFFECTIVE PLANNING FOR DISASTER READINESS

The Phases of Disaster

Disasters go through phases that have been labeled as: (1) *threat*, (2) *warning*, (3) *impact*, (4) *inventory*, (5) *rescue*, (6) *remedy*, and (7) *recovery*.[1] All disasters pass through most of these phases. The phases, however, may not be easily distinguished from one another since there is a great degree of overlapping, especially of phases 4, 5, and 6.

Threat Phase

People tend to disregard the threat of disaster. There is a natural human protective mechanism that gives man a sense of invincibility. This "it can't happen to me" feeling makes people delay their preparation, sometimes until it is too late to reach safety.

An awareness of this natural reaction may make it easier to accept the necessity of emergency and disaster planning.

The threat phase is that period of time during which a particular disaster is likely to occur. It may last from a few minutes to an entire year.

During the threat phase, these actions should take place:

(1) *Assess your situation:* Identify the types of disasters that are apt to occur in your area and the conditions that signal a warning of those disasters. Be alert to the changes in social and political climate in your community and throughout the nation.

(2) *Formulate a plan:* Make a plan of action for each type of emergency or disaster that you might reasonably expect to occur to your family.

(3) *Implement the plan.*

---

[1] Solomon Garb and Evelyn Eng, *Disaster Handbook* (New York: Springer Publishing Co., Inc, 1964), pp. 12-13.

(4) *Practice carrying out your plan.*

When the warning comes, your family will be prepared to act without delay.

The Assessment

Find out from long-time area residents and local officials what hazards your family faces because of your geographical location. Become aware of the disaster history of your own neighborhood or your immediate locality.

Determine what times of year natural disasters such as flood or storm are most likely to occur.

Your family will need to know what services are available to give needed assistance and how help is summoned. They will also need to find out how long it takes for assistance to arrive.

Nearby physical hazards such as dams, rivers, sea coasts, power lines, large trees, gasoline or chemical storage tanks will need to be considered when making your plan.

Determine which kinds of disasters will require you to evacuate your home and which ones will allow your family to shelter at home.

The Plan

1. *Shelter:* To be prepared for unexpected circumstances during an actual emergency, make plans for sheltering at home and for evacuation.

For sheltering at home, office, etc., decide:

——What the effects of the impact will be.
——What must be done to the surroundings to reduce hazards and increase protection during and after impact.
——Where the occupants of the structure should station themselves for greatest protection during and after impact.
——If members of the family who are away from the prepared shelter when warning is given should attempt to reach that shelter or seek shelter elsewhere.

To make an evacuation plan you will need to decide:

——If there will be warning.
——How much time there will be between warning and impact.
——When you must prepare to leave.
——When you must leave to ensure safety.
——Where you will go.
——How you will get there.
——What you will need to take.

——How long you can expect to be away from home.

——Since all members of the family will most likely not be at home together, how you will become advised of each other's safety and how you will get together.

——Where you will go for safety if you are at home, school, work or elsewhere.

——What one person least likely to be affected by the disaster will always know where you are after evacuation.[2]

——How you will contact persons who might be concerned about your safety and need to know that you have safely evacuated.

——What responsibilities each member of the family will have during evacuation.

——Where the best medical attention will be available.

In the event that you are caught away from shelter when warning is given:

——What your best course of action is.

——What you should do during impact.

——How soon it will be safe to seek shelter or go home after impact.

Implementation: A Planning Checklist

(Not all items apply to all situations)

Shelter: (home, office or elsewhere)

1. Modifications to make
    _____ Barricade doors and windows
    _____ Board up or cover windows
    _____ Draw drapes
    _____ Place sandbags or barricades to protect foundations, basement from flooding
    _____ Turn off water and gas and electric appliances as if preparing to leave home for the day. Do not turn off at the meters.

2. Other preparations
    _____ Tools and supplies ready for constructing, protecting or evacuating the shelter
    _____ Ventilation system planned and ready to initiate.
    _____ Firefighting tools and supplies on hand

---

[2] A family member in another town or another neighborhood, your pastor or the local Red Cross unit are good clearing houses for this purpose.

Food and Water:

_____ Flight kit prepared (see page 23 for a list of contents)
_____ Adequate food and water stored in the shelter for the expected sheltering period.
_____ Water purification supplies on hand
_____ Tools and supplies for digging a well or otherwise obtaining water available

Cooking, Heating and Lighting:

_____ Provisions made in shelter and checked periodically for proper functioning
_____ Portable stove, fuel, matches in flight kit
_____ Flashlight, batteries and extra bulbs available and functioning

Clothing:

_____ Adequate clothing or sewing supplies stored for the sheltering period
_____ 1 extra set of clothing for each family plus extra diapers for baby stored with the flight kit

Bedding:

_____ Sleeping bags or blankets packed in flight kit

Sanitation:

_____ Sewage and garbage disposal containers and supplies stored and ready to use
_____ Water for washing and cleaning provided for
_____ Supplies for cleaning and disinfecting stored

Medical Attention:

_____ Emergency first aid supplies in flight kit and all supplies kept fresh
_____ Well-stocked first aid kit in shelter and all supplies fresh
_____ First aid and home nursing training given to all members of the family according to their age and condition
_____ Supplies for care of the invalid or chronically ill available in the shelter
_____ Family members trained to recognize signs of disease
_____ Family members aware of how to obtain medical aid if needed

_____ Isolation techniques for home care of persons with infectious disease learned

Transportation:

_____ Auto gas tank full
_____ Auto functioning well
_____ If no auto is available, alternate means of transportation arranged

Protection:

_____ Plans made for the protection of life and property from looters and marauders
_____ Radiation detection equipment available

Special Needs of Baby:

_____ Special food, clothing, bedding available in shelter
_____ Supplies available for emergency childbirth
_____ Family members trained to handle emergency childbirth

Communication:

_____ Portable radio and extra batteries stored in flight kit and functioning properly
_____ Radio or TV tuned to local civil defense radio station or local TV channel for latest bulletins
_____ Citizen band radio and batteries available if shelter is in remote area

The Flight Kit

The flight kit is a portable kit to be taken in the car in the event evacuation of the home is necessary. It should be as compact and as portable as possible. Keep it assembled and ready to load into the car. The following are suggested contents.

Food and Water: (per person)

The food in the kit should require no cooking. Dehydrated fruits and vegetables can be eaten raw, if necessary.

3 (No. 3) cans DH vegetables
3 (No. 3) cans DH fruits
1 lb. fruit-flavored breakfast drink
3 lb. non-instant milk powder
14 servings canned meats (in small cans to be used at one meal)

14 servings canned prepared dinners and soups (in small cans to
     be used at one meal)
1 lb. sugar
1 small jar peanut butter
2 jars cheese spread
1 can nuts
1 package hard candy
2 lbs. crackers
2 lbs. ready-to-eat cereals
3 lbs. canned bread, steamed puddings and cakes
1/2 gallon water (for cooking purposes for one day) in unbreak-
     able containers

Since some of these items are difficult to obtain in sealed containers, rotate them often to keep them fresh. Additional water will
have to be obtained after evacuation. Water is too heavy to include in
quantity in the flight kit.

Other Items:

Matches
Can opener
Set of nested kettles for cooking, mixing, and washing
Paper plates and cups
Knife, fork and spoon for each person
Portable stove and fuel
First Aid Kit including:
     Antiseptic solution (3 to 6 oz.)
     Adhesive bandages, asst. sizes, large tin
     Sodium Bicarbonate tablets (for shock, nausea, burns)
     Soda and salt
     12 gauze pads, 3" x 3"
     3 roller bandages, 1" wide and 10 yds. long
     Triangular bandage and 2 safety pins
     4 large bandages
     Eye drops
     Water purification tablets
     Aspirin
     Safety pins
     Scissors
     Splints, tongue blades
     Special medicines for you or your family
     Needle

Flashlights and extra bulbs and batteries
Battery operated radio and extra batteries
Change of clothing for each person
Blankets or sleeping bags
Heavy gloves
Shovel, hand ax
Hand tools (pliers, wrench, screwdriver, crowbar, hammer)
Recreation kit (see page 255)
Clock, calendar, maps, important personal papers
Sanitation Supplies
Covered pail
Paper bags and bundle of newspapers
Toilet tissues and facial tissues
Paper towels and other towels
Soap and detergent
Tooth brushes
Disposable diapers
Sanitary pads
Nail brush, clippers, and tweezers
Insecticide and deodorizer
Household bleach

Practice

"Practice makes perfect." There was never a more appropriate slogan for emergency preparation. Disaster drills held regularly with your family members will make their responses to disaster warnings more automatic and will better enable the family to safely endure the impact.

Small children can be taught the essentials of disaster drills in the form of a game and will eagerly particiapte. They should be taught that these drills are serious, however, to help them to respond appropriately in a real emergency.

Warning Phase

The nature of the emergency situation will determine the length of the threat and warning periods. The time for you to make actual modifications to your shelter or for you to seek other refuge will depend on the duration of the threat and warning phases.

Usually, preparations for sheltering or evacuation are made during the threat phase and actual seeking of shelter is done during the warning period.

Delays in preparation and evacuation can catch your family unprepared and vulnerable during the impact.

Once warning is received, follow through with your sheltering plans. Act calmly and do not panic. Your practiced plan will see you safely through the crisis.

Keep tuned to the local civil defense radio station for accurate, up-to-the-minute details of the disaster situation.

Impact

What to do during the impact of any particular disaster will be discussed in detail in the next chapter.

The most important thing to remember for safety during the impact of a disaster is to seek the best shelter available, well in advance of impact, and to stay there as long as you are safe there and until the impact period is clearly over.

If you have been able to reach a designated public shelter or are safely sheltered in a home or other structure that has the necessary emergency supplies, remain where you are throughout the impact phase and until you are certain it is safe to leave.

If your shelter is makeshift or you are caught out in the open and are in immediate danger, seek better shelter as soon as it is reasonably safe to do so without submitting yourself or your family to greater danger.

Usually it is best to wait until the impact phase is clearly over before moving, if you were unable to do so before impact. The danger of injury is greatest during impact and diminishes with time after impact.

Be prepared for secondary impacts such as aftershocks or tidal waves that often follow earthquake.

In all disasters where there is property damage, expect some degree of disruption of:

Transportation
Emergency services (fire, police, etc.)
Utilities
Housing
Communications
Employment and business
Sanitary sewer facilities
Clean water supplies
Distribution of food and goods
Manufacture and production of food and goods
Water supplies for fire fighting

Epidemic often accompanies disaster because of disrupted sanitation services and lack of medical assistance.

Looting may occur in areas of heavy damage if police protection is inadequate.

Inventory

After impact it is necessary to assess your situation to determine dangers, first, to your family, then to your property.

First, assess immediate dangers that you face, such as building collapse, fire, explosion, or death from severe injuries.

If there are severe injuries as well as any of the other immediate dangers, risk further injury from moving the victim rather than jeopardize the lives of victim and rescuers from the other hazards.

One quick tour of the shelter, starting at the top and working down, will enable you to make this immediate assessment.

Never turn on electricity or use matches until you are sure there is no danger of explosion from gas leaks. Use a flashlight instead.

If gross examination reveals no further dangers to persons, take care of emergency first aid and then proceed to assess dangers to property.

During the assessment tour be alert inside for:

> Broken wiring, water pipes, and gas pipes
> Smoke
> Gas odors
> Collapsing structures, chimneys, power poles or trees
> Severe personal injuries
> Strong chemical odors
> Sewage odors

Outside be alert for:

> Blowing, floating or falling debris
> Broken utility lines or mains
> Damaged sewage systems
> Damaged exterior trim that might fall or collapse
> Damaged and leaking chemical or gasoline storage or transportation tanks
> Radioactivity from atomic blast

After assessing these immediate hazards and needs, assess the general situation of your family to determine how prepared you are for the total sheltering period and what will need to be done to improve the situation, if possible.

Following the impact of any disaster, avoid unnecessary travel in the impact area. Allow emergency vehicles to have the right-of-way, and cooperate with the authorities.

The Rescue Phase

The principle activity of the rescue phase is removal of persons from danger.

Extreme caution must be exercised during this phase to avoid further injury to the rescuers or the victims.

The buddy system should be used so that one rescuer can summon further assistance if the other rescuer should get into trouble or more help is needed to free victims.

The Remedy Phase

During this phase of a disaster, first aid is given, the injured are evacuated and definitive medical care is sought. Also during this phase, protection of property from secondary impact can be accomplished.

Shut off the gas at the meter if house piping has been broken or a strong odor of gas is present. Shut off main water valve if piping is leaking.

The utility company should be notified of any broken utility pipes or lines so that steps can be taken to prevent injury or property loss.

Stay clear of downed power lines and do not stand on wet ground or in water near a downed line.

The Recovery Phase

The recovery phase is the period of rebuilding and return to normalcy.

If previous examination of the home and premises revealed no immediate danger, now is the time to make a more thorough examination to be sure that no hidden damage exists.

To test for hidden damage to gas lines, turn off all gas appliances and watch the meter. If the meter dials turn, gas is leaking somewhere.

Very small gas leaks can be plugged by rubbing a bar of soap over the rupture until the hole is plugged. Permanent remedy should be sought as soon as possible.

The same temporary remedy will work on water pipes. Larger water leaks can be temporarily plugged by tying rags tightly around the rupture and covering them with a waterproof covering.

To check out the electrical circuits, try each outlet and switch. If fuses blow or outlets fail to work, there is damage somewhere that must be evaluated by a competent electrician. Do not attempt to use electricity if any part of the circuitry fails to function properly.

Many factors combine to create a housing problem after a major disaster involving structural damage. The lack of building materials and skilled labor can delay rebuilding for extended periods.

Restoration of normal utility and sewage and water service, manufacturing and distribution of food and goods, and repair of roads and airposts can be expected to take many months following a major disaster.

Most major disasters will affect not only those in the impact zone, but others for many miles around. Because the segments of our society are so interdependent and because our mobility has resulted in a city-suburb pattern in metropolitan areas, essential services may be unavailable to many living well outside the impact area.

Shortages of crops and manufactured goods that often result from disaster have far-reaching effects.

CHAPTER II

PLANNING FOR COMMONLY OCCURRING DISASTERS

Snow Storm or Blizzard

Those who live in colder areas of the country soon learn how unpredictable winter storms can be. During the winter months, residents of these areas should always be prepared for the worst.

Weather conditions often change very rapidly in snow and ice country. Whenever snow is predicted, preparations should be made. The warning phase may last from a few minutes to many hours.

Snow and rising wind presage blizzard conditions.

High winds and blowing snow during the impact phase of a blizzard can reduce visibility to zero. Anyone caught out during this period risks becoming lost with resultant frostbite injury or death from freezing. The danger of falls is also very great when the visibility is poor.

Falling snow-laden limbs are often a hazard.

The snowfall period is often followed by a period of extreme cold.

Travel during the impact of a severe storm is extremely hazardous due to high wind, decreased visibility and icy roads, and it should be avoided.

Winter travelers through areas prone to heavy snowfall or blizzard should take along emergency supplies of food and water and sleeping bags or blankets in case they should become stranded away from shelter.

Anyone stranded or snowbound should remember that foot travel through deep snow is extremely exhausting. The exhausted individual risks injury or death from falling, frostbite or freezing.

Blowing snow or ground blizzards that follow the storm can be as hazardous as the storm itself.

Persons snowbound at home are usually best off if they stay put. Even a cold house offers a better shelter than the out-of-doors. There is enough clothing and bedding in the house to keep the occupants reasonably warm. Water can be melted from snow and food supplies can be rationed, if necessary.

Persons stranded on a major highway can expect help to arrive as soon as the snowplows can reach them. The rescue crews must be able to locate the stranded vehicle. Drifted snow may have to be cleared from part of the car to make it visible.

Warmth, food and water will be the major concerns of persons who are snowbound. Care of injuries can often wait until these needs are taken care of.

Use the buddy system when seeking help. Never send out a person alone if two are able to go.

Two good sources of outdoor survival information are included in the recommended library on page 256. They are *Outdoor Survival Skills* and *How to Stay Alive in the Woods*. For information on the recognition and treatment of frostbite see the *American Red Cross First Aid Textbook*.

After debris is removed and snow is either removed or melted, normal living usually resumes immediately. Restoration of interrupted utility services usually is completed within a day or two after the storm passes. Heavy damage to utilities may prolong this recovery period.

Protecting Stored Food and Supplies:

The primary cause of loss in stored food due to snow storm would be freezing. Insulating the storage area or covering the food with blankets would help to keep it from freezing in case the heat to the storage area goes out.

Earthquake

The threat of earthquake always exists in areas along earth faults. Past earthquake activity in an area is an indication that future earthquakes are likely to occur there.

Although small foreshocks often accompany major earthquakes, there is no way to distinguish these foreshocks from minor earthquakes. They are therefore not reliable warning signals. Many major earthquakes occur without forewarning of any sort.

To minimize property damage and injury from earthquake:

1. Be sure that your home conforms to building codes and is earthquake resistant in construction.
2. Bolt down gas appliances.
3. Place large and heavy objects on low shelves.
4. Brace or securely anchor all high or top-heavy objects.
5. Securely anchor overhead fixtures.
6. Do not stack glass or china objects.
7. Remove all structural hazards that might fall or collapse during an earthquake.
8. Bolt pictures and mirrors to the wall.

9.   Draw drapes across windows.

Most damage and injuries from earthquake occur because of falling debris and breaking glass. The trembling and quaking of the earth causes building collapse and causes trees and power poles to topple. Seldom does the earth open and swallow people or buildings.

Fires caused by broken gas and electric lines are a major hazard and can constitute a secondary impact.

Aftershocks, some of major intensity, usually follow a major earthquake. Tidal waves and flooding can be expected after earthquakes that occur at sea or near sea coasts.

Damage to sanitary sewerage facilities and pure water supplies necessitates strict sanitation after an earthquake to prevent the spread of disease. (See pages 240 to 243.)

Good places to seek shelter during the impact of an earthquake are a bathroom, an inside hallway, a doorway, or under a desk, bed or sturdy table. Persons caught outside during a quake should stand in a doorway or get completely clear of buildings, trees and power poles or lines and other hazards.

Rebuilding and removal of debris can begin almost immediately after an earthquake but this period is often prolonged due to inadequate supplies and building materials and lack of skilled labor.

Protecting Food and Stored Supplies:

1.   Store everything in unbreakable containers, if possible.
2.   Do not stack boxes, cans, etc. Put only one layer of objects on a shelf or on the floor.
3.   Build sturdy storage shelves. Enclose the fronts of the shelves with doors that are securely closed with latches or hooks. A piece of lath nailed across the front of each shelf opening about 2 inches above the shelf will keep the contents on the shelves.
4.   Home canned foods packed in jars can be stored in cartons. Stuff newspapers between the jars.
5.   Store water in plastic bottles or buckets or metal barrels lined with heavy plastic liners, or store cans or bottles of distilled water.
6.   Store your food and supplies in the sturdiest part of your home. A room with an outside entrance is desirable. If your house collapses on your storage, part of the storage might be lost. But, if there is no fire or explosion, you should be able to salvage much of it, if you can get to it. Be cautious during salvage attempts to avoid risk of further collapse.

Epidemic

Today, in the United States, epidemics are very uncommon. Good sanitation, vaccination, and good nutrition have made this country a very healthy place in which to live. The lack of these favorable living conditions after a disaster can lead to the outbreak of disease.

Epidemics are sometimes caused by unvaccinated persons reentering this country after travel abroad.

The U.S. Public Health Service will notify the public of serious outbreaks of infectious disease and will advise of proper disease preventive measures and necessary vaccinations. Generally, they will advise the public to:

1. Observe good sanitation practices.
2. Eat and drink only food and water that you are certain is uncontaminated.
3. Become vaccinated or, in some cases, revaccinated.
4. Stay away from crowds.
5. If someone in your home becomes ill, isolate the individual and obtain medical aid.

Often persons with contagious diseases must be isolated and the entire household may be quarantined for a certain period of time. If the disease spreads among the quarantined members of the family, the quarantine period could last for several weeks.

During the worst stages of an epidemic, the family may be advised to remain inside its own house and avoid all contact with others. You will most likely not be allowed to leave the epidemic area.

Secondary epidemics often accompany epidemics because the weakened population has become susceptible to other diseases.

The impact phase may last from a few days to several weeks.

Fire

Most major disasters involving property damage are also accompanied by fire.

There is no time for preparation after a fire has started. A delay of more than a few minutes in fighting the fire may allow the fire to get out of control.

Always practice good fire prevention measures:

1. Keep the premises free of litter and debris.
2. Store flammable liquids and fuels away from heat and flames.
3. Check wiring and cords. Repair or replace any that are worn or frayed.

4. Never run electric cords under rugs or furniture.
5. Plug no more than two appliances into one outlet.
6. Use the proper sized fuses or breakers. Never put pennies under fuses.
7. Discard paint rags.
8. Store treated dust cloths in closed metal containers.
9. Never store items close to the furnace or water heater.
10. Keep matches away from children.
11. Use a fireplace screen across the fireplace when there is a fire burning.

If you suspect a fire, first get anyone in the building to safety, then call the fire department. If the fire department is unable to respond, try to determine the exact location of the fire and extinguish it. Even if the fire department is able to respond, the homeowner can often put out a small blaze before the fire department arrives and prevent further damage.

There are several principles to be remembered about fire fighting. First, life is more precious than property. Second, fire needs air, heat and fuel to burn and cannot burn if any one of these is missing. Third, time is on the side of the blaze. Do not waste it gathering supplies and equipment or trying to salvage the contents of the building.

For a list of fire-fighting supplies and equipment the homeowner will need, see page 199. Keep these supplies throughout the house so that they will be readily accessible when needed. It should take no more than two minutes to get the equipment and start fighting the fire.

During a fire, especially one that follows a disaster, you can not rely on the water supply for putting the fire out. Have alternate means of extinguishing the fire.

Type of Fire	Water, aimed at base of flames	Foam or CO_2 Extinguisher	Dry powder Extinguisher	Smother with dirt, sand, wet rug, etc.
Solid materials: wood, paper, fabric	XX	XX	XX	XX
Electrical fire			XX	XX
Chemical or flammable liquid		XX	XX	XX

Table 2.1 How to Extinguish a Fire

After the flames are out, stir up the ashes and charred material and soak with water or completely cover with dirt. Do not leave the burned area unattended until the ashes and all charred materials are completely cold.

Some pointers to remember when searching for victims or when attempting to leave a burning building:

1. The heat and toxic gases from the fire are more dangerous than the flames.
2. Stay close to the floor. The smoke and heated gases will rise.
3. In smoke-filled rooms, move along a wall toward the safest exit.
4. If a doorknob is hot, there are flames or heated gases on the other side. Seek another exit if possible. If you must go through that door, stand to the side of the door nearest the knob, well out of the doorway. Open the door and duck back against the wall. The flames and heated gases might explode through the door when it is opened.
5. Cover the mouth and nose, preferably with a damp cloth.
6. Move quickly.
7. If you must go through flames, remove all clothing that would easily ignite. Douse hair and clothing with water, if possible.
8. If hair or clothing should ignite, immediately roll on the floor or ground to extinguish the flames. Remove smoldering clothing as quickly as possible, then drench the skin with water to cool the burned areas and prevent further tissue damage.
9. To escape from a second story window, lower yourself completely out the window until you are hanging full length from the ledge. Then drop to the ground. This shortens the drop by about 6 feet for an adult.
10. To escape from third story windows, tie sheets or blankets together with square knots. Tie one end to a radiator or heavy piece of furniture. Lower the other end out the window and let yourself down to the ground.
11. Never enter a burning building alone when it can be avoided. Use the buddy system.
12. Look in closets and under beds and in other hiding places for victims, especially children.

Fire increases the damage in any disaster situation and delays recovery.

Protecting Stored Food and Supplies:

It is difficult to protect storage against fire. Sometimes it is possible to enter the building and save some of the storage before the fire gets too large. This involves great risk to life, however, and the author does not recommend this to the reader.

Choose the most fire resistant area of your home for your storage. Outside access to the storage area is recommended. Store the goods in containers that can be easily and quickly moved.

Practice good fire prevention.

Flood

Flooding most often occurs in low-lying coastal areas and in areas near rivers, streams and lakes. Hurricane, earthquake, heavy rain, heavy snow-melt runoff and ice jams in rivers are the most common causes of flooding.

Persons living in flood-prone areas should be always aware of weather conditions and forecasts. These warnings of impending flooding usually occur far enough in advance of the flooding to allow safe evacuation. Flash flooding may occur with little or no warning, however.

Household goods and food storage can be moved to high ground as soon as the likelihood of a flood exists. The flight kit should be loaded into the car and the gas tank kept full so that evacuation can be accomplished quickly when the time comes. Tie down or store anything that might float away during the flooding. Board up doors and windows. Move all unnecessary vehicles from the flood area.

Erect barriers with lumber or sandbags to protect basement windows, doors, and other openings from flooding. Sandbags or barriers placed around the foundation of the house, on the sides expected to receive the greatest force from the flood waters, will help to prevent undermining of the foundation.

Shut off water and appliances before evacuating.

Clean-up supplies should be gathered before the flooding begins and stored either in the car or in a part of the house that will not become flooded, such as the attic. For a list of clean-up supplies see page 196.

In homes with basements, to prevent sewage backup, have ball-check valves installed in all sewer traps.

It is very unwise to remain in the flood-prone area after warning has been given to evacuate. Flood waters can rise swiftly, cutting off the escape route. Flood waters are powerful enough to move boulders weighing up to 100 tons. Once the flood waters become deep enough the engine of the auto will not function due to wetting of the electrical system.

Never attempt to wade through flood water above the knees.

The two biggest dangers from flooding are drowning and disease. Flooded sewers allow sewage to contaminate the flood water, clean water supplies and anything that the flood waters touch.

Fire danger is high during and after a flood. Caution should be exercised to prevent explosion of leaking natural gas or spilled gasoline.

Persons stranded by flood waters should seek the highest ground around and wait for rescue.

Once you have evacuated the flood area, do not attempt to re-enter it until advised that it is safe to do so. Avoid all unnecessary travel in the impact area.

After the flood, strict sanitation is necessary to prevent disease. (1). Avoid all unnecessary contact with flood water and items contaminated by flood water. (2). Eat no food that has been in contact with flood water. All food containers that have been contaminated by flood water should be washed thoroughly with a disinfectant solution before they are opened. (3). Purify any water that you are not sure is safe. The water from your taps may be contaminated.

Do not handle live electrical wires or stand in water or on wet ground near a downed electrical wire. Report all disrupted utilities. Use flashlights to check for damage or to search for victims. Do not attempt to operate or handle live electrical equipment while wet or while standing in a wet area. Check for structural damage before entering any building.

Clean-up should begin as soon as possible after the flood waters subside.

1.   Open all doors and windows to air out the structure.
2.   Stuck doors can be removed from their frames by removing the hinges, then allowed to dry.
3.   Use flashlights to inspect the premises.
4.   Before trying to salvage any damaged building, have it inspected by a qualified inspector. Be alert for hidden damage.
5.   Break down any loose or wet plaster to prevent it from falling and causing injury.
6.   Remove and discard wet sidewall insulation.

7. To prevent spontaneous combustion, clean out and discard all water-soaked and unsalvageable items (especially clothing, drapes, papers, books, magazines) before they begin to dry and rot. Any salvageable items should be kept wet until you are ready to salvage them.
8. Immediately pump out water from basements.
9. Remove mud while wet. Do not allow it to dry inside the building.
10. Clean mud out of furnace, flues and chimneys.
11. Check chimneys for damage.
12. Do not waste time trying to salvage items that are unsalvageable.
13. Disinfect everything.
14. Drain standing water from property as soon as possible to minimize problems with disease and mosquitoes.
15. Turn on the heat and dry out the structure as soon as the furnace is clean and safe to use.

Items of paper, fabric, or wood are often damaged beyond repair.

Discard all stored food items that are water-soaked. Disinfect outsides of jars, cans and other containers. Dry all cans and move storage to the driest area possible to prevent rust and deterioration.

Protecting Stored Items From Flooding:

An insulated attic is the best place to store food and supplies to protect them from flooding. Put all items in watertight containers. Avoid breakable containers. Do home canning in cans rather than jars.

Hurricane

Tropical storms often develop into hurricanes that strike the Gulf Coast and the Atlantic seaboard of the United States.

A hurricane usually proceeds forward at a speed of 10 to 25 miles per hour. Since the path and progress of the hurricane are somewhat predictable, weather watchers can give warning hours or even days in advance of the impact. Hurricane warning is almost 100% effective in saving lives.

During the warning phase, board up doors and windows. Tie down or store any loose objects in the yard. Roll up or take down awnings. Sandbag doors and basement windows in flood prone areas. Check stores of food and water. Fill the gas tank of your auto and load in the flight kit. Move objects away from windward windows and doors. Remove pictures and mirrors from walls. Draw the drapes across the windows and clear away any objects that might be blown around. Ready fire-fighting equipment. Turn off electric and gas appliances and water.

Check with local civil defense officials to learn the best plan of action for your neighborhood.

A sturdily-built home on high ground is usually adequate shelter during a hurricane.

All low-lying coastal areas and areas along coastal rivers for several miles inland should be evacuated.

If evacuation is necessary, it should be accomplished well in advance of the predicted impact time to avoid being caught out in the open during impact.

The impact of a hurricane passes through three distinct stages: (1) High winds in one direction; (2) a period of calm (the "eye" of the hurricane); (3) high winds in the opposite direction. The winds of a hurricane will blow in excess of 73 miles per hour.

The path of a hurricane can be several thousand miles long and several hundred miles wide. In fact the entire Atlantic Seaboard can be stricken by a single hurricane.

Impact will last anywhere from a few hours to several days.

The biggest dangers during a hurricane are the high winds and the high tides that accompany the storm. The water level along coasts and coastal rivers will rise as much as 16 to 18 feet above high tide level. This high water area will extend several miles inland and the tide will rise rapidly, as much as 6 - 8 feet in a few minutes.

The high winds of a hurricane create a suction that pulls the roofs off of houses and causes buildings to collapse. These winds are usually accompanied by torrential rains.

Flooding that accompanies hurricane causes a multitude of problems. The sewers are flooded and contaminate flood water and clean water supplies with sewage. In swampy areas, snakes and other animals will be driven out of their natural habitat by the rising waters and become a hazard to persons.

During the major impact period of the storm, stay inside in the most protected area of the shelter. Stay away from doors and windows. Get under a heavy desk or table or under a bed.

Don't be fooled by the calm that occurs as the eye of the storm passes over your area. The high winds will return very suddenly after the eye passes and there will not be time to return to shelter if you are outside.

After the storm it is important to stay out of disaster areas. Travel cautiously, watching for such hazards as undermined roads, debris and broken power lines. Stay away from rivers and streams and away from the coast.

Protecting Stored Food and Supplies:

The most protected area of the home would be a corner of the basement on the windward side of the house. An outside entrance with some sort of wind baffle to protect the entrance would make the supplies more accessible in the case of structural damage. Do not store supplies in an area having unprotected windows.

See also Flood and Fire.

Tornado

Tornadoes can occur anywhere and at any time of the year but are most prevalent in the middle third of the United States during the spring and summer months.

Hot, sultry weather accompanied by electrical storm is tornado weather. Tornado watches are usually issued by the weather bureau when tornadoes are likely to occur.

The sight or sound of the tornado funnel may be the only warning that is received. If the funnel is in the distance, there is usually enough time to get to a nearby shelter. If the sound of the tornado resembles a passing freight train, the tornado will strike in a few seconds.

Tornadoes travel forward at speeds of 35 to 70 miles per hour. The path may be from a few feet to a mile in width and from a few yards to 200 miles in length. A tornado usually lasts less than an hour.

The southwest corner of the basement is usually the safest place to take shelter during a tornado. If caught out in the open, a person should never try to outrun a tornado. Travel away from the funnel at right angles to its path. Lie down in a depression or ditch as the storm passes over.

Damage and injury are caused by the high wind. The force of the wind creates a suction that lifts very heavy objects such as railroad cars and autos. Buildings literally explode from the force of the suction.

Be alert for additional tornadoes in the area.

Protecting Stored Food and Supplies:

The southwest corner of the basement will be a good place to construct a tornado shelter and store your supplies. Be sure that the door to the outside is sturdy and has a wind baffle to protect it. Sturdy shutters should protect the windows during a tornado.

Riot

It is difficult to write about riot and civil disturbance because there is so much differing opinion on the subject. Therefore, I am including only a few general comments and the reader must formulate his own plan of action.

Discontent, demonstration and civil disobedience have become household words in this country in the past few years. Riots, such as occurred in Watts, are one of the biggest fears of many city dwellers today. There is no way to predict the outcome of a demonstration. This uncertainty has made police and citizens fear any signs of unrest or demonstration of discontent. Fear leads to overreaction and over-reaction feeds fuel to the fire. It seems that too often peaceful demonstrations erupt into violence due to the overreactions of those not involved.

My first suggestion would be to be fully aware of the social and political climate of your area. If signs of violence begin to appear, remain calm. Avoid any action that calls attention to yourself or your family, and avoid violence on your part.

I do not mean to suggest that one should not defend his home and family, but I feel that premature displays of violence and hostility toward the demonstrators can only fan the fire and lead to more trouble.

Needless injury and death often result from amateurs "defending" their homes, especially where firearms are involved.

Protecting Food and Stored Supplies:

(1) Do not tell people that you have food.
(2) Store at least part of your supplies and food in hidden areas without obvious entrances.
(3) If looters break into your home, let them have what they can find.
(4) Keep in mind that life is more important than property.

War and Atomic Blast

It is not within the scope of this book to enter into a detailed discussion of the consequences of war or atomic warfare. But the reader should be aware that much of the literature about atomic warfare tends to gloss over the lasting effects of fallout radiation.

It is commonly reported that after two weeks victims will be able to leave shelter safe from further radiation danger. However, residents of areas close to the blast site may find that radiation levels can remain at dangerously high levels for several months. After a few weeks it will be safe to leave the shelter for periods of only minutes without receiving dangerous doses of radiation.

Since radiation doses are cumulative, it is not advisable to leave shelter before the radiation level drops to the point where an individual will not receive an excess of radiation during the rest of his lifetime.

With this in mind, the sheltering preparations should include stores sufficient for a full year, at least.

For further information see:

1. Eugene P. Wigner, *Survival and the Bomb: Methods of Civil Defense*, (Bloomington, Ind.: Indiana University Press, 1969).
2. Solomon Garb, M.D. and Evelyn Eng, R.N., M.A., *Disaster Handbook* (New York: Springer Publishing Co., Inc. 1964).
3. Richard J. Healy, *Emergency and Disaster Planning* (New York; John Wiley and Sons, Inc., 1969).

Drought and Famine

Because of the present mobility and highly-developed state of our economy, these disasters have only slight effect on our country when they occur. But during time of war or following a major disaster, they could have a great impact on us.

Drought hits agriculture hard. Crops and animals die from lack of water and food.

Food stores in the home would have to be heavily depended upon during a period of drought.

PART TWO

FOOD STORAGE

CHAPTER III

WHAT TO STORE

An Introductory Note

The idea of a home storehouse is not new. For most of us it is a relic of bygone days. When our economy was largely agricultural, it was the established practice for families to set aside food from one year's harvest to feed the family until the next harvest. Before the age of the supermarket, a housewife filled her fruit cellar with home-canned fruits and vegetables. The hog was slaughtered, smoked and hung in the smokehouse all winter, being used as needed.

There is a difference between storing and hoarding. Hoarding is the greedy gathering of material belongings, including food, without plan or good reason. Hoarding is the result of panic. Storing is the planned, sensible accumulation of goods during times of plenty to prepare for times of need.

The farm family with a freezer full of home-grown beef and full root and fruit cellars is not accused of hoarding, but praised for wisdom and forethought. The urban family with a full pantry of either home-canned or commercially-processed foods and a full freezer should be considered equally wise.

Panic buying does not prevent price increases. On the contrary, by producing false shortages, it drives prices higher.

No one can devise the perfect storage plan that will suit the needs of every individual or family. Therefore, the plans in this book are meant to serve only as guides. You will be able to determine from them the types of goods and quantities that some families have found to be adequate for their needs.

The first step in determining what to store is to decide whether you want a storage plan that will require continual rotation, or one that will require infrequent rotation, or a combination of the two. Most families will find that a combination plan offers the greatest amount of flexibility.

Long-term Storage

This type of plan relies heavily on wheat, beans and other dried seeds and grains. Also included in a long-term storage plan are the low-moisture, dehydrated foods.

The relatively small amount of storage space required for these items in comparison with wet pack foods is the principle advantage of this plan. Also, these foods require little maintenance and can be held in storage for extended periods with little deterioration.

The low cost of these foods is a definite advantage. One recent comparison of cost-per-serving of low-moisture and wet-pack canned foods shows that the low-moisture foods cost substantially less. Because of regional variations in prices and the present inflationary trend in food prices, you should make your own comparison, taking into account any waste in fresh foods or wet-packed canned foods.

The major disadvantage is that few of us are accustomed to this type of diet. Also, large amounts of water are needed to prepare these foods. In the event of a major disruption of the water supply, these foods would be virtually useless without having significant quantities of water stored. Once a can of low-moisture food is opened, the contents must be used within a certain period of time to prevent deterioration. Beans, wheat and other such products are quite inexpensive and pack a great deal of nutrition. However, one must accustom his body to eating large quantities of these foods.

Rotation Storage

This type of plan calls for the storage of canned foods, fresh fruits and vegetables, and frozen foods.

The major advantage of this storage program is that one can store the foods he is accustomed to eating. Stores of large quantities of water are not needed in order to make good use of these goods. Most canned foods are packed with water in some form. The water in them can be used for drinking and preparation of foods that require the addition of water.

It is the water in these foods that constitutes the major disadvantage, however. Because of weight and bulk they require more space and are harder to move than the long-term storage foods. There is a certain amount of maintenance needed to keep these foods in good condition. Most must be rotated periodically, and some foods must be inverted or shaken at regular intervals to maintain quality. Attention must be paid to keeping your stock fresh. With this type of storage plan, you cannot just purchase the supply, store it and forget it.

Combination Plan

Let us assume that your goal is to have a one year's supply of food on hand. First, purchase a 6 months' supply of long-term storage items. Then purchase a good variety of foods that require rotation.

This way you will have a good supply of nourishing and inexpensive foods available while you are purchasing the more costly foods that require rotation. By incorporating the rotated foods in your daily meal planning you can keep them in constant rotation. Regularly including the lont-term storage items in your meals will help your families to become accustomed to eating those foods.

Now after you have decided which type of a storage program to use, the next step is to decide what and how much to store.

To determine how much will be needed for a rotation program, the best method is to keep a record of everything you use for a certain period of time, such as two weeks. Then multiply that to obtain the amount needed for a year or whatever period of time for which you desire to maintain stores. This requires very detailed records of everything used, right down to the 1/2 teaspoon of soda used in Sunday's pancakes. Place a chart on the refrigerator or some convenient place and record what you use as you use it. Be sure to include all exhaustable supplies such as food, soap, paper products, medicines, light bulbs and baby supplies. Then inventory your closets and cupboards to determine what additional supplies you may need that were not used during the period for which you kept record. While taking your inventory, record what supplies you have on hand.

Some Tips on Storage

The prime rule of food storage is:

STORE WHAT YOU USE AND USE WHAT YOU STORE

—Test *all* products before purchasing large quantities for storage. If you don't like a product, or you can't eat it or wear it, it will do you no good to have it on the shelf.

—Tests have shown that a person will sometimes starve himself rather than eat an unfamiliar food. This is especially true of children. Serve the foods that you store so that your family will be accustomed to them. There will be fewer problems maintaining good health on your storage diet. When you throw away 20 cents worth of food, you might as well be throwing away 20 cents in cash. It amounts to the same thing.

—Purchase basic items first. Then add frills, if desired. Always keep in mind the goal is to be as adequately prepared as possible at all times, should an emergency arise.

—Make a month-by-month purchasing plan that will maintain

adequate balance among the foods that you have stored so that you can use your storage conveniently and have proper nutrition and variety at any time while you are building up your supply.

—Plan for variety. Monotony can lead to loss of appetite and eventually to malnutrition from improper eating.

—Don't forget to include in your storage plan the supplies that you have on hand for current use.

—Take advantage of sales. But be aware that many items placed on sale may be old stock that is being cleared to make way for new. Sales of canned fruits and vegetables during the summer may be just such a clearance. Allowances for the time already stored before purchase must be made in determing the shelf life of the product.

—Shelf life as given in tables is not absolute. Most foods will keep much longer. The tables will help you to use your food while it has the best quality and the highest nutrition. Do not feel that food has to be thrown out if it has been stored longer than the table advises.

—Inspect your storage frequently to avoid costly losses from insects, rodents, rusting cans, water seepage into the storage area, or other causes.

—Avoid dented or rusted cans, regardless of cost. These should never be purchased for storage. Likewise, be wary of merchandise on the merchant's half-price table. These items may be near the end of their storage life. If in doubt, ask the manager why the item has been reduced in price.

—Buy the item that will give you the most nutrition for the least price. Regular low-moisture foods will give you many more servings per dollar than will freeze-dried foods. However, some foods are available only in the freeze-dried form. Where you have a choice, regular low-moisture food is generally the better buy. Always compare cost per serving.

—Similarly, dried beans cost much less per serving than do cooked, canned beans. The basic ingredients for baked goods or casseroles are less costly than the prepared mixes. When you consider the total cost of a year's supply of food, those pennies saved on each item can add up to a lot of dollars on the total supply.

Food Storage Plans

The plans included in this book are only suggestions. Use them as a starting point to develop your own plan.

Any storage plan should be designed to give adequate nutrition. The basic four food groups will serve as a guide.

FOUR BASIC FOOD GROUPS

    Meats and Other Protein Foods: Two servings daily

1 serving equals:	3 oz. lean meat
	3 eggs
	3 ox. yellow cheese
	1 to 1 1/2 c. cooked dried beans
	1/3 c. peanut butter

    Fruits and Vegetables: Four servings daily
    (At least 1 citrus, or tomato, and 1 dark green or yellow)

1 serving equals:	1/2 c. canned or cooked fruit
	1 fresh fruit
	1 c. berries or cherries
	1/2 c. cooked or canned vegetables
	1 c. raw leafy vegetables

    Breads, Cereals, Pastas: Four servings daily

1 serving equals:	1 slice bread
	1 roll or muffin
	1/2 c. potatoes, pasta, or rice
	3/4 to 1 c. flaked or puffed cereal
	1/2 c. cooked cereal
	1/4 c. granola

Milk or Milk Products:	Adults: Two servings daily
	Children: Three to four servings daily
	Teens: Four servings daily
1 serving equals:	8 oz. milk
	1 oz. cheese
	1/2 c. cottage cheese

    The following are suggested storage plans based on varying types of foods:

PLAN A

A SUGGESTED STORAGE PLAN BASED ON WHEAT, HONEY, SALT, AND POWDERED MILK

Amount needed for one person per day, for a balanced diet:

1-1/2 oz. honey	salt
1 lb. wheat	Vitamin C - from wheat sprouts
1 qt. reconstituted	or greens or vitamin tablets
non-fat milk	

This requires these amounts per adult per year:

365 lbs. wheat	5 lbs. or more of salt
35 lbs. honey	365 vitamin C tablets
60 lbs. powdered milk	

Variation: For 2300 calories per day per adult store:

    300 lbs. wheat   5 lbs. salt
    100 lbs. powdered milk   365 vitamin C tablets
    100 lbs. sugar

The preceeding plan is based primarily on information found in *Passport to Survival* by Esther Dickey (Salt Lake City, Utah: Bookcraft, Inc. 1969).

PLAN B

A Suggested Food Storage Plan Using Dehydrated Foods

Item   *Number in Family*

	1	2	3	4	5	6	7	8	9	10
Wheat—5-gal. cans	5	10	15	20	25	30	35	40	45	50
Milk—quarts	365	730	1095	1460	1825	2190	2555	2920	3185	3650
Gelatin—24-oz. cans	4	8	12	16	20	24	28	32	36	40
Eggs—1-lb. cans	3	6	9	12	15	18	21	24	27	30
Boullion—1-lb cans	2	4	6	8	10	12	14	16	18	20
Cereal—No. 10 can	4	8	12	16	20	24	28	32	36	40
Peas—No. 10 can	5	10	15	20	25	30	35	40	45	50
Beans—No. 10 can	5	10	15	20	25	30	35	40	45	50
Rice—No. 10 can	5	10	15	20	25	30	35	40	45	50
Potatoes—No. 10 can	4	8	12	16	20	24	28	32	36	40
Vegetables—No. 10 can	4	8	12	16	20	24	28	32	36	40
Stew—No. 10 can	4	8	12	16	20	24	28	32	36	40
Onions—No. 10 can	2	4	6	8	10	12	14	16	18	20
Tomato crystals—No. 10 can	2	4	6	8	10	12	14	16	18	20
Fruit—No. 10 can	5-6	10	15	20	25	30	35	40	45	50
Juice crystals—24 oz.	4	8	12	16	20	24	28	32	36	40
Sugar or honey—lbs.	60	120	180	240	300	360	420	480	540	600
Salt—lbs.	5	10	15	20	25	30	35	40	45	50

The above plan is adapted from Chart 7 in the book, *Just Add Water*, by Barbara D. Salsbury (Bountiful, Utah: Horizon Publishers). Used by permission.

PLAN C

ONE YEAR'S SUPPLY OF LOW-MOISTURE FOODS

The following is the suggested supply for one adult for one year:

    5 - No. 10 cans leafy green or yellow vegetables, to provide 2 servings daily.

    12 lbs. juice crystals, to provide 1 serving daily or 30 - 50 mg. vitamin C daily.

    8 - No. 10 cans of potatoes, fruit, and rice, to provide 2 servings daily.

    185 quarts milk (37 lbs. non-instant dry milk), to provide 2 servings daily.

8 - No. 10 cans MPF *(Multi-Purpose Food)*

3 lbs. eggs
1 can gelatin
1 jar bouillion } To provide four servings daily
2 No. 10 can beans
25 regular canned meats

4 (5 gal.) cans flour or
    wheat (about
    165 lbs.)
1 - No. 10 can cereal or } To provide four servings daily
    macaroni, or corn-
    meal
1 lb. dried yeast

25 lbs. sugar, honey, molasses, etc., to provide 2 T. daily.
25 lbs. fats and oils, to provide 2 T. daily.

(The above plan is recommended by Perma-Pak, a low-moisture foods distributing company based in Salt Lake City, Utah.)

PLAN D

FOUR MONTH'S SUPPLY OF LOW-MOISTURE FOODS FOR A FAMILY OF FIVE

6 - No. 10 cans fruits
12 - No. 10 cans cereals and grains
    3 cornmeal (13.5 lbs.)
    3 oatmeal (8.25 lbs.)
    3 rice (16.5 lbs.)
    2 elbo spaghetti (7.5 lbs.)
    1 popcorn (5.5 lbs.)

6 - No. 10 cans protein foods
    2 whole egg solids
    1 chicken chunks
    1 red beans (5 lbs.)
    1 white beans (5 lbs.)
    1 split peas (5.5 lbs.)

24 cans powdered milk (54 lbs.)

12 - No. 10 cans vegetables
    1 cabbage   4 potato granules
    1 carrots   1 potato dices

1 corn	1 tomato flakes
1 peas	1 celery
1 onion slices	

165 lbs. wheat or flour

(The above plan is recommended by Sam-Andy, a low-moisture foods distributing firm, based in Beaumont, California.)

Consult your distributor of low-moisture foods for more detailed and varied plans.

COMBINATION PLAN E

MY PERSONAL STORAGE PLAN FOR ONE YEAR

Plan I feeds 1 adult, 1 teenager or 2 small children
Plan IV feeds 4 adults, or teenagers or 8 small children

DH = Dehydrated
D = Dried

	AMOUNT NEEDED	
Meats and Other Protein Foods	*PLAN I*	*PLAN IV*
Salmon	6 (1 lb.) cans	26 (1 lb.) cans
Ham, canned or frozen	12 lbs.	45 lbs.
Bacon, canned	10 lbs.	39 lbs.
Chicken, canned or frozen	6 whole	26 whole
Luncheon meat	13 cans	52 cans
Corned beef	6 cans	26 cans
Tuna	20 cans	78 cans
Roast beef, canned	6 cans	26 cans
Stew beef, frozen	7 lbs.	26 lbs.
Roasts, frozen	10 lbs.	40 lbs.
Ground beef, frozen	10 lbs.	40 lbs.
Dried beef	13 lg. jars	52 lg. jars
Sausage, canned or frozen	6 lbs.	26 lbs.
Textured Vegetable Protein (TVP), DH	1 (No. 10) can	1 (No. 10) can
Pork and beans	13 (1 lb.) cans	52 (1 lb.) cans
Chili with beans	6 (1 lb.) cans	26 (1 lb.) cans
Limas, DH	6 lbs.	25 lbs.
Lentils, DH	6 lbs.	25 lbs.
Soybeans, DH	12 lbs.	45 lbs.
Pinto beans, DH	14 lbs.	55 lbs.
Eggs, DH	3 (No. 10) cans	11 (No. 10) cans

Milk and Milk Products

Evaporated milk	18 lg. cans	70 lg. cans
Pineapple cheese spread	6 jars	26 jars
Cheese	16 lbs.	65 lbs.
Powdered milk	70 lbs.	280 lbs.

Pasta

Macaroni	4 lbs.	15 lbs.
Noodles	6 lbs.	25 lbs.
Rice	10 lbs.	40 lbs.

Fats

Shortening (for baking and frying)	9 (3 lb.) cans	35 (3 lb.) cans
Margarine (for eating)	6 lbs.	26 lbs.
Peanut butter	1 - 3 lg. jars	6 - 12 lg. jars

Fruits

Pie fillings	6 cans	26 cans
Grapefruit segments, canned	6 cans	26 cans
Assorted canned fruits	40 cans *or* 20 quarts	156 cans *or* 78 quarts
Fresh apples	1/2 bushel	2 bushels
Apple granules, DH	1 (No. 10) can	1 (No. 10) can
Apple slices, DH	1 (No. 10) can	3 (No. 10) cans
Prunes, DH	xxxxxxxx	2 (No. 10) cans
Fruit blend, DH	1 (No. 10) can	2 (No. 10) cans
Peach slices, DH	1 (No. 10) can	2 (No. 10) cans
Date bits, DH	xxxxxxxx	1 (No. 10) can
Banana slices, DH	xxxxxxxx	1 (No. 10) can
Juice or juice substitute	54 quarts	215 quarts
Raisins, D or DH	4 lbs.	20 lbs.

Sugars

Granulated, for cooking and eating	37 lbs.	150 lbs.
Granulated, for canning	25 lbs.	100 lbs.
Powdered sugar	6 lbs.	25 lbs.
Brown sugar	6 lbs.	25 lbs.
Honey	2 lbs.	10 lbs.

Flour and Grains

Flour or wheat for baking	100 lbs.	400 lbs.
Wheat, for cereal, etc.	10 lbs.	40 lbs.
Oatmeal	4 lbs.	15 lbs.
Cornmeal	4 lbs.	15 lbs.
Rolled wheat	1 lb.	5 lbs.
Cracked wheat	3 lbs.	10 lbs.
Wheat germ	1 lg. jar	3 lg. jars
Rye flour	4 lbs.	15 lbs.

Vegetables

Tomatoes, canned	45 (1 lb.) cans	182 (1 lb.) cans
Tomato sauce	13 cans	52 cans
Enchillada or taco sauce	4 cans	12 cans
Canned vegetables, assorted	26 cans	104 cans
Green beans, canned	6 cans	26 cans
Corn, canned	7 cans	26 cans
Spinach, canned	13 cans	52 cans
Yams, canned	6 cans	26 cans
Potatoes, fresh	15 lbs.	50 lbs.
Hash browns, DH	1 (No. 10) can	2 (No. 10) cans
Mashed potatoes, DH	1 (No. 10) can (173 servings)	3 (No. 10) cans (519 servings)
Onions, fresh	6 lbs.	25 lbs.
Carrots, fresh	16 lbs.	65 lbs.
Assorted vegetables, DH	2 (No. 10) cans	8 (No. 10) cans
Cabbage, DH	1 (No. 10) can	1 or more (No. 10) can
Celery, DH	1 (No. 10) can	1 (No. 10) can
Green beans, DH	1 (No. 10) can	1 (No. 10) can

Soups

Vegetable	13 cans	52 cans
Mushroom	6 cans	26 cans
Tomato	6 cans	26 cans
Cream of chicken	7 cans	26 cans

Adjuncts

Yeast	2 cups	8 cups
Molasses	2 quarts	8 quarts

Seasonings:
    Cinnamon
    Maple Flavoring
    Vanilla
    Italian seasoning
    Caraway seed
    Chili powder

Salt (for seasoning and canning)	6 to 10 lbs.	25 to 35 lbs.
Pepper		
G. Washington Broth	2 pkgs.	8 pkgs.
Bouillon	1 sm. jar	1 lg. jar
Mustard	1 pint	2 quarts
Garlic powder	1 sm. jar	2 lg. jars
Dry mustard	1 sm. can	1 lg. can
Pudding mix	13 pkgs.	52 pkgs.
Sour cream	6 sm. cans	26 sm. cans
Chocolate chips	6 pkgs.	26 pkgs.
Mayonnaise	4 quarts	13 quarts
Jello	13 pkgs.	52 pkgs.
Plain gelatin	6 envelopes	26 envelopes
Vinegar	1 pint	2 quarts
Nuts for cooking and snacks	4 lbs.	15 lbs.
Pickles and relishes	3 jars	12 jars
Tortillas	3 cans	12 cans
Cocoa	1 can	3 cans
Coconut	1/2 lb.	2 lbs.
Catsup	3 lg. bottles	12 lg. bottles
Baking powder	1 - 2 lg. cans	3 - 6 lg. cans
Baking soda	1 - 2 lbs.	3 - 6 lbs.
Vitamin C tablets	365 tablets	1460 tablets

Nice To Have

Condensed milk	3 cans	12 cans
Mushrooms	6 cans	24 cans
Gravy mixes	12 pkgs.	50 pkgs.
Popcorn	1 - 2 cans	6 cans
Koolaid	25 pkgs.	100 pkgs.
Candy	3 pkgs.	12 pkgs.
Corn starch	1 - 2 boxes	6 boxes
Whipped topping mix	6 boxes	24 boxes
Worchestershire sauce	1 bottle	2 bottles
Soy sauce	1 bottle	2 bottles

Salad dressings	3 bottles	12 bottles
Olives	3 cans	12 cans
Chow mein noodles	3 cans	12 cans
Green pepper, DH	1 (No. 10) can	1 (No. 10) can

I have purposely avoided any mention of cost because of the currently unstable condition of food prices. I would estimate that Plan IV would cost about as much as the average family of 4 or 5 spends on a year's groceries.

Suggested Food Items Suitable for Storage

Cereals and Grains

wheat
cracked wheat
bulgar wheat
rolled wheat
oatmeal
rice
wheat flour
other flours and grains
corn starch
corn
cornmeal

Leavenings

yeast - active dry
soda
baking powder
cream of tartar

Sugars

granulated sugar
powdered sugar
brown sugar
raw sugar
honey
maple syrup
molasses
sorghum
jams and jellies

Adjuncts

cocoa
gelatin, flavored or un-
    flavored
drink mixes
sauce and flavoring mixes
salt
pepper
spices
maple flavoring
vanilla
vinegar
bouillon cubes
mayonnaise
catsup
salad dressings
mustard

Beans, peas, etc.

pinto beans
lentils
split peas
lima beans
kidney beans
other beans
nuts

Fats

peanut butter
margarine

butter
shortening
oil

Pasta

macaroni
spaghetti
noodles

Fresh, Dried or Canned
Vegetables, Fruits and Meats

peas
green beans
corn
tomatoes
tomato sauce
tomato juice
tomato crystals
carrots
spinach
beets
cabbage
asparagus
green peppers
sauerkraut
potatoes
hominy
onions
yams
pumpkin
okra
lima beans
raisins
apricots
applesauce
apples
peaches
pears
figs
pineapple
berries
cherries

fruit cocktail
soups, dry or condensed
roast beef
corned beef
turkey
chicken
pork
meat loaf
meat balls
sandwich spreads
tuna
salmon
crab
clams
oysters
mackarel
sardines and kippers
ham
luncheon meat
dried beef
jerky
deviled meats
beef stew
pork and beans
lima beans and ham
chicken and noodles
spaghetti and meat or cheese
    sauce
ravioli
macaroni and cheese
baked beans
beans and franks
tamales
salad tomatoes
artichoke hearts
mushrooms
canned salad vegetables
orange juice
grapefruit juice
grape juice
apple juice
pineapple juice

Fruits, Vegetables and Meats,
    continued

    lemon juice
    vegetable juice
    juice crystals
    punch
    juice drinks

Eggs

    powdered eggs
    fresh eggs

Milk and Milk Products

    powdered milk
    canned milk
    condensed milk
    powdered buttermilk
    infant formula
    canned sour cream

Cheese

    cheese spreads
    dried cheese
    brick cheeses:
        Cheddar
        Swiss

Mixes

    pancake mix
    cake mix
    cookie mix
    all-purpose baking mix
    main dish mixes
    muffin mix
    macaroni and cheese dinner
    pizza mix
    spaghetti dinner

CHAPTER IV

STORAGE CONDITIONS

There are three conditions which are necessary for successful long-term storage of food. The storage area must be (1) cool, (2) dry, and (3) dark.

Temperature

Extremes of temperature must be avoided when storing most foods. Unless food is properly prepared and packaged for freezing, significant losses in food value and palatability can result from freezing.

If canned foods become frozen, they are still edible as long as the cans remain sealed and do not become bulged. Any cans that are bulged or leaking should be discarded without tasting. Freezing of canned foods will cause changes in the texture of the foods and their taste may be affected. Canned foods that have become frozen should be used as soon as possible. Be especially alert to signs of spoilage as you use these foods.

High temperature accelerates the rate of chemical and physical change that occurs in stored foods.

Most foods store best at temperatures between 40º F. and 70º F. High temperatures accelerate vitamin losses and encourage insect infestation. At 48º most insects become active. Activity increases as the temperature increases. Fat melts at 95º F.

Never store foods near radiators, furnaces, or steam pipes. Do not store foods in the furnace room. An unheated basement room or insulated garage will meet the temperature requirements for storing most foods.

Moisture

Moisture can cause many undesirable changes in stored foods. Moisture encourages insects and molds. Cans will rust and cloth or paper containers will rot in the presence of moisture. Flour, wheat and milk will pick up musty flavors. Many foods would have to be discarded if they became wet.

Choose a storage area that is as dry as possible. If there are flooding problems in your storage area, correct the problems before storing food there. Never store food directly against earth, concrete, stone or masonry walls or floors. Paint or other coverings on these surfaces are no guarantee against moisture damage. Use wooden pallets or strips of wood to hold storage containers up off the floor.

Ventilation

Good ventilation is necessary to help control temperature and moisture in the storage area.

Light

Light will cause deterioration in foods. All foods should be stored in light-proof containers or in a dark storage area. If the storage area has windows for ventilation, they should be covered to admit as little light as possible.

Odors

Never store food near paints, paint thinners, kerosene, fuels, or any strong-odored substance. Flour, wheat and milk, especially, will pick up off-flavors.

CHAPTER V

WHERE TO STORE

Your food and other supplies can be stored any place where correct storage conditions exist.

Containers

Store food in containers that will protect the foods from light, air, moisture, insects and rodents. Use containers that are small enough to be easily moved. Some foods, such as honey, should be stored in small containers so that they can be conveniently used. Avoid spoilage and waste by purchasing foods in the sized containers that suit the size of your family.

Wooden, metal, fiber, and plastic barrels make convenient storage containers for bulk purchases of grains and beans. Lined with a plastic liner, these containers also make ideal storage containers for flours, meals, powdered milk and bulk purchases of low-moisture foods, macaroni, rice, sugars and salt. Plastic containers can be used without the plastic liner. Tight fitting lids are a necessity.

Lids can be sealed with a coating of parafin or a strip of tape. Heat duct tape is excellent for this purpose.

Attics

Attics may be used for storage only if well-insulated to maintain a temperature of 70° F. or below. The temperature within an attic during the summer can approach 150° F., if uninsulated. The heat rising from within your home during the winter should protect your food from freezing. If in doubt, check the attic temperature during a winter cold spell.

Basements

Basements make excellent storage areas if they are cool and dry. The excess humidity in a damp basement can cause deterioration in the stored food. Never store foods in a damp area for more than very short periods of time, and then, only if in moisture-proof containers.

Garages

Incorrect temperature and excessive moisture are usually the problems one encounters in using a garage for storage. If the temperature remains in the acceptable range in your garage and there is no moisture problem, it will make an excellent storage area.

Food stored in a cold garage can be protected from freezing. Place the container of food in a larger container. Insulate the space between the two containers with straw or crumpled newspapers. Cover the top of the containers with a thick layer of newspapers or an old blanket This, however, would be quite impractical for storing large quantities of food.

Root Cellars and Pits

These areas are excellent for storing many varieties of fresh fruits and vegetables during the late fall, winter and early spring.

Freezer

Do not overlook the freezer as a place for storing emergency food supplies. Most emergencies which one will face will not affect the power for your freezer. One must be prepared, however, to take care of any frozen food should the freezer fail to function or should a power failure occur.

Crawl Space

The crawl space under the house or mobile home could be utilized for food storage. Sheets of plywood could be propped up on concrete blocks to provide clean, dry storage space for foods. All foods would have to be in air-tight, insect, rodent and moisture-proof containers. Because the crawl space might be damp, canned foods should not be stored there for long periods, as the cans might rust. Cross-ventilation should be provided to maintain low humidity and low temperature.

Under Beds

Put casters and pulls on sheets of plywood or construct shallow wooden boxes on casters to slide under beds, where space permits. Boxes of canned foods can be placed on the sheets of plywood or individual cans of food can be stored on end or on their sides in the wooden boxes. Food stored this way can be easily pulled out from under the bed for use and cleaning. A cover of closely woven fabric or plastic would help to keep the dust out of the food. The corners of the cover can be fitted and elasticized.

If the space under the bed is too short, the bed could be raised up on supports to provide more space.

In "Tables"

Barrels of grains or stacks of food in cases can be covered with floor length cloths and used as occasional tables.

Chests, Trunks, Cabinets, and Shelves

1.   Chests of drawers make excellent places to store canned foods. Be sure that the drawers have stops to prevent them from coming all the way out. When full, the drawers will be quite heavy. The bottoms of the drawers should be sturdy enough to hold the weight.

2.   Foot lockers and trunks can be made into attractive accent items and used to store food. An old foot locker, covered with adhesive backed paper or plastic, or painted and decorated, could be used as an occasional table, or topped with a cushion to become a stool, bench, or hassock. Remember that these will not be very portable when full because of the weight.

3.   Cabinets can be constructed in any unused corner or on any unused wall. In many homes the space above the kitchen cabinets can be converted into storage space with the addition of doors or curtains. Cabinets near the ceiling do not make good storage areas for food because of the high temperature. Seldom used items from other closets and cabinets could be stored there, however, thus freeing the more suitable spaces for food storage.

Boxes or barrels of food can be stacked in a corner or along a wall and hidden with a curtain. If this method is well-planned, these curtains could add to the room decor.

4.   Additional shelves can be built into many closets and cupboards. Utah State University Extension Services Bulletin, *More Storage Space in Your Kitchen* will give you some good ideas.

By rearranging the clothes in the closet so that all the short clothes are hung together, room can be found for the storage of boxes or barrels or for the addition of shelves, drawers, or cupboards.

5.   Special shelving units can be constructed for the rotation storage of canned foods. (See figure 5.1 next page.)

6.   Use the space within your walls. Several feet above the floor, cut slots between the studs, large enough for the cans to be slipped through. Further down the wall, cut slots for the removal of the cans. Cover the slots with a hinged decorative trim and fasten it with magnetic catches. Drop the cans in through the top slot and remove the cans from the lower slots. The cans are automatically rotated. Do not place the top slot too far above the bottom one or

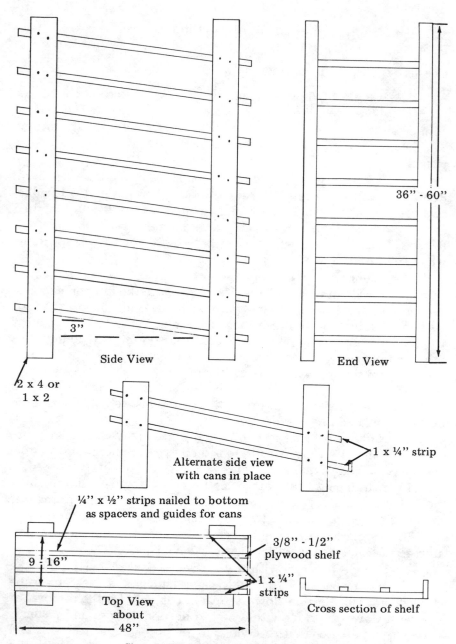

3"

Side View   End View

36" - 60"

2 x 4 or
1 x 2

Alternate side view
with cans in place

1 x ¼" strip

¼" x ½" strips nailed to bottom
as spacers and guides for cans

3/8" - 1/2"
plywood shelf

9 - 16"

1 x ¼"
strips

Top View
about
48"

Cross section of shelf

Shelves for Canned Good Storage
Figure 5.1

the cans may be dented dropping to the bottom. Be sure that the bottom slot is just above a crossbrace or the floor and that there are no cross braces between the top and bottom slot. Check with your local building department to be sure that your alterations are within the building code.

7. Furniture built upon an enclosed box base may be used to store food. The pull-out drawer of a captain's bed would be a good storage area. Be sure to use nylon drawer glides so that the heavily filled drawer will glide in and out easily. A sofa built on a plywood box base with a hinged, cushioned top, or a window seat would hold a lot of food. Low, cushion-topped seating could be built along a wall in almost any room and used for storage. (For plans and designs, consult books on furniture building and storage.) Lift-out trays or shelves positioned within these cabinets will help you to make the most efficient use of the space.

CHAPTER VI

WHERE TO OBTAIN STORAGE ITEMS

Group-Buying Plans

Commercial group-buying plans can be a good source of food to store. Be sure to investigate the plan before using it. Be wary of plans that require you to sign a long-term contract, purchase a freezer, or finance your purchase. Choose a plan that offers national brands and avoid off-brands that may be second or third quality. Check the reputation of the firm with the Better Business Bureau.

Group Purchases and Grocery Co-ops

A group of individuals can band together to purchase large quantities of food from the grocery wholesaler. This kind of a purchase can often results in a substantial savings.

The group can organize itself as a grocery co-op and arrange to purchase groceries on a regular basis. This cuts out the middle man and will save the members most of the middle man's markup.

Freight Salvage Outlets

Always compare prices. At some outlets, the prices charged are as high as or higher than the prices for the same articles in top condition at the local grocery store. Avoid any merchandise that looks shopworn or dented, rusted or watersoaked. These are signs of poor handling and poor storage conditions. And these signs may indicate that the item is at or near the end of its shelf life. Consult the yellow pages of the telephone book for the addresses of freight salvage outlets.

Grain Mills and Feed Stores

Good buys on grains can often be made at the grain mill or the feed store. Be sure to indicate to the salesperson that you want the grain for human consumption. This may make a difference in which product you buy.

Consult the yellow pages of the telephone book for addresses.

Wholesale Grocers

Many wholesale grocers will sell directly to the public if large quantities are ordered. Consult the yellow pages of the telephone directory.

Farmers

Buying directly from the farmer can save money and, at the same time, provide you with better quality merchandise than is available at the market. For a list of organic farmers and organic farming associations where you can do your shopping, send a stamped self-addressed envelope to:

> Reader Service Department
> Organic Gardening and Farming
> Emmaus, Pennsylvania 18049

To locate additional sources, ask the woman who cans, the small corner grocer, the county agricultural agent or the farmers' co-op. Consult the newspaper want-ads under produce. Drive through rural areas looking for farms that produce the foods that you want. Then talk to the farmer.

MANUFACTURERS AND SUPPLIERS
OF FREEZE-DRIED AND DEHYDRATED FOODS

KEY: (For those companies for which the information was available use the following key to the code that follows the company name. Omission of a code does not necessarily indicate that the category does not apply.)

DH -	dehydrated	No. 10 -	No. 10 cans available
FD -	freeze-dried	NA -	nitrogen atmosphere in cans
W -	wholesale	RO -	Sell to retailers only
R -	retail	WO -	Sell to wholesalers only
BP -	bulk pack	EO -	Sell through established outlets
I -	sell to individuals		only
G -	sell to groups		

CALIFORNIA

Sam-Andy
DH, FD, W, R, I, G, No. 10
Full line of low-moisture foods

P. O. Box 2125
(149 East Third St.)
Beaumont, Calif. 92223
Phone: (714) 845-1691

E.Y.F.S. Company
   BP
   Livermore, California

Wheat Kernel
   BP
   Stanton, Calif.

Bernard Food Industries
   DH, FD, W. R, No. 10, I, G
   Full line of low-moisture food for home use and storage.
   Individual serving packs and camp packs also available. Lots
   of variety. Only water needed to prepare any of the foods.

   Box 487
   San Jose, Calif. 95103

Vacu-dry Company
   DH, WO, RO, EO, BP, No. 10
   Low-moisture fruits and specialty food products

   P.O. Box 8277
   Emeryville, Calif. 94662

FLORIDA

Plant Industries
   FD, W, BP
   Sell to manufacturers and distributors and to buyers of
   $600.00 or more.

   1111 W. Haines St.
   Plant City, Florida 33566

ILLINOIS

Sokol and Co.
   DH, WO, BP, No. 10
   Solo Cake and Pasty Fillings

   5325 Dansher Rd.
   Countryside (La Grange), Ill. 60521

MASSACHUSETS

Eastern Food Storage Division
Stow-A-Way Industries

DH, FD, R, No. 10, NA, I, G

Stow-a-way Freeze-dried foods for campers, Mountain House Freeze-dried foods (pre-cooked) for campers and in No. 10 cans, backpacking and camping equipment (many items suitable for emergency supplies).

10% discount on orders of $100, 20% discount on orders of $300 or more.

166 Cushing Highway
Cohasset, Mass. 02025
Phone: (617) 383-9116

NEBRASKA

Wilson and Co.
DH, FD, W, R, BP, No. 10, NA, I, G,
Campsite low-moisture foods, sold in case lots only

27th and Y St.
Omaha, Nebraska 68107

OHIO

Glidden-Durkee
DH (onions, garlic), FD (chives, celery flakes, bell peppers), RO, WO

900 Union Commerce Bldg.
Cleveland, Ohio 44115
Phone: (216) 771-5121

OREGON

Oregon Freeze Dry Foods, Inc.
FD, RO, WO, EO, No. 10, NA
Manufacturer of Mountain House and Tea Kettle FD foods (Vegetables, fruits, meats, prepared entrees, and snacks)

P.O. Box 1048
Albany, Oregon 97321

TEXAS

The Right-Away Foods Company
FD, W, BP, No. 10, NA, G
Also available in flexible packaging

P.O. Box 184
Edinburg, Texas 78539

UTAH

Perma-Pak

DH, FD, W, R, BP, I, G, No. 10, NA
Full line of low-moisture foods

40 East Roberts Ave.
Salt Lake City, Utah 84115

For names and addresses of other companies consult the yellow pages of *Thomas Grocery Directory*, available at the public library.

SUPPLIERS AND MANUFACTURERS
OF EQUIPMENT AND SUPPLIES

Perma-Pak (see above)

Stow-a-way Industries (see page 66)

Stak-On International (can storage racks and cabinets)
P. O. Box 17075
Salt Lake City, Utah 84115

Barrels, Drums, and Plastic Pails

Consult the yellow pages of the telephone directory for local distributors.

69

CHAPTER VII

INVENTORY CONTROL

In order to be useful, any system of inventory control must be simple.

The method I prefer uses 3" x 5" or 5" x 7" index cards and a chart.

Make a card or cards for each food or category of foods, for example: vegetables, meats, non-food items, wheat.

Sample Card

Vegetables	Amount Needed	Amount Bought	Amount Still to Buy
Green Beans	26 cans	12	14
	(in pencil)		

The cards serve as a record of your total supply. To know how many of each item is used, so that they can be replaced, I use a chart. I have found both of the following methods satisfactory:

1. Tack up a piece of paper in the storeroom and hang a pencil near it. Each time an item is removed from storage, record it on the paper. Take the list with you to the store.

2. Make a list of all of the foods stored. Tack it to the storeroom wall and cover it with a piece of clear acetate. Each time an item is removed from storage, put a checkmark with a grease pencil or washable marking pen next to the appropriate entry on the chart. As the items are replaced, erase the check marks.

CHAPTER VIII

HOW TO STORE

Some General Information

- Store a good can opener to open canned foods.
- Date and label all items. Maintain an inventory and regularly rotate all foods that require it.
- Replace food as it is used.
- Use the food within the recommended storage life.
- Inspect regularly for signs of rust, spoilage, moisture damage, heat or freezing damage, insect or rodent infestation.

For all the foods listed, remember the general storage conditions outlined in Chapter Four.

Ascorbic Acid Compounds for Use in Canning

Store in airtight containers in a cool, dark, place. These products will cake if they absorb moisture. They can be broken up and pulverized or dissolved in the container, if they become hard. Never store any product to which you have added water. Rotate every one or two years.

Baking Powder, Baking Soda

Store double-acting baking powder. Store soda and baking powder in glass or metal containers. If kept cool and dry they should keep indefinitely.

Beans, Peas, Lentils, Rice, Soybeans

These foods store best in moisture-proof, rigid containers such as metal, fiber or plastic barrels. They can be stored in sacks, however.

A fumigant is generally not needed in these products. They should be watched for any signs of insect infestation, nonetheless.

Store beans in a cool, dry place.

If these are stored in sacks, stack them alternately with sacks of sugar on wooden pallets. This will help to reduce the chance of insect infestation.

These foods have a long shelf life. They have been successfully kept for as long as twenty years. However, after one or two years many of them will lose their ability to germinate. They will become drier with age and may require special handling in cooking.

Beans may be planted in the garden if they are not too old to germinate.

Dried peas, split or whole, green or yellow, can be used interchangeably. However, only whole peas will sprout.

Lentils are a very nutritious legume. Like beans, they are high in protein and low in fat. They are rich in minerals, iron, calcium, phosphorus and B vitamins and they contain some vitamin A.

Small amounts of animal proteins such as meat, cheese or milk should be added to the diet in addition to beans or lentils to satisfy the body's complete protein needs.

Sprouted beans, peas or lentils are a rich source of vitamin C. Sprouting will reduce the gassy effect of beans.

Soybeans are very versatile. They do not produce gas as much as other beans do.

Kinds of beans and Their Common Uses:

White: Marrow, Great Northern, Navy, Pea Beans - Baked
Pinto: These are speckled - served in stews and chili
Kidney: Red or white varieties - chili, soups, salads
Limas: Large, small or Calico (speckled) - combine with meat or corn
Red Beans: Chili
Black-eye or Yellow-eye: Hoppin John
Chick Pea or Garbanzo: Salads, stews, soups or pureed for dips
Black or Turtle: Soups
Cranberry Beans: Like pintos, only these have pink markings - succotash

Rice: Store only white rice. Because of the high fat content of brown rice it becomes rancid within a short time.

Bouillon Cubes, Soup Mixes, Gravy Mixes

Keep cool and dry. Protect from insects. Rotate after one year.

Canned Foods (except meat)

Definitely rotate your supply of canned goods so that no cans are older than one or two years. This will result in maximum nutrition and quality. Do not discard cans of food that have exceeded their recommended storage life. They will usually still be edible, but perhaps not as palatable as fresh canned goods.

It is safe to leave canned foods in the opened can in the refrigerator. Acid foods will dissolve some of the iron from the can, turning the inside of the can black. This is harmless, but may cause a metalic taste.

The law prohibits use of food containers that would transfer a poisonous or harmful substance to the food in the can. A discoloration on the inside of the freshly opened can is usually the result of the action of the sulfur in the food on the metal of the can. This is harmless.

Cans that are leaking or bulged should be discarded. Rust on the outside of the can is harmless. Any can that has rusted through should be discarded.

Inspect cans for signs of rust, regularly. Use the food as soon as possible, if rust is found, in order to avoid having the can rust through and spoil the food. Correct any moisture problems that are causing rusting.

To help prevent cans from rusting: Paint the entire can with varnish or oil-based, lead-free paint.

Badly dented cans, especially if dented near the seam, may have lost their seal. Therefore, never store dented cans.

Home canned foods or other foods stored in glass jars should be stored in the dark to avoid deterioration of the contents.

Fruits and Vegetables

"Only small losses of vitamin C, about 10%, occur when these foods [canned fruits and vegetables] are stored for a year at 65° F. When the temperature is 80°, losses may reach 25 percent in one year. Canned citrus juices hold vitamin C especially well. Carotene, a precurser of vitamin A, is well retained in canned fruits and vegetables. Losses average only about 10% in a year when cans are stored at 80° F. Canned tomato juice, a particularly stable, year-round source of carotene, shows no loss of this nutrient. Thiamine in canned fruits and vegetables is well retained when stored for one year at 65° F. When stored at 80° for one year, losses may increase to 15 percent in canned fruits, and 25 percent in canned vegetables . . . Losses accelerate at higher temperatures."[1]

Cans should be inverted every six months to redistribute the solids in the liquid.

Canned Soups

Store 6 to 8 months. The starches in some soups deteriorate

[1]U.S. Dept. of Agriculture, *Conserving the Nutritive Value in Foods,* Home and Garden Bulletin No. 90, (Washington, D.C.: U.S. Government Printing Office, 1963), pages 8-9.

rapidly. The storage life of cream soups can be extended if they are inverted every 30 days to redistribute solids. Shake the cans before opening. Other soups should be inverted at the end of 6 months.

Canned Juices

See table for storage life. Invert every 30 days to maintain quality.

Cereals and Cereal Products

These products must be protected from moisture, odors and insects. Generally, they should be kept in rigid, moisture-proof containers. They store best in a cool, dark place.

Flour

Store only that amount of flour that you will use in a year. Old flour takes on an off-flavor. The longer flour is stored, the more apt it is to become infested with insects.

Flour loses only slight amounts of nutrients on storage.

Store flour in airtight, metal or plastic cans. Seal the lids well. Bread made from freshly milled flour is ordinarily inferior in volume, grain and texture to bread made from the same flour after a period of aging. Aging for a certain period improves the action of the gluten in the flour. Longer aging leads to a deterioration in the action of the gluten.[2]

If flour takes on an off-flavor from long storage, sifting several times to aerate will improve the flavor.

Whole wheat flour can become stale very quickly because of the high fat content. It loses only small amounts of nutrients under ordinary storage conditions. It is best to purchase or mill whole wheat flour in small amounts that will be used within a few weeks. It should be stored in the refrigerator or freezer. The colder it is kept, the longer it will remain fresh. Whole wheat flour has the best flavor when ground just before using. Such fresh flour often makes a crumbly bread, however.

Wheat Germ

Wheat germ for storage should be purchased in vacuum sealed jars and stored in a cool place. Because of the vacuum seal the freshness is prolonged. If frozen, wheat germ will remain fresh for quite a

---

[2]J. A. Anderson and A. W. Alcock, eds., *Storage of Cereal Grains and Their Products,* Monograph Series, Vol. II, (St. Paul, Minnesota: American Assn. of Cereal Chemists, 1954.)

long time. On the shelf it will store for about 1 year, if kept cool and unopened. After opening it will store for about 6 months in the refrigerator or 1 month on a cupboard shelf.

Pasta

Pasta can be stored indefinitely if kept cool and dry and protected from insects.

Cake, Muffin, Pancake, Cookie and Pastry Mixes

Those mixes containing eggs or fat should be used up within 12 months to insure freshness. The boxes and bags that mixes are packaged in provide little protection against insects and moisture. If mixes will not be used within a few days of purchase, it is a good idea to put them into insect-proof containers. Sometimes insects are brought into the home hidden either in the packaging or the contents of pre-mixed foods. Mixes are generally not meant to be stored for extended periods. Those mixes packaged in No. 10 cans and sold by low-moisture food distributors have a longer shelf life. Consult your distributor.

Store mixes in a cool, dry, dark place.

Cornmeal

Cornmeal is available in several forms. It is ground from white or yellow corn. The yellow cornmeal has slightly more nutritional value. The major difference between the two is that white cornmeal contains only a trace of vitamin A, while yellow cornmeal contains 610 international units per cup of dry meal.

Types of cornmeal:
   grits - the coarsest grind
   cornmeal - finer than grits
   corn flour - the finest grind

Grits are often used as a vegetable or starch in meals or as a cereal. Cornmeal is a versatile cereal product that stores well. The enriched degermed meal should be stored. For best results, store for no more than one year.

Whole Dried Corn

Any whole grain stores longer than the milled grain product. Corn will store at least 5 years and probably longer. It should be kept in a rigid insect-proof container. Fumigation is not necessary. Whole corn can be sprouted to eat, or the corn can be planted. Long storage will affect the ability to germinate. Corn will usually germinate for two years after harvest.

Wheat

Wheat is an important staple in the storage program. Because of its versatility large amounts should be stored. It can be cooked whole, cracked, or as bulgar. It can be ground into flour for baking, sprouted for use as greens, planted and allowed to mature. Wheat can be used at any meal. Made into gluten, flour can replace meat.

Important: If you plan to use your wheat for flour, purchase a *good quality stone* wheat grinder. Do not waste your money on a cheap metal grinder. Cheap metal grinders leave metal flakes in your flour. These metal flakes can cause intestinal disturbances and even lead to ulcers. If you purchase a metal grinder, buy the kind that has steel cutters, such as those found in electric coffee mills. You will need to purchase the special pulverizing blades for an electric coffee mill. It is advisable also to have some means of converting your electric mill to manual use in case of a power failure. The electric mill will be the most effortless means of grinding or cracking your wheat. Electric mills are quite expensive, however.

If you already have an inexpensive metal grinder, investigate the possibility of converting it to a stone grinder.

Store only hard winter or spring wheat that has a moisture content of 10% or less. Insects have a hard time reproducing in such wheat. Turkey Red, Cheyenne, and Marquis are desirable varieties. Marquis is a hard spring variety. Your wheat should be No. 1 grade, that is, not less than 60 pounds per bushel and with a protein content of 11.5% or better. The wheat should be cleaned and fumigated.

Wheat needs to be protected from insects, rodents and moisture. It should be stored in sealed cans or barrels that will support its weight.

Wheat will absorb odors and take on off-flavors. Therefore, it is important to store wheat away from any odor-producing substances, especially paint and kerosene.

A good container for wheat is a 50 gallon steel drum with a tight-fitting lid. Near the bottom on the side of the drum, make an opening with a metal cover that can be slid aside to allow the wheat to flow out of the opening, as needed. Be sure that the cover over the opening fits tightly enough to prevent the entry of insects. Set the drum up on 18" concrete blocks for ease in dispensing. Fresh wheat is added at the top as the wheat is used, thus creating a constant rotation of the wheat.

1/2 pound of wheat provides the following nutrients:

- 30 grams protein
- 1 mg. thiamine
- 8 mg. niacin
- 6 mg. iron
- a trace of riboflavin

Amount to store: The amount that you decide to store will depend on the uses that you intend to make of it. For use as cereal and for baking in a normal diet, about 175 pounds would be adequate for an adult. If wheat is to be the major part of the diet, about 300 to 400 pounds per adult and about 70 pounds per child will be needed.

For an adequate and balanced diet based on wheat, an adult will need to consume daily: 1 pound of wheat, 1 quart non-fat milk, 1-1/2 ounces of honey and salt, as desired, plus some source of vitamin C, such as sprouted wheat or vitamin tablets.

Wheat Dispenser

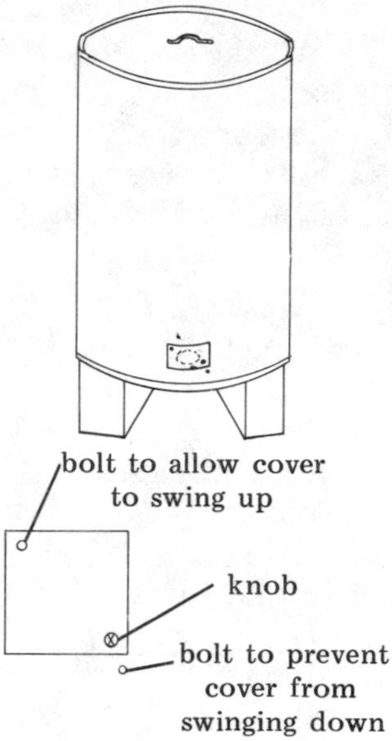

bolt to allow cover to swing up

knob

bolt to prevent cover from swinging down

Detail of Cover for Opening

Figure 8.1

Never store wheat where it will pick up moisture. Moisture encourages insect activity which in turn encourages heating of the wheat. This leads to the growth of bacteria and fungi which will spoil the wheat.

In moist climates, a sack of salt should be placed in the center of each wheat container to absorb moisture. Moisture-proof containers and fumigation are essential in moist areas.

After fumigation and storage in moisture-proof containers, wheat should require no further attention, if stored in a cool, dry place. Wheat stored in sacks or under adverse conditions should be examined regularly for insects. It should be turned and aerated every 6 months to keep the moisture content at the proper level. A convenient method for doing this is to shake the sack then place the vacuum cleaner hose on the blower end of the vacuum cleaner and blow air through the wheat.

Fumigation is essential for wheat. Remember that if the container in which you are storing your wheat is not insect-proof, the wheat may need refumigation at intervals to keep it insect-free. (For methods of fumigation, see chapter twelve.)

One method of fumigating wheat is to heat it. Wheat so treated will not sprout, and the quality of baked goods made of the flour ground from such wheat may be severely affected. The wheat is still good for many other uses, however. If necessary this flour can be mixed with other flour and used for baking.

Never throw out wheat that has become infested with insects. They will, in fact, add protein to your diet. In our culture we are not accustomed to eating insects. However, many peoples of this world eat insects as a regular part of their diet. If the idea of eating insects seems repulsive to you, there will probably be someone nearby who will use what you will not. If you are really hungry, those bugs may not seem so bad to you, after all.

However, do not let an insect infestation go uncorrected. The longer you wait, the worse the problem becomes.

Low temperature leads to inactivity in insects and inactivity leads to death from starvation. Therefore, the lower the storage temperature of wheat, the better. Most insects become active at about 48° F. A grain temperature of 70° F. is considered to be the danger line. At that temperature or higher, severe damage to stored grain from insects may be expected, whereas below this temperature level no serious damage is likely to occur.

The bread-baking quality of wheat improves with storage up to 4 or 5 years, then slowly deteriorates. Freshly-harvested wheat makes the least desirable bread.

Cheese

Cheese may be stored in any of these forms:
> dry, grated
> cheese spreads in jars and boxes
> brick cheese - cheddar, Swiss, etc.
> soft cheese - ricotta, cottage cheese, cream cheese

Many cheeses may be frozen. Experiment to see if your favorite brand freezes well. Do not freeze cheese spreads packed in jars because the jars will break. Soft cheeses and cheese spreads do not usually freeze well because of their high water content. However, even these soft cheeses may be frozen in an emergency. They should be used in cooked dishes after thawing. Uncreamed cottage cheese or farmer's cheese will freeze satisfactorily.

Some brick cheeses become crumbly after freezing and others remain unaffected.

Freezing will not kill molds. It will slow them down, however.

Dry, grated cheeses may be frozen if protected from moisture. If they absorb moisture, they will cake. These cheeses may be stored on the shelf in a cool, dry place for about 6 months.

To freeze cheese, wrap well in plastic or foil to prevent drying and absorption of odors. Store for 1 to 2 years.

Cheese spread in jars keeps for several months on the shelf. If packaged in boxes, these spreads may be stored for limited periods on the shelf in a cool, dry place. For longer storage, refrigerate. Because of high water content these cheeses mold easily.

To store brick cheeses: Wrap the cheese in a cloth that has been soaked in vinegar and allowed to dry. The vinegar will retard mold and the cheese will not need to be rewrapped for 6 to 8 months. To prevent drying, dip the cheese in parafin or wrap in foil or heavy plastic.

When brick cheese is in current use, a thick coating of butter spread on the cut end will prevent drying.

Mold on cheese is not harmful and can be eaten if you do not mind the musty taste. Otherwise, wash the cheese with water to remove the mold and pat dry. This will only remove the mold. It will not prevent regrowth.

Keep all cheeses cool and dry. Storage at 35° F. will preserve the cheese longest without freezing.

Cottage cheeses will store about 1 week in the refrigerator. Cream cheese will keep about two weeks.

Cocoa and Chocolate

Store at 60 to 70 degrees, away from heat and in glass, plastic, or metal containers. Keep the containers tightly capped. Cocoa will lump if it absorbs moisture. A grey film will form on chocolate that has been exposed to heat. The film is some of the cocoa butter that has separated out; it is harmless.

Dutch process cocoa has been treated with alkali to remove the acids.

Corn Syrup, Molasses and Maple Syrup

Store these products in tightly-capped jars in a cool, dark place. Corn syrup can become moldy after opening when stored at room temperature. Refrigerate these products after opening.

Types of corn syrup:

Light corn syrup - has sugar, salt and vanilla added

Dark corn syrup - has refiners' syrup added for a dark color

Dark and light corn syrups can be used interchangeably except in light candies and baked goods where the dark syrup would give the product a dark color.

Unsulfured molasses is best for storing. Sulfur gives molasses a bitter taste. Blackstrap molasses "is defined as the 'dark, thick syrup remaining after the economic exhaustion of crystaline sugar.' It is the third extraction frequently called the 'dregs from sugar making!'" "The first and second extractions of molasses have slightly less mineral content, and are much more palatable than blackstrap."[3]

Molasses will keep 5 years or more.

Dried Foods

Dried foods should not be confused with dehydrated or low-moisture foods. Dried foods have had some of the moisture, about 75%, removed as a method of preservation. They are such foods as raisins, apricots, apples, and dates which can be purchased at the retail grocer. They are usually sold in plastic or cellophane bags or in boxes. They are soft and moist to the touch.

Store in airtight, rigid, plastic, metal or glass containers, in a cool, dry, dark place. If kept cool and dry, dried fruit will keep at least 5 years. Oxidation in dried fruits turns them dark. (See Low-Moisture Foods) In warm, humid climates, dried fruits will become moldy. They should be refrigerated to avoid this. Sometimes, particularly after long storage, the fruits will become sugary. This does not harm the fruit. Dried fruit can be stored in the freezer, if properly wrapped.

Dried fruits that become hard can be softened by soaking overnight in lukewarm water or they may be stewed. A cut apple placed in the container will help to soften them. Keep the container tightly closed to prevent drying out.

Fruits and vegetables dried at home may not keep as long as those that are commercially processed and chemically treated. Store home-dried vegetables up to eight months. Home-dried carrots, onions and cabbage store well for only a short time.[4]

Dry Yeast

Dry yeast will keep its leavening ability up to 5 years under proper storage conditions. Yeast will keep longest if left in its unopened, vacuum-sealed jar or can. Foil-packaged yeast is not recommended for storage. Yeast should be stored in a cool, dry place. The freezer is an excellent place to store it. Keep yeast tightly capped.

---

[3]Edna Miller, *Facts About Food and Nutrition*, Utah State University, Extension Circular No. 302 (Logan, Utah), p. 25.

[4]W.V. Creuss, Hilda Faust and Vera Greaves Mrak, *Home Drying of Vegetables and Fruits*, University of California Agricultural Extension Service Bulletin (Berkeley, California) p. 5.

Do not try to store compressed yeast cakes. They may be frozen, but they will not keep as long as dried yeast. Compressed yeast has no advantage over dry yeast.

Dried eggs

Dried eggs are produced by removing 90% or more of the water from fresh eggs. They are available as whole egg solids, egg white solids, egg yolk solids and in various blends. They are also available as freeze-dried, pre-mixed dishes, such as scrambled eggs.

Many of these products make good-tasting scrambled eggs and omelets. When good quality dried eggs are used in baked goods, the results are as satisfactory as with fresh eggs.

Eggs can harbor the food poisoning organism, salmonella. Some dried eggs are pasteurized to sterilize them. These products may be used for making scrambled eggs, omelets and other dishes in which the eggs are not thoroughly cooked. If eggs are not pasteurized, use only in thoroughly-cooked dishes. Scrambled eggs may be made from them if they are made in small batches and cooked dry.

Store dried eggs at 50º or below. They keep best when refrigerated. They may be stored for about one year, if kept cool.

After opening, they should be refrigerated and kept tightly capped.

If an off-flavor develops, dried eggs can still be used in baked goods, especially highly-flavored ones.

Quick mixes made with powdered eggs should be stored in a cool place, tightly capped. They can be stored for about 6 months. They will keep best in the refrigerator.

1 pound of egg powder = 32 to 36 whole medium eggs.

2 1/2 tablespoons egg powder + 2 1/2 tablespoons water = 1 egg.

Fresh Eggs

Method One - Refrigeration: Store in the refrigerator for up to 6 weeks. Store in the original container and do not wash the eggs. They have been lightly coated with mineral oil to retard evaporation of moisture from the eggs. As the eggs age, the white becomes watery and the eggs are less satisfactory for some uses.

Method Two - Freezing: Break the eggs and separate the yolks and whites. To whole eggs, add 1 teaspoon salt or 1 tablespoon sugar or corn syrup to each 2 cups of eggs. To egg yolks, add 2 teaspoons salt or 2 tablespoons sugar or corn syrup to each 2 cups of yolks. Nothing needs to be added to the whites.

Package in jars or plastic containers with tight-fitting lids, leaving

1" head space. Seal and label with the number of eggs in the container. Freeze at 0° F. or below. Frozen eggs can be stored for 6 to 8 months.

They should be thawed before using by placing the container in a pan of cold water and letting it thaw slowly. Refrigerate after thawing and use within 12 hours.

A convenient method of freezing eggs would be to freeze them in ice cube trays. Measure the eggs so that each cube will contain one or two eggs. Store in plastic containers or heavy plastic bags in the freezer. Remove only the amount needed at one time.

2 tbsp. egg white − white of one egg.
1 tbsp. egg yolk = yolk of one egg.

Method Three - Water Glass: Place the whole, unwashed, unbroken eggs in plastic pails or parafined wooden kegs. Mix sodium silicate as directed on the package. Sodium silicate may be obtained at the drugstore. Pour sodium silicate solution over the eggs. Cover the eggs completely. One quart of sodium silicate will store 18 dozen eggs. Place a lid on the container and store at 50° F. or below. Eggs packed this way will store for 9 to 12 months. The solution can be re-used if uncontaminated.

Evaporated Milk, Canned Liquid Baby Formulas and Condensed Milk

Recommended storage period for these products is no more than 6 months. They will keep up to about 3 years. The cans should be inverted every 30 days to help prevent separation. If the milk separates or becomes lumpy it is still usable. Shake the can well before opening. As the milk ages, it will darken. This is not harmful, but will affect the taste.

Fats, Shortening and Peanut Butter

Brown and green glass will keep these products fresh longer than clear glass. If vacuum packed in cans and treated with an anti-oxidant, they will keep for many years. Anti-oxidants are added to oils, fats, and peanut butter to retard oxidation and thus delay rancidity. Moisture and air encourage rancidity. Once opened, fats should be used as soon as possible. Whenever possible, keep these products in the original, unopened containers. Fats and oils in partially-filled containers will keep longer if transferred to smaller containers in which there is little or no air space. Light hastens deterioration of these products.

Fats can be melted and poured hot into sterile jars and sealed. They will keep from 5 to 8 years in a cool place.

Recommended storage period for these products if treated with an anti-oxidant is 1 year. They will keep, under good storage conditions, for about 3 years.

Most fats melt at 95 degrees and heat hastens rancidity. Store fats in a cool, dark place. After opening, store in the refrigerator.

Oil may become cloudy at low temperatures. This is harmless and the cloudiness will disappear when the oil is warmed to room temperature.

Whole peanuts will store better than peanut butter. They can be made into peanut butter in the blender. Store peanuts in the freezer for longest freshness.

Rancid peanuts and peanut butter can be made more palatable by baking in a 150° F. oven for about 20 minutes. Spread them out on a pan before baking.

If lard is rendered at home be sure that all the moisture is boiled off before packing it in sterile jars. To test, place a lid on the pot. If moisture condenses on the under side of the lid, the lard needs further rendering.

Fresh Fruits and Vegetables

These foods can be stored in the basement, in root cellars or pits, or in unheated garages. They need to be protected from freezing and dehydration. Nutrients are lost as these foods wither. For information on root cellars, consult the sources listed in the *Readiness Library* (page 256). See information on trenches and pits at the end of this chapter.

Handle gently to prevent bruising. Sort before storing and remove any bruised or decayed fruits or vegetables. Inspect often.

Tomatoes, Cucumbers, Summer Squash, and Other Vine-ripened Vegetables

Pack in dry sand in the basement or garage. They will store for several weeks. Green tomatoes should never be refrigerated. Keep them out of direct sunlight and away from heat.

Cabbage

Store heads down in a trench in the garden or in a root cellar. Cabbage keeps well in the refrigerator. Do not allow to dry out.

Oranges and Other Citrus Fruits

Keep in a hydrator in the refrigerator or in a milk can with the cover placed on loosely. Store in a cool place. Storage at 60 to 70 degrees is best, but they will keep longer if kept cooler.

Green-tipped oranges are ripe.

Apples

Store them in a garage or root cellar. In the garage, they should be left in their box. Place the box inside a larger box and insulate the space between the two boxes with straw or crumpled newspaper. Insulate the top and throw an old blanket over the whole thing. Best storage temperature is about 35º F.

If you have room in the refrigerator, apples will store well in plastic bags. Always poke several holes in the bags to allow the apples to breathe.

Firm apples store best. Do not plan to store soft apples.

Garlic

Store in an open jar in the refrigerator.

Carrots, Parsnips, Beets, Turnips, and Other Root Vegetables

Wash, cut off the tops leaving 1". Place in a covered milk can. Leave the cover on loosely. Store at about 32º F. for best results. Sprouting and rooting indicate too high a storage temperature. Young carrots resist rooting and sprouting longer than more mature carrots.

These vegetables can be stored in a root cellar or in a box of dry sand in a cool place. They can also be mulched with a foot or more of straw to prevent freezing and be left in the ground to be dug as needed. If the ground freezes even under a mulch, these vegetables should be dug while the ground still can be worked.

Onions

Onions store best in mesh bags that let the air circulate freely around them. Let the tops die before digging and then allow them to dry thoroughly before storing. Hang them on a nail in the garage until the temperature in the garage dips below freezing. Then hang them in a cool basement room. Check occasionally for spoiled or soft onions. Remove those and discard. Store from October to May at the longest. Sprouted onions may be planted in the spring and allowed to go to seed, or they can be used for eating or cooking. The tops are good in salads.

Onions may be chopped and frozen. Freezing makes them less potent in flavor. Use them for cooking after thawing because they will be soft.

Onions can be chopped or sliced, then dried. Dehydrated onions store for 5 years or more.

Winter Squash and Pumpkins

Allow the vines to die before picking. Harden the squash by exposure to a temperature of about 75 to 80 degrees for a few days. Then store in a cool, dry place. Best storage temperature is 50 to 60 degrees. Do not refrigerate.

Potatoes

Store in perforated plastic bags or burlap sacks on slats of wood on the floor of an unheated basement room from October to May.

Keep potatoes cool but avoid storage below 40º F. for long periods. Cold storage turns the starch in the potatoes to sugar and makes them taste sweet. Storage at room temperature for a few days will remove the sweet taste. Best storage temperature is 45 to 50 degrees. High temperature causes shriveling and encourages sprouting.

Light turns potatoes green and gives them a bitter taste. Remove the sprouts as they form. The sprouts use the food energy stored in the potato for growth and cause the potato to shrivel and eventually to become worthless.

Potatoes may also be stored in a root cellar, garden pit or in a box of sand in a cool basement.

Store a few apples with potatoes to discourage sprouting.

Eggplant, Rutabagas, and Sweet Potatoes

Store at 50 to 60 degrees.

Gelatin Dessert and Pudding Mixes

These products must be kept cool, dry and insect-free. They should be stored in glass or metal. Gelatin can be stored about two years. Puddings should be used within one or two years.

Plain gelatin can be flavored with soft drink mix powder or fruit juice.

Honey

If the moisture content of honey is 18% or below, and the honey is unpasteurized, the honey will crystallize rapidly. Crystalline honey will keep indefinitely. Commercially-packed honey has been pasteurized to prevent it from crystallizing for at least one year. It may also have water added up to the legal limit of 20% moisture content.

Raw, strained honey has the highest nutritive value. If allergies are a problem in your family, only small amounts of this unfiltered honey should be consumed until it is determined that a reaction does not result from the pollen in the honey.

Since it is difficult to use honey that has crystallized in a large container, honey should be stored in small containers. Pint or quart jars are convenient to use. Crystallized honey can be liquified by placing the open jar in a pan of warm water. The honey can be used in its crystalline state in many recipes.

To prevent recrystallization of honey, add 2 tablespoons of Karo syrup to each quart of liquified honey. Keep tightly capped.

Honey has fewer calories than sugar, yet honey tastes sweeter than sugar. Therefore, less honey is needed for sweetening.

Honey should be packed in glass or stoneware, never plastic or metal, for long-term storage. The acids and enzymes in the honey can cause undesirable reactions with plastic or metal containers. Store honey in a cool, dry place. Keep it tightly capped and protected from light. Honey loses flavor rapidly if stored at 75º F. or above. Honey will become dark and strong-flavored with age. This does not render the honey useless. Refrigeration helps to prevent mold and fermentation in liquid honey.

The cap on molasses and honey jars will not stick as easily is you rub a little salad oil around the rim and on the jar threads before pouring anything from the jar. Always wipe off any drips before replacing the cap.

Jam and Jelly

It is important to store these in a cool, dark place to preserve their quality. For extended storage, two-piece metal lids are recommended. Parafin seals tend to loosen with changes in temperature. As jam and jelly ages it will darken, especially if stored at too high a temperature. This darkening is not harmful. Jam or jelly that has sugared is usable. If you do not like the sugary texture, stir in an equal amount of water and heat to dissolve the sugar. Use as a pancake syrup or dessert topping. Mold that forms on top of jelly or jam is not harmful. Remove the mold from the surface or it will flavor the product.

Store jams and jellies in the refrigerator after opening.

Low-Moisture Foods

Low-moisture foods have been dehydrated to remove 90 to 98% of the moisture. These include the dehydrated or freeze-dried foods. These products are hard, shriveled and dry. Dehydrated potatoes, macaroni and dried beans are probably the most familiar of these foods. A wide variety of foods are available, preserved in this manner.

Low-moisture foods are frequently sold in No. 10 cans. They should be kept in a cool, dry place. Many of these products will keep indefinitely, if unopened. Consult your distributor for specific storage information about the products that you purchase. See the table on pages 88 - 92 for a partial list of products and their storage lives.

It is usually most suitable to leave these cans in their original cartons and stack the cartons on wooden pallets. Label and date each can and also label and date the outside of the carton so that you can tell at a glance what is in each carton.

Oxidation will sometimes take place in unopened cans. The food will darken when this occurs. There is some loss of nutrients due to oxidation, but the food can still be eaten even if it has turned completely black. The flavor may change as oxidation progresses. Many manufacturers are now injecting an inert gas into the can to retard oxidation. Ask your supplier about this. He will be able to tell you which of his products have been treated in this manner.

Oxidation and moisture absorption will occur after the can has been opened. To prolong the shelf life of the opened product, cover the can with a tight-fitting lid or place the contents in a canister or jar with a tight lid. For best results, use the product within one year after opening.

Any foods with a high fat content, such as whole milk solids, powdered infant formula, butter solids, or powdered eggs, should be refrigerated after opening to preserve flavor and they should be used up as quickly as possible.

Never let opened cans sit, unused, on the shelf. You are inviting waste.

Moisture absorption may cause the opened product to cake. Break the chunks apart or soak them in water when you are ready to use the food. Powdered products that cake can be pulverized with a hammer or ground up in a grinder or blender. A cut apple placed in the top of the can may soften some caked powdered items. This adds more moisture, however, and may necessitate using up the remainder of the product as soon as possible in order to avoid spoilage.

To reduce moisture absorption, place a cloth bag of rice, salt, silica gel or activated charcoal in the top of the can. Remove the bag occasionally and dry it out in the oven at a low temperature. When cool, replace.

Check your plastic lids occasionally to make sure they are tightly sealed and not split. Insects and moisture can get into the food if the lid is not tight.

Low-moisture foods are frequently packed in heavy-duty cans that will resist rusting and will not dent easily. Cans are sometimes coated too prevent rusting. If you plan to store unenameled cans for long periods, paint the entire outside surface with varnish or lead-free oil-base paint. Make frequent checks for signs of rust.

Margarine or Butter

If packed in sealed cans and kept cool, margarine will keep for quite a long time. Consult your supplier for recommended length of storage.

If tightly wrapped, butter or margarine can be frozen for 1 year. In the original package it can be frozen for about two months. It may also be stored in the refrigerator for about two weeks.

To store these products on the shelf, heat just enough to melt. Separate the fat from the solids and seal the fat in sterile jars, while hot. Store in a cool dark place for up to 1 year. Use the solids in cooking. Do not store the solids.

Exposure to heat and light hastens rancidity in butter and margarine.

Butter powder is available through suppliers of low-moisture foods. Consult your supplier for the recommended storage period.

Meats

Canned Meats

Like all canned foods, canned meats should be stored in a cool, dry place. A temperature of about 40° F. to 60° F. is best. Some canned meats require refrigeration. The label will indicate if refrigeration is needed. Meats requiring refrigeration are not intended for long-term storage.

After opening, canned meats should be treated like fresh meats. Home-canned meats have a recommended shelf life of 1 year. Commercially canned meat can be kept longer. (See chart on pages 95 - 96)

Some thiamine is lost during storage. Up to 30% may be lost in six months' storage, especially at high temperatures.

Read Labels: The product labeled gravy and meat is mostly gravy. Meat and gravy is mostly meat.

Fresh Meat

How to judge spoilage:

1. Use your nose. Spoiled meat has an off-odor.
2. Color change from bright red to pale pink or dull brown-grey indicates loss of freshness.
3. A slippery surface on meat in the unopened package in-

dicates spoilage. Fresh meats will keep from 1 to 7 days in the refrigerator. They should be stored in the coldest part of the refrigerator. Loosen the wrapping around the meat. Consult a good cookbook or USDA Bulletin, *Storing Perishable Foods in the Home*, for further information. Chopped or sliced meats should be kept no more than one or two days. A meat keeper drawer in the refrigerator will keep most meats fresh at least a week.

Frozen Meat

Freeze the meat as quickly as possible and be sure to wrap it properly for freezing. Freeze only fresh, sound meat. Freezing will not improve the quality of the meat stored. Do not put large quantities of unfrozen food into the freezer at one time. If the food is not frozen quickly, deterioration or spoilage may result. For proper methods of freezing, see *Use Your Freezer* (page 136) or consult *Putting Food By*, listed in the Readiness Library on page 257.

Store frozen meat at 0° F. or lower.

Length of Storage for Frozen Meat[5]
(in freezer wrapping)

Beef	(roasts and steaks)	12 months
Ground Beef		3 months
Lamb.	(roasts)	12 months
	(patties)	4 months
Veal	(cutlets, chops)	6 months
	(roasts)	8 months
Fresh Pork		8 months
Chicken	(cut-up)	6 months
	(whole)	12 months
Turkey		6 months
Smoked meats and sausage		2 months
Cooked meats		3 months
Cooked chicken or turkey	(and gravy)	6 months
Fried chicken		3 months

[5]U.S. Dept. of Agriculture, *Home Care of Purchased Frozen Foods*, Home and Garden Bulletin No. 69, 1960, p. 3.

Bacon

Bacon should be stored in the refrigerator. It should be eaten within a week to ensure best quality. Mold that forms on bacon is not harmful. Simply scrape it off before it flavors the meat. Canned bacon can be stored on the shelf, unless the label indicates that refrigeration is needed. Refrigerate after opening. Rancid bacon should be discarded.

Jerky

Jerky is meat that has been cut into thin strips, seasoned, smoked and then dried to remove most of the water. Four pounds of fresh meat will make about one pound of jerky. This product may be stored in a cool, dark place and needs no refrigeration. Any fat in the meat will eventually turn rancid, but jerky can be stored for several years, if kept cool. Even if the fat does become rancid, the meat is still edible. Jerky should be stored in airtight jars.

Nuts

Shelled nuts are best for storage because they require less space than nuts in the shell. Shelled nuts can be canned, frozen or refrigerated for storage. To freeze, place the nut-meats in heavy plastic bags and seal. They will keep for 12 to 18 months. Salted or roasted nuts should be frozen no longer than 3 months.

Store home canned nuts in a cool, dark, dry place. They will keep for several years. Commercially-canned nuts are usually vacuum-sealed and will store for several months. Unsalted and dry-roasted nuts seem to keep best.

Nuts can be refrigerated in jars, cans or plastic bags. They will keep for about 1 year.

Nuts can be stored on the shelf for short periods. Cool temperatures retard rancidity.

If nuts become rancid, the flavor can be improved by baking in a 150° F. oven for 20 to 25 minutes, in a shallow pan.

Pectin

This product is available in liquid and powder. The liquid pectin is packed in brown bottles and should be stored in the dark. Powdered pectin must be protected from moisture, insects and rodents. Store all pectin in a cool place and rotate every one or two years.

Powdered Milk

Store extra-grade, spray process, low-heat, low-moisture (4% or less) non-fat milk powder. This is a non-instant milk. Instant milk is more convenient to use, but it has a shorter shelf life. Many people prefer the taste of the non-instant milk.

Non-instant milk is usually mixed 3/4 cup powder to 1 quart of water. Instant milk is usually mixed 1-1/3 cups powder to 1 quart of water. One pound of either kind of milk makes 5 quarts.

Store milk in a cool, dry place away from odor-producing substances. Keep it in tightly closed containers at no higher than 75⁰ F.

If stored at:	It will keep:
40⁰ F.	36 to 60 months
70⁰ F.	12 to 24 months
90⁰ F.	3 months

When vacuum packed and kept cool, it will keep at least 5 years.

As powdered milk becomes old it darkens in color and develops an off-flavor. It is still edible, but will not be as palatable.

Whole milk solids will not keep for very long because of the fat content. They should be purchased in small quantities and stored in the refrigerator in a tightly-closed container. Powdered baby formulas are whole milk products and should be stored like whole milk solids.

Powdered buttermilk is a non-fat milk product so it should keep as well as non-fat milk.

Salt

In areas where iodine is deficient in the diet, iodized salt should be stored for eating. Iodized salt may turn yellow with age. This is caused by the iodine in the salt and is not harmful.

Table salt contains a dessicant to keep it free flowing.

For pickling, store pickling salt. This salt is non-iodized and has no dessicants added. It will absorb moisture and become caked.

Pack salt in glass or plastic containers. It will corrode some metals. Store it in a cool, dry place and keep it tightly covered. A few grains of rice placed in with the salt will prevent caking. Salt stored in the top of the wheat can will not cake, it the wheat is dry.

Salt will keep indefinitely.

Spices, Condiments and Flavorings

Spices should be stored in a cool, dry, dark place to prolong freshness. When spices become odorless or tasteless they should be discarded. Most spices can be stored about 1 or 2 years.

Catsup will oxidize and turn dark when stored on the shelf for long periods. This will result in a slight change in flavor but it is harmless. The cooler the temperature at which catsup is stored, the longer it will remain fresh. Refrigeration will prolong the storage period.

Mayonnaise and salad dressings should be stored like fats. Refrigerate after opening.

Mustard should be stored in a cool, dark place. It will remain fresh for a long time.

Flavorings must be kept tightly capped. They will become more concentrated due to evaporation.

Sugar

Beet and cane sugar are identical, chemically. They can be used interchangeably.

Types of sugar:

> Superfine sugar - very finely granulated sugar. It is especially good to use in making cakes. 1 cup superfine can replace 1 cup granulated.
>
> Granulated - also called white sugar.
>
> Powdered and confectioner's sugar - very fine powdery sugars, used in baking and frostings.
>
> Brown sugar - less refined than granulated; higher in some mineral elements than granulated. Dark brown sugar has a stronger flavor than light brown.
>
> Raw sugar - the least refined form of sugar. Contains one-fourth of the minerals found in brown sugar. Can be used in place of brown sugar.

Sugar must be protected from heat and moisture. Sugar will cake if it absorbs moisture. Under dry conditions, granulated and powdered sugars can be stored in the original package. If moisture is a problem, they should be repacked into moisture-proof containers. A cloth bag of salt, rice or silica gel placed in the top of the closed container will help to prevent caking.

Brown and raw sugars will store well if placed in a plastic bag inside a plastic or metal barrel with a tight fitting lid.

To remedy caked sugar: Sometimes tapping the container will loosen the contents adequately. A moistened paper towel or a cut apple placed in the top of the container will often do the trick. Placing the sugar in an open container in the refrigerator is another possible remedy. A brick of sugar can be pulverized with a hammer or mallet. If all else fails, place the hard sugar in water and make syrup out of it.

Vinegar

Vinegar will keep indefinitely if tightly capped and stored in a cool place. It may become more concentrated if allowed to evaporate.

Types of vinegars:

> Cider vinegar - made from apples; used in salad dressings, cooking, and pickling.
> White vinegar - distilled from cereal grains; used in salad dressings, cooking and for pickling.
> Wine vinegars - made from wine; used in salad dressings and marinades.

All vinegars can be used interchangeably. However, dark vinegars will darken pickles. Each type of vinegar has a distinct flavor.

Storing Vegetables And Fruits In Basements And Pits

(excerpts from *USDA Home and Garden Bulletin No. 119*)

You can store vegetables and fruits without refrigeration in basements, cellars, outbuildings and pits, but you need cool outside air to cool the stored products.

Storage Facilities

Storage facilities described in this publication are not practical unless you live in an area where outdoor temperatures during the winter average 30⁰ F. or lower.

House Basement

A well-ventilated basement under a house with central heating may be used for ripening tomatoes and for short-term storage of potatoes, sweet potatoes and onions.

But to store vegetables and fruits over winter (long-term storage) in a basement that has a furnace, you will need to partition off a room and insulate it. Build the room on the north or east side of the basement, if practicable, and do not have heating ducts or pipes running through it.

You need at least one window for cooling and ventilating the room. Two or more windows are desirable, particularly if the room is divided for separate storage of fruits and vegetables. Shade the windows in a way that will prevent light from entering the room.

Equip the room with shelves and removable slatted flooring. These keep vegetable and fruit containers off the floor and help circulation of the air. The flooring also lets you use water or wet materials (such as dampened sawdust) on the floor to raise the humidity in the room. Store vegetables and fruits in wood crates or boxes rather than in bins.

Cellar Under House Without Central Heat

Cellars under houses without central heat have long been used successfully for winter storage of fruits and vegetables in colder parts of the United States.

These cellars usually have an outside entrance and a dirt floor. The door is a means of ventilating the cellar and regulating the temperature. Some cellars have no windows. If there is a window, it aids in ventilating and in temperature control.

You need at least one window, if the cellar has separate compartments for vegetables and fruits. Shade the windows in a way that will prevent light from entering the cellar. Insulate the ceiling so that the cold air will not chill the house.

Pits

Cone-shaped outdoor pits are often used for storing potatoes, carrots, beets, turnips, salsify, parsnips and cabbage. (See Figure 8:2) They are sometimes used for storing winter apples and pears. The pit may be built on the ground, or in a hole 6 to 8 inches deep in a well-drained location. Build the pit as follows:

*Spread a layer of straw, leaves, or other bedding on the ground.
*Stack the vegetables or fruits on the bedding in a cone-shaped pile.
*Do not store vegetables and fruits in the same pit.
*Cover the vegetables or fruits with more bedding.
*Cover the entire pile with 3 or 4 inches of soil.
*Firm the soil with the back of a shovel to make the pit waterproof.
*Dig a shallow drainage ditch around the pit.

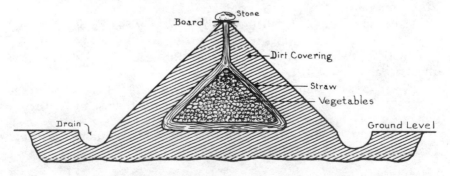

Cone-shaped Pit Showing Details Of Construction
Figure 8:2

Small pits containing only a few bushels of vegetables or fruits will get sufficient ventilation if you let the bedding material over the vegetables extend through the soil at the top of the pile. Cover the top of the pile with a board or piece of sheet metal to protect the stored products from rain. A stone will hold the cover in place.

To ventilate large pits, place two or three boards or stakes up through the center of the pile of vegetables or fruits to form a flue. Cap the flue with two pieces of board nailed together at right angles.

It is difficult to remove vegetables and fruits from cone-shaped pits in cold weather, and once a pit is opened its entire contents should be removed. For these reasons it is better to construct several small pits rather than one large one. Put a small quantity of different vegetables in each pit. This makes it necessary to open only one pit to get a variety of vegetables. When several vegetables are stored in the same pit, separate them with straw or leaves. Do not store apples and pears in vegetable pits.

Another type of pit is made simply of a barrel covered with several layers of straw and earth. (Lay the barrel on its side.)

Pits should be made in a different place every year. Leftovers in used pits usually are contaminated.

(Long, narrow pits can be made and it is not necessary to remove all the contents from these once the pit is opened. Simply open one end, remove the amount needed and close it back up.)

Maintenance

Keep storage facilities for vegetables and fruits clean. Get rid of vegetables and fruits that show signs of decay. At least once a year, remove all containers from your storeroom. Then clean them and air them in the sun. Wash and whitewash the walls and ceiling of your storeroom before you put the containers back into storage.

Regulate storage temperature by opening and closing doors, windows and other openings used as ventilators.

Without proper moisture, stored vegetables and fruits shrivel, lose quality, and eventually become unfit to eat.

Two ways of maintaining proper humidity are (1) the use of water to raise the humidity of the storage air, and (2) the use of ventilated polyethylene bags and box liners.

(For further information consult the USDA Bulletin, *Storing Vegetables and Fruits in Basements, Cellars, Outbuildings and Pits.*)

Ripening Fruits

1.   The best way to ripen fruits at home is to place them in a paper or plastic bag or a box along with a ripe apple.

2. Tomatoes, peaches, pears and apples ripen best in transparent containers.
3. Do not ripen fruit in a window sill. This dries and shrivels the fruit. Avoid direct sunlight and heat. Temperatures of 80º F. or above will cause some fruits to become soft and watery.
4. The container used should not be airtight. Punch a few holes in it. The ripe apple gives off ethylene gas which stimulates ripening. Fruit breathes in oxygen and gives off carbon dioxide. A build-up of carbon dioxide will slow down ripening. Air holes also prevent high humidity that encourages growth of decay organisms.
5. Hold at a temperature of 65 to 75 degrees. At lower temperatures the fruit will ripen slowly. Some fruits will not ripen if refrigerated when still green.
6. Refrigerate the fruits when ripe. To enjoy the fruits at their best, use them within a few days after ripening.

Recommended Replacement Periods For Foods Stored[6]

FOOD	MONTHS TO STORE
Milk	
Evaporated milk	6
Non-fat dry or whole dry in metal container	6
Canned Meat	
Meat, poultry	18
Fish	12
Condensed meat and vegetable soups	8
Fruit and Vegetables	
Berries and sour cherries	6
Citrus fruits and juices	6
Other fruits and juices	18
Dried fruit in metal container	6
Dehydrated (low-moisture) fruits and vegetables	Consult supplier
Tomatoes, sauerkraut	6
Other vegetables (including dry beans and peas*)	18

[6]U.S. Department of Agriculture, *Family Food Stockpile for Survival,* Home and Garden Bulletin No. 77 (Washington, D.C.: U.S. Government Printing Office, 1969), p. 7.

Cereal and Baked Goods

Ready-to-eat cereals in metal container	12
in original package	1
Uncooked cereal in metal container	24
in paper package	12

Hydrogenated or Antioxidant Treated Oils and Fats ... 12

Sweets, Sugars, Nuts

Sugar	Keeps indefinitely
Hard candy, gum	18
Nuts, canned	12
Instant pudding	12

Miscellaneous

Cocoa	18
Dry cream product	12
Bouillon products	12
Flavored beverage powders	24
Salt	Keeps indefinitely
Spices; flavorings, extracts	24
Soda, baking powder*	12

Approximate Shelf Life For Typical Dehydrated Foods And Related Items
(If product is sealed in vacuum-sealed cans)

Items	Years
Baking powder and soda	5 to 10
Barley	10 plus
Cornstarch	5 to 10
Flour, white	2
Flour, wheat	2
Honey	Indefinite
Milk, instant, non-fat	2
Milk, regular, non-fat	2
Multi-Purpose Food	Indefinite
Onions, DH	10 plus
Peppers, green DH	10 plus
Potatoes, DH	10 plus
Rice, brown	2

---

* These can be kept indefinitely if properly stored.

Rice, white	10 plus
Salad blend, DH	10 plus
Salt	Indefinite
Shortening	5 plus
Sugar, white	Indefinite
Tomato crystals, DH	10 plus
Wheat, whole kernel	Indefinite
Yeast, dry	2 plus
Bouillon, cube	3 to 5
Bouillon, granule	5
Gelatin, unflavored	Indefinite
Gelatin dessert	10 plus
Macaroni products	5
Soup blend, DH	10 plus
Stew blend, DH	10 plus
Meat substitutes	10 plus
Spices	Indefinite
Vegetables, DH	10 plus
Beans and peas, dried	10 plus
Eggs, whole, DH	2 to 5
Fruit, DH	2 to 5

(Reproduced from the book, *Just Add Water*, by Barbara D. Salsbury, by permission of Horizon Publishers, Bountiful, Utah.)

CHAPTER IX

EMERGENCY WATER SUPPLIES

A person can go five weeks or more without food but can survive only a few days without water. Since water is essential for life, we should always have an adequate supply on hand to provide for an emergency that might interrupt the safe water supply to our homes.

It is recommended that two weeks' supply of water be stored for cooking and drinking. Additional pure water should be available for tooth brushing, dish washing and bathing. Use of contaminated water for these purposes can result in illness.

One-half gallon of water per day per person is needed for drinking and cooking. Another one-half gallon per day per person is needed for washing and bathing, if used sparingly. If most of your stored food supply is dehydrated food, store more water.

Sources of Water

When the water supply is disrupted, clean water will be available in your hot water tank and in the toilet tanks in your home, if you take the precaution of turning off the inlet valve to your home before drawing water from these sources in order to prevent contamination.

Also, turn off the gas line on the hot water heater as a precaution against overheating and explosion. Repeated reheating of the water in the tank will cause it to become cloudy. Have a competent service man restore the gas service to the hot water heater when water supplies are restored.

To obtain water from the hot water tank, open the drain valve at the bottom of the tank. To get a free flow of water you may need to vent the tank by opening a faucet somewhere along the water line. Some tanks are automatically vented.

Another source of water that is often overlooked is the liquid in canned fruits and vegetables and fruit juices. If you can your own fruit, use a light syrup. This will save on sugar and the light syrup is more easily used as an emergency water supply than is a heavy syrup.

If you have no clean water stored, you may use any water that is available, if you purify it first.

If your water supply runs out before water service is restored, there are alternate sources of water.

(1) *Lakes, rivers, ponds, creeks, streams, ditches, and even*

puddles. Purify before using.

(2) *Rainwater.* Rainwater is simple to collect. If your house has gutters and downspouts, simply place buckets or barrels under each downspout.

If you have no gutters, use one of these methods to collect rainwater:

(a) Construct a large trough in which to collect your rain-water supply. Stretch a large tarp or sheet of plastic between the edge of the roof and the trough in such a way that the water will run from the roof, down the tarp and into the trough.

(b) Use a small trough or rain gutter with one open end. Set it up on supports and place a barrel or bucket under the open end. Stretch the tarp or sheet of plastic between the roof and the trough. The water collects in the bucket.

Purify water collected in these ways.

(3) *Wells.* A simple well can be dug with a shovel, if the water table is high. Simply dig until you reach water in adequate quantities to meet your needs. Observe caution to prevent cave-in.

Do-it-yourself well drilling equipment is available from large catalog department stores.

Any well should be covered to protect stray children and pets.

Sometimes well water is contaminated. Purify your well water until you can have its purity certified.

(4) *Water in the air and soil.* Water can be wrung from mud wrapped in a cloth or distilled from the air in a pit or around the branch of a tree. For further information see: *Outdoor Survival Skills* or *How To Be Prepared.* [1]

How To Store Water

Plastic bleach bottles or similar containers make the most ideal water storage containers. They are clean, unbreakable and portable. If the water is accidentally spilled, only a small amount is lost.

Metal containers will give the water a metallic taste. Glass containers would break during many kinds of disasters.

---

[1] Larry Dean Olsen, *Outdoor Survival Skills*, (Provo, Utah: Brigham Young University Press, 1973), p. 33-34.

Roland Page, *How To Be Prepared* (Provo, Utah: Jefferson House, 1974), p. 17.

If you store your water supply in glass jars, put them in boxes with cardboard dividers or wrap each jar in several layers of newspaper. Then place the boxes on the floor. This will minimize the possibility of breakage.

Place two drops of chlorine bleach per quart of water into the water when it is stored. Check stored water periodically. If you detect cloudiness, unpleasant taste or odor, throw out that water, wash the containers and refill. Date your water containers and refill them about every three months.

Water Purification

First, strain dirty water through a cloth to remove sediment. Then, treat it in one of the following ways:

(1) *Boiling:* Boil vigorously for 1 to 3 minutes to destroy bacteria. Cover the kettle with a lid, if you have one, and splash water on the rim and sides of the kettle several times during the boiling to sterilize these areas. They might have become contaminated when the kettle was filled. To improve the flavor, aerate by pouring the water back and forth between two clean containers, after cooling.

(2) *Bleach:* Any household bleach that contains hypochlorite as its only active ingredient will purify water. Ordinary liquid household bleach with 5.25% sodium hypochlorite is added to water as follows:

Amount of Water	*Amount of Bleach To Add To*	
	Cloudy Water	*Clear Water*
1 quart	4 drops	2 drops
1 gallon	16 drops	8 drops
5 gallons	1 teaspoon	1/2 teaspoon

Add the bleach to the water and stir. Let stand for 30 minutes. A distinct odor or taste of chlorine should remain. If not, add another dose of bleach. Let stand 15 minutes and test again for taste or odor. Repeat until you can either taste or smell the chlorine. The taste or smell of chlorine is a sign of safety. If you cannot detect chlorine in the water that you purify this way, do not use it. The bleach that you are using may have weakened from age or some other reason.

(3) *Iodine:* Use a 2% tincture of iodine. Add 3 drops per quart of clear water or 6 drops per quart of cloudy water. Stir

thoroughly.
(4) *Water Purification Tablets:* These tablets release either iodine or chlorine. Follow package directions. Usually 1 tablet per quart of clear water or 2 tablets per quart of cloudy water is used.

CHAPTER X

TECHNIQUES FOR HOME FOOD PRESERVATION

This chapter provides instructions for preserving foods in the home using a variety of preservation techniques. Included are charts and reference information on yield and procedures.

APPROXIMATE YIELDS OF A BUSHEL

	Lbs./ Bushel	Yield
Apples	48	16 to 20 qts.
Apricots	50	20 to 24 qts.
Berries, except strawberries	24 qt. crate*	12 to 18 qts.
Cherries	56	22 to 32 qts.
Peaches	48	18 to 24 qts.
Pears	50	20 to 25 qts.
Plums	56	24 to 30 qts.
Strawberries	24 qt. crate*	12 to 16 qts.
Tomatoes	53	15 to 20 qts.
Asparagus	45	11 qts.
Lima beans, in pod	32	6 to 8 qts.
Snap beans	30	15 to 20 qts.
Beets, without tops	52	17 to 20 qts.
Carrots, without tops	50	16 to 20 qts.
Sweet corn, in husks	35	8 to 9 qts.
Okra	26	17 qts.
Peas, in pod	30	12 to 15 qts.
Pumpkins	50 lbs.*	15 qts.
Spinach	18	6 to 9 qts.
Summer squash	40	16 to 20 qts.
Sweet potatoes	55	18 to 22 qts.
Dried beans	60	
Cabbage	50	
Cucumbers	50	
Grapes	50	
Onions	55	
Peanuts	22	
Dried peas	60	
Potatoes	60	
Rutabagas	60	
Walnuts	50	

*Not sold by the bushel.

HOME CANNING

Water-Bath Canner

Any large metal container that is at least three inches deeper than the height of your canning jars and large enough for the water to boil briskly around the jars can be used as a water-bath canner. This height will allow you to fill the canner with water to 1 to 2 inches above the tops of the jars without boiling over when the water bath is at a full boil. The canner must have a tight-fitting cover and a wire or wooden rack.

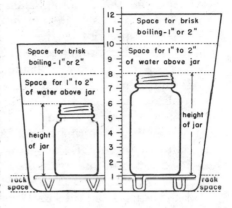

Water-Bath Canner
Figure 10:1

The steam-pressure canner can be used as a water-bath canner if it is deep enough to cover the jars with water. Place the cover on the canner and tighten. Leave the petcock open to allow the steam to escape.

The Boiling-Water Bath

Place the filled jars on a rack in the water-bath canner. Cover the jars with hot water to 1 to 2 inches above the tops of the jars. Bring the water quickly to a boil, with the lid on the canner. Keep the water boiling gently throughout the processing. Start timing the processing as soon as the water has reached a full rolling boil.

Remove the jars from the boiling-water bath as soon as the processing time is up.

The Steam-Pressure Canner

This is a large pressure cooker, not a pressure saucepan. It must be deep enough that the lid does not touch the tops of the canning jars and large enough to allow plenty of room for the circulation of the steam around the jars. Before using the canner, run a string or pipe cleaner through the petcock and the safety valve openings. Be sure that there is no food trapped in the dial gauge or the gauge opening. Check the accuracy of the steam pressure dial gauge every year to assure proper processing of the food you are canning.

Jars are placed on a rack in the canner. About 2 or 3 inches of water is poured into the canner and the lid sealed tightly. If your canner has a dial gauge, be sure that it is on tight. Leave the steam pet-cock open or the weighted gauge off until the steam starts to flow steadily from the opening. Then allow the steam to escape for 10 minutes before closing the petcock or putting on the weighted gauge. Let the pressure rise to the proper level for the food that you are processing. Start timing as soon as the pressure reaches the proper level. Keep the pressure constant by regulating the heat under the canner. Fluctuations in pressure can result in over or under-processing. They also cause food and liquids to be drawn from the jars and can interfere with proper sealing.

When the processing time is up, remove the canner from the heat and allow it to cool. Do not speed cooling by running water over the canner or opening the steam petcock or removing the weighted gauge to allow the steam to escape. Sudden release of pressure will draw food and liquid from the jars. When the pressure has returned to zero, open the petcock or remove the weighted gauge. Open the lid of the canner and remove the jars. Set them in a draft-free place to cool.

High Altitude Adjustments for Pressure Canning

Pressures given in canning instructions are for canning at sea level. Add one pound pressure for every 2000 feet above sea level that you live. The processing time remains the same.

High Altitude Adjustments for Boiling-Water Bath Processing [1]

Times given in canning instructions are for sea level. If you live above sea level you must add time to the processing time given in the instructions. For every 1000 feet above sea level, if the processing called for is: *20 minutes or less*, add 1 minute; *more than 20 minutes*, add 2 minutes.

Glass Canning Jars

Any glass jar that will fit a canning lid may be used. Check the jars for cracks and chips. Pay particular attention to the rims where the lids will seal. Glass jars manufactured for home canning will give the most satisfactory results since they are generally heavier and will withstand more heat than jars such as mayonnaise jars.

Lids

Glass Lids: This type of lid is one of the oldest types of canning

---

[1] *Home Canning and Freezing Methods Sketch Book*, Ball Brothers Company Inc., p. 11.

closures. The glass lid is sealed with a rubber ring that fits over the rim of the jar. A wire bale usually holds the lid tight. This type of lid is left loose during processing and tightened when the jars are removed from the water bath. Place the long wire loop over the top of the lid but do not snap the short loop down until after processing. Rubber rings should not be reused.

Zinc Lids: These lids require a rubber ring that fits over the jar rim. The lids should be screwed down firmly, then turned back 1/4 turn before processing. They are tightened after removing the jars from boiling water bath. Rubber rings should not be reused.

Two-piece Metal Lids: Tighten before processing. Only the rings are reusable.

Cleaning and Sterilizing the Lids and Jars

Most canned products are put into clean jars that have not been sterilized. To clean jars, wash well in hot, soapy water and invert to drain. For hot-packed foods, leave the jars in a pan of hot water until filled. This helps to minimize breakage.

If the instructions call for sterilized jars, after washing the jars in soapy water and rinsing, place them in a pan of hot water on the stove and boil for 15 minutes. Leave them in the sterilizing water until ready to use. Usually sterilized jars are suggested when canning juices, pickles, jams and jellies and any other product that requires little or no processing.

Glass and zinc lids can be sterilized in the same way as jars. In contrast, flat metal self-sealing lids and rubber rings should never be boiled. To clean these, wash them in hot, soapy water. Then put them in a pan or bowl and cover them with boiling water. Let stand in the water until you are ready to use them.

Cooling Canned Food

Glass jars will break if exposed to sudden changes of temperature. Cool jars on a rack or folded towel. Never set hot jars on a cold surface or expose the jars to cold water. Keep jars away from drafts. Leave them uncovered so that they will cool rapidly.

Testing the Seal

Zinc or glass lids: Tip the jar and check for leaks.

Two-piece metal lids: If the center of the lid remains depressed when you press on it, the lid is sealed. If a lid was not depressed and it pops down when you press it, turn the jar upside down and shake it to be sure that the lid is going to stay down.

Always wait until the jars are completely cold before testing the seals.

CANNING FRUITS

Sugar Syrups

Sugar helps the fruit to retain its shape, color and flavor. To make syrup combine:

4 cups water or juice	2 cups sugar	for thin syrup
	3 cups sugar	for medium syrup
	4 3/4 cups sugar	for heavy syrup

Honey Syrup

Honey can be used to flavor and sweeten canned fruit. Mild flavored honey is best for canning. To make syrup combine:

4 cups water or juice   4 cups honey

How to Can Fruits

1. Use firm, ripe fruit. Green or overripe fruits can be mixed with other fruits when making jams or jellies, but they do not make a satisfactory canned product. Avoid using fruits that are beginning to spoil. They can cause the whole jar or batch to spoil.
2. Wash, peel and pit fruit. In general, apricots, cherries, plums, figs, grapes and berries are the only fruits canned unpeeled.
3. Slice the fruit as desired.

Raw Pack

Pack prepared fruits loosely in jars, leaving 1/2" headroom. Add boiling syrup, leaving 1/2" headroom. Tighten lids. Process in boiling water bath.

Headroom: space left at the top of the jar to allow for expansion of the food during processing.

Hot Pack

1. Heat syrup to boiling. Add fruits and continue heating just until fruits are heated through.
2. Drain, reserving syrup.
3. Pack fruit loosely into jars. Leave 1/2" headroom.
4. Fill jar with syrup, leaving 1/2" headroom.
5. Tighten lid.
6. Process in boiling-water bath.

PROCESSING TIME FOR FRUITS IN BOILING-WATER BATH [2]

Type of fruit	Raw Pack		Hot Pack	
	Pints	Quarts	Pints	Quarts
Apples (see note 1)			15 min.	20 min.
Applesauce (see note 2)			10 min.	10 min.
Apricots	25 min.	30 min.	20 min.	25 min.
Berries, except strawberries				
(see note 5)	10 min.	15 min.	10 min.	15 min.
Cherries	20 min.	25 min.	10 min.	15 min.
Fruit juices			5 min.	5 min.
Peaches	25 min.	30 min.	20 min.	25 min.
Pears	25 min.	30 min.	20 min.	25 min.
Plums (see note 3)	20 min.	25 min.	20 min.	25 min.
Rhubarb (see note 4)			10 min.	10 min.
Tomatoes	35 min.	45 min.	10 min.	10 min.
Tomato juice			10 min.	10 min.

Notes for directions above:

1. Boil for 5 minutes in thin syrup or water, then pack in jars.
2. Pack hot applesauce to 1/4" of the top of the jar.
3. Prick skins of whole plums before canning.
4. In saucepan, add 1/2 cup sugar to each quart of cut-up raw rhubarb. Let stand to draw out juice. Bring to a boil.
5. To hot pack berries and cherries, combine raw fruit with 1/2 cup sugar for each quart of fruit. Cover pan and bring to a boil. Shake pan to prevent sticking. A little water can be added, if desired.

Some hints:

1. Use a thin syrup whenever possible to reduce calories, save sugar, reduce the sugar intake of persons consuming the canned fruit, and make the syrup more usable as a source of water in an emergency. Certain fruits, such as apricots, are more palatable when canned in heavy syrup.
2. To prevent cut fruit from turning brown, drop pieces into a solution of 1 gallon water mixed with 2 tablespoons salt and 2 tablespoons vinegar, or into a solution prepared from a commercial ascorbic acid compound meant especially to prevent oxidation of fruit. Drain just before heating or

---

[2]U.S. Department of Agriculture, *Home Canning of Fruits and Vegetables*, Home and Garden Bulletin No. 8, (Washington, D.C.: U.S. Government Printing Office).

packing raw.

3. To peel tomatoes, peaches and apricots: Dip the fruits into boiling water for a few seconds to loosen skins. Cool at once in cold water. Slip the skins off the fruit. If they fail to slip right off, dip them in the boiling water again.

HOME CANNING OF VEGETABLES

1. Select only fresh, sound vegetables to can. Wilted vegetables or vegetables that show signs of spoilage will result in an inferior canned product that is very likely to spoil after processing. The less time between picking and canning, the higher quality the product and the less chance of spoilage.
2. Wash and trim the vegetables as you would to prepare them for the table.
3. Cut the vegetables into pieces or leave small vegetables whole, if desired.
4. Blanch or precook, if needed.
5. Pack into jars.
6. Add salt, if desired. The salt in ordinary canned vegetables is for seasoning, not for preservation.
7. Add boiling liquid.
8. Wipe tops of jars and seal.
9. Process in the steam pressure canner for the required length of time. *All vegetables except tomatoes, pickled & brined vegetables, and acidified vegetables must be processed in the steam pressure canner.* Never try any other method.

Note of caution: (see page 123).

Directions for Specific Vegetables [3]

Beans, fresh Lima: can only young, tender beans.

Raw pack: shell and wash beans. In glass jars: pack beans into clean jars. For small-type beans, fill to 1" of the top of jar for pints and 1 1/2" for quarts; for large beans, fill to 3/4" of top for pints and 1 1/4" for quarts. Beans should not be pressed or shaken down. Add 1/2 teaspoon salt to pints; 1 teaspoon to quarts. Fill jar to 1/2" of the top with boiling water. Adjust jar lids. Process in pressure canner at 10 pounds pressure (240° F.): pint jars - 40 minutes; quart jars - 50 minutes. As soon as you remove jars from canner, complete seals, if necessary.

---

[3]U.S. Department of Agriculture, *Home Canning of Fruits and Vegetables*, Home and Garden Bulletin No. 8.

Hot Pack: shell the beans, cover with boiling water and bring to a boil. In glass jars: pack hot beans loosely to 1" of top. Add 1/2 teaspoon salt to pints; 1 teaspoon to quarts. Cover with boiling water, leaving 1" space at top of jar. Adjust jar lids. Process in pressure canner at 10 pounds pressure: pint jars - 40 minutes; quart jars - 50 minutes. As soon as you remove jars from canner, complete seals, if necessary.

Beans, snap

Raw pack: wash beans. Trim ends; cut into 1" pieces. In glass jars: pack raw beans tightly to 1/2" of top. Add 1/2 teaspoon salt to pints; 1 teaspoon to quarts. Cover with boiling water, leaving 1/2" space at top of jar. Adjust jar lids. Process in pressure canner at 10 pounds pressure: pint jars - 20 minutes; quart jars - 25 minutes. As soon as you remove jars from canner, complete the seals, if necessary.

Hot pack: wash beans. Trim ends; cut into 1 inch pieces. Cover with boiling water; boil 5 minutes. In glass jars: pack hot beans loosely to 1/2 inch of top. Add 1/2 teaspoon salt to pints; 1 teaspoon to quarts. Cover with boiling-hot cooking liquid, leaving 1/2 inch space at top of jar. Adjust jar lids. Process in pressure canner at 10 pounds pressure: pint jars - 20 minutes; quart jars - 25 minutes. As soon as you remove jars from canner, complete seals if necessary.

Beets

Sort beets for size. Cut off tops, leaving an inch of stem. Also leave root. Wash beets. Cover with boiling water and boil until skins slip easily 15 to 25 minutes, depending on size. Skin and trim. Leave baby beets whole. Cut medium or large beets in 1/2" cubes or slices; halve or quarter very large slices. In glass jars: pack hot beets to 1/2 inch of top. Add 1/2 teaspoon salt to pints; 1 teaspoon to quarts. Cover with boiling water, leaving 1/2 inch space at top of jar. Adjust lids. Process in pressure canner at 10 pounds pressure: pint jars - 30 minutes; quart jars - 35 minutes. As soon as you remove jars from canner, complete seals if necessary.

Carrots

Raw pack: wash and scrape carrots. Slice or dice. In glass jars: pack raw carrots tightly into clean jars, to 1 inch of top of jar. Add 1/2 teaspoon salt to pints; 1 teaspoon to quarts. Fill jars to 1/2 inch of top with boiling water. Adjust jar lid. Process in pressure canner at 10 pounds pressure: pint jars - 25 minutes; quart jars - 30 minutes.

Hot pack: wash and scrape carrots. Slice or dice. Cover with boiling water and bring to a boil. In glass jars: pack hot carrots to 1/2 inch of top. Add 1/2 teaspoon salt to pints; 1 teaspoon to quarts. Cover with boiling hot cooking liquid, leaving 1/2 inch space at top of jar. Adjust jar lids. Process in pressure canner at 10 pounds pressure: pint jars - 25 minutes; quart jars - 30 minutes. As soon as you remove jars from canner, complete seals, if necessary.

Corn, whole-kernel

Raw pack: husk corn and remove silk. Wash. Cut from cob at about two-thirds the depth of kernel. In glass jars: pack corn to 1" of top; do not shake or press down. Add 1/2 teaspoon salt to pints; 1 teaspoon to quarts. Fill to 1/2 inch of top with boiling water. Adjust jar lids. Process in pressure canner at 10 pounds pressure: pints - 55 minutes; quarts - 85 minutes. As soon as you remove the jars from canner, complete seals if necessary.

Hot pack: husk corn and remove silk. Wash. Cut from cob at about two-thirds the depth of kernel. To each quart of corn add 1 pint boiling water. Heat to boiling. In glass jars: pack hot corn to 1 inch of top and cover with boiling hot cooking liquid, leaving 1 inch space at top of jar. Or fill to 1 inch of top with mixture of corn and liquid. Add 1/2 teaspoon salt to pints; 1 teaspoon to quarts. Adjust jar lids. Process in pressure canner at 10 pounds pressure: pints - 55 minutes; quarts - 85 minutes.

Peas, fresh green

Raw pack: shell and wash peas. In glass jars: pack peas to 1 inch of top; do not shake or press down. Add 1/2 teaspoon salt to pints; 1 teaspoon to quarts. Cover with boiling water, leaving 1 1/2 inches of space at top of jar. Adjust jar lids. Process in pressure canner at 10 pounds pressure: pints - 40 minutes; quarts - 40 minutes. As soon as you remove the jars from the canner, complete seals if necessary.

Hot pack: shell and wash peas. Cover with boiling water. Bring to a boil. In glass jars: pack hot peas loosely to 1" of top. Add 1/2 teaspoon salt to pints, 1 teaspoon to quarts. Cover with boiling water, leaving 1 inch space at top of jar. Adjust jar lids. Process in pressure canner at 10 pounds pressure: pints - 40 minutes; quarts - 40 minutes.

Pumpkin, strained

Wash pumpkin, remove seeds and pare. Cut into 1 inch cubes. Steam until tender, about 25 minutes. Or wash pumpkin, cut in half, and remove seeds. Place on baking sheet and bake in 400º F. oven until tender, about 45 minutes. Scoop flesh out of skin. After pumpkin is cooked, put through food mill or strainer. Simmer until heated through; stir to keep pumpkin from sticking to pan. In glass jars:

pack hot to 1/2 inch of top. Add no liquid or salt. Adjust jar lids. Process at 10 pounds pressure: pints - 65 minutes; quarts - 80 minutes.

Spinach and Other Greens

Can only freshly picked, tender spinach. Pick over and wash thoroughly. Cut out tough stems and midribs. Place about 2 1/2 pounds of spinach in a cheesecloth bag and steam about 10 minutes or until well wilted. In glass jars: pack hot spinach loosely to 1/2 inch of top. Add 1/4 teaspoon salt to pints, 1/2 teaspoon to quarts. Cover with boiling water, leaving 1/2 inch space at top of jar. Adjust jar lids. Process in pressure canner at 10 pounds pressure: pints - 70 minutes; quarts - 90 minutes. As soon as you remove jars from canner, complete seals if necessary.

Squash, Winter

Follow instructions for pumpkin.

Sweet Potatoes, wet pack

Wash sweet potatoes. Sort for size. Boil or steam just until skins slip easily away. Skin and cut into pieces. In glass jars: pack hot sweet potatoes to 1 inch of top. Add 1/2 teaspoon salt to pints; 1 teaspoon to quarts. Cover with boiling water or medium syrup, leaving 1 inch space at top of jar. Adjust jar lids. Process in pressure canner at 10 pounds pressure: pints - 55 minutes; quarts - 90 minutes.

Nutmeats

Place raw nutmeats in clean jars and cap with two-piece metal lids. Bake at 250º F. for 20 minutes. Cool, test seals and store.

Alternate method: After packing and capping, process in pressure canner for 15 minutes at 5 pounds pressure. Processed this way the nuts will have a fresh taste. However, they will not store well unless kept in a cool, dark place. To keep in hot weather or under adverse storage conditions, process at 10 pounds pressure for 45 minutes. This will roast the nuts. These instructions are for pint jars.

PREPARING ACIDIFIED VEGETABLES [4]

Non-acid vegetables can be made more resistant to spoilage by the addition of acid during canning.

Once acidified, they can be processed either in a boiling-water

[4]W. E. Pyke and Elizabeth Dyer, *Wartime Food Processing Aids,* (Ft. Collins, Colo.: Colorado Agricultural Experiment Station Press, Bulletin No. 97, June 1943).

bath for the times given below or in the pressure canner for the times given in the canning instructions on pages 108 to 111.

Pressure processing is preferable to water-bath processing for these products as a safety precaution.

Always boil these vegetables for 15 minutes before tasting or eating.

General Directions

1. Prepare vegetables as instructed on page 108.
2. Blanch.
3. Pack in quart jars.
4. Add acid.
5. Add liquids and seasonings.
6. Process.

ACID NEEDED TO PRESERVE NON-ACID VEGETABLES

Vegetable	Citric Acid * USP Granular	Vinegar 5% acidity
Asparagus, snap beans, beets, broccoli, celtuce, carrots, corn, cauliflower, greens, peas, peppers, pumpkin, squash, eggplant.	1 teaspoon per quart	4 tablespoons per quart
Shell beans	2 teaspoons per quart	6 tablespoons per quart
Shell beans with tomato sauce and molasses added	1 teaspoon per quart	3 tablespoons per quart

Citric Acid USP is available at the druggist.

PROCESSING PROCEDURE FOR ACIDIFIED VEGETABLES

Vegetable	Preliminary Preparation	Processing Time (in quart jars) in Boiling-Water Bath
Asparagus	Wash. Blanch in boiling water or live steam. For hot-water blanch, tie in bundles and set in boiling water 2/3 of length for 3 min. Tip over and blanch 1 minute more. For steam blanch, steam 5 min. or until wilted. Remove and pack, tips upward. Add acid. Fill jar with boiling water used for blanching.	Altitude: 5000 ft.: 65 min. 7500 ft.: 80 min. 10,000 ft.: 105 min.

Snap beans: Wash. Pack whole, in strips or cut. Blanch for 3 min. in boiling water, or steam for 5 min. or until wilted. Pack loosely in hot jars. Add acid. Fill jars with boiling water used for blanching.

Altitude:
5000 ft.: 65 min.
7500 ft.: 80 min.
10,000 ft.: 105 min.

Lima beans
Shell beans Wash. Shell. Discard overly-mature beans. Blanch 3 min. and pack into hot jars. Add acid. Fill with water used for blanching.

Altitude:
5000 ft: 90 min.
7500 ft: 110 min.
10,000 ft.:125 min.

Beets Wash. Boil or steam 10 min. or until skins slip easily. Skin. Pack whole or cubed. Add acid. Fill with boiling water.

Altitude:
5000 ft.: 65 min.
7500 ft.: 80 min.
10,000 ft.. 105 min.

Broccoli
Lettuce Wash. Blanch 3 min. in open pan of boiling, salted water. Pack in hot jar. Add acid. Fill jar with water used for blanching.

Altitude:
5000 ft.: 65 min.
7500 ft.: 80 min.
10,000 ft.: 105 min.

Carrots Scrub. Boil 3 min. Pack hot. Add acid. Fill with boiling carrot water.

Altitude:
5000 ft.: 65 min.
7500 ft.: 80 min.
10,000 ft.: 105 min.

Corn, off cob Cook on cob until tender. Cut off. Reheat, then pack hot. Add acid. Cover with hot juice. For succotash, add baby lima beans before packing.

Altitude:
5000 ft.: 65 min.
7500 ft.: 80 min.
10,000 ft.: 105 min.

Cauliflower Florets canned in pint jars for salad. Wash in cold water. Blanch 2 minutes in boiling salted water. Pack loosely. Add acid. Cover with blanching water.

Altitude: *(pints)*
5000 ft.: 65 min.
7500 ft.: 80 min.
10,000 ft.: 105 min.

Greens Wash thoroughly in cold water. Blanch until wilted in boiling water or by steaming. Pack loosely in hot jars. Don't mash. Add acid. Cover with boiling water. Use fork or spatula to release entrapped air bubbles.

Altitude:
5000 ft.: 65 min.
7500 ft.: 80 min.
10,000 ft.: 105 min.

Peas — Shell. Blanch 3 min. in boiling, salted water. Pack loosely in jars. Add acid. Fill with blanching water.

Altitude:
5000 ft: 65 min.
7500 ft: 80 min.
10,000 ft: 105 min.

Peppers — Quarter. Scrape out seeds. Blanch 1 min. Pack in half pints or pints. Add acid. Fill with blanching water.

Altitude: *(Pints or Half Pints)*
5000 ft: 65 min.
75000 ft: 80 min.
10,00 ft: 105 min.

Pumpkin
Squash
Eggplant — Scrub, peel, slice or cut into cubes. Blanch in boiling salted water for 1 to 10 minutes. Pack hot. Add acid. Fill with boiling water used for blanching.

5000 ft: 65 min.
7500 ft: 80 min.
10,000 ft: 105 min.

Tomatoes
(no acid
needed) — Wash, scald, peel. Pack whole or cut. Shake jar to release trapped air bubbles. Fill with boiling water or tomato juice or pack solidly without added liquid.

Cold Pack
Altitude:
5000 ft: 65 min.
7500 ft: 80 min.
10,000 ft: 110 min.
Hot Pack
5000 ft: 45 min.
7500 ft: 45 min.
10,000 ft: 45 min.
Cold Pack Puree
5000 ft: 90 min.
7500 ft: 100 min.
10,000 ft: 110 min.

PICKLING AND BRINING VEGETABLES

Pickling[5]

The term "pickling" is generally applied to the process of preserving food in brine or acid solution, either with or without subsequent fermentation. When the salt or acid content reaches a sufficiently high percentage, fermentation will no longer occur. Heavily-brined vegetables are usually used in soups or for later conversion into special pickled products. Mold growth may be minimized or eliminated by various handling methods.

When the salt content is low, fermentation occurs. When properly controlled, the fermentation, usually of the lactic-acid type, may serve as a means of food preservation. Dill pickles, snap beans, and

---

[5] *Wartime Food Processing Aids, op. cit.*

leafy green vegetables, except spinach, are readily preserved in this manner.

Since the fermentation processes use up a portion of the nutrients in the food, it is often more desirable to add to the brine, at the start, the acid normally formed in the fermentation process. Edible lactic acid, vinegar, or sometimes citric acid, may be used to furnish the acidity.

Pickled foods are stored in sealed containers to eliminate possible contamination from the air and to prevent evaporation.

Brining[6]

A brine of high salt content, 15 percent by weight, does not permit the growth of micro-organisms. Trials at the Colorado Agricultural Experiment Station indicate that a 15 percent brine solution is sufficient to preserve foods. Fifteen percent brine is made by dissolving 3 cups salt in 1 gallon of water.

If the preserved material is weighted down below the surface of the brine, and the surface is covered with a thin layer of mineral oil, evaporation of the brine becomes negligible. The objection to this type of brining is the limited use of the food because of its high salt content.

When the salt content of a brine solution is 4 1/2 to 5 percent of the weight of the material, a lactic-acid type fermentation follows. If edible acid is added in appropriate amount, this fermentation is held to a minimum and comparable food preservation occurs. A 3-minute steam blanch before brining is desirable.

Foods preserved in this low-salt-sour brine should be stored in sealed containers. Foods preserved this way may be held at least 9 months before using if kept in a cool place.

No "freshening" is needed for foods preserved in the low-salt-sour brine. They are simply washed free of the brine, cooked and seasoned. Bacon, salt-pork, ham hocks or butter may serve as seasonings.

The products do not have a flavor identical with fresh cooked vegetables but they are very palatable. Nutritive values are well-retained in this type of brining.

All brined foods should be cooked before being tasted or eaten.

General Directions[7]

Good quality vegetables, carefully and quickly handled, proper

[6]Ibid.
[7]Inez M. Eckblad, Preservation of Vegetables by Salting or Brining, (Ft. Collins, Colorado: Extension Service of Colorado State College, Colorado Farm Victory Program, May 1942.)

equipment and a good grade of salt are essential for satisfactory pre-servation.

Scald crocks, cover, weights and cutting utensils. Do not use a crock with cracks in it. Use clean, white muslin or cheesecloth and a hardwood board or a plate for covering the crock. Weigh it down with clean stones, use a clean brick that has been dipped in melted parafin to form a waterproof film, or fill a glass jar with water and tightly cap it to serve as a weight.

Some vegetables are dry-salted without fermentation. Others, such as cabbage, contain enough sugar to cause fermentation, making an acid brine. Other products may have water and vinegar added for variation.

Dry-Salting without Fermentation: (No acid added at the start of brining)

This method can be used for string beans, corn, peas, turnip tops and other greens.

1. Prepare vegetables by washing and cutting. Greens and corn are better with a 5-minute steaming or blanching period.
2. Weigh salt and vegetables. Use 3 pounds salt to 17 pounds vegetables.
3. Put a 1-inch layer of vegetables in crock and sprinkle with salt.
4. Continue alternating layers of vegetables with sprinklings of salt. Put any salt left on top.
5. Cover with cloth and plate or board fitting the inside diameter of the crock. Put weight on top.
6. Pour a thin layer of tasteless mineral oil over the top to shut out air and prevent molding after bubbling ceases.
7. Store container in a cool room. If salted product is put into glass jars, be sure food is packed down. Dip rubber rings in mineral oil to keep salt solution from being lost around the rubber.

Dry-Salting with Fermentation:

Cabbage, cauliflower, string beans and turnips are frequently preserved this way.

1. Carefully wash and cut vegetable. Weigh ingredients.
2. Use same method for salting and packing as for dry-salting without fermentation.
3. Allow product to stand in a warm room to ferment until bubbling stops. Time for fermentation usually varies from

1 to 4 weeks.

Brining:

>   Brining is more satisfactory than dry salting for some products.

>   1.   Make the solution of salt and water, or salt, water and vinegar. Proceed as for salted products.

>   Cucumbers - Add dill and spices. 1 ounce of spices for 4-gallon crock; 1/2 lb. or more dry dill, as desired.

PROCEDURES FOR PICKLING AND BRINING[8]

High Salt Brining

>   Cauliflower florets, cucumbers, unshelled peas or lima beans, seeded peppers, celery.

Pretreatment:

>   Wash and cleanse thoroughly, then drain; do not cut peas or beans.

Brine: 15% by weight, 1 1/2 pounds salt per gallon water, or 3 cups salt per gallon water.

>   For each 10 pounds unshelled peas and beans preserved this way, 1 1/2 pounds additional salt should be added a few days later.

Storage: In storage jars, in cool place, covered with film of tasteless mineral oil. Cover jar.

To serve: Freshen by soaking overnight in 1 gallon of fresh water to each pound of material. Cook and serve.

Low-Salt-Sour Brining

>   Snap beans, shell beans, cauliflower, greens, except spinach, green tomatoes, carrots, beets.

Pretreatment: Wash and cleanse. Stem and cut snap beans. Steam blanch cauliflower, snap beans, shelled beans, greens, for three minutes; carrots and beets for 5 minutes.

Brine: 4 1/2% by weight, 1/2 pound salt per gallon water, about 1 cup salt per gallon.

Acid to be added to brine at start: 8 ounces vinegar per gallon or 1/2 ounce edible lactic acid of 87 1/2% strength per gallon.

Storage: Allow to stand 10 days covered. Heat, pack in glass con-

---

[8]*Wartime Food Processing Aids, op. cit.*

tainers with glass-top seals. Process in boiling water bath till heated to boiling throughout. Keep in a cool place.

To use: Wash products when removed from container. Add water and seasoning before cooking. Resalting is unnecessary.

Dry-Salt Brining with Acid

Snap beans:

Pretreatment: Wash, blanch 5 minutes, cut.

Brine: 5% salt, 1/2 pound for each 10 pounds beans. Use layer pack. (Pack a layer of beans, then a layer of salt; repeat until all beans are packed.)

Acid to be added to brine to start: 8 ounces of vinegar for each 10 pounds of material.

Storage: Weight down so that brine formed will cover food in 24 hours. Cover with muslin cloth tied to the jar. Store in cool place.

To use: Ready for use in about 3 weeks. Keep scum removed. Products may be canned after fermentation. Food should be thoroughly heated before or after packing to prevent further fermentation.

Cabbage, Cauliflower, Lettuce (No acid needed)

Pretreatment: Wash, trim, shred or slice, then pack.

Brine: 3 percent salt, 5 ounces for each 10 pounds of material. Use layer pack. (See snap beans, above.)

Storage and Use: Same as snap beans, above.

Beets

Pretreatment: Wash, steam until peeling slips, then peel slice or shred.

Brine: Same as for snap beans.

Acid to be added to brine to start: 8 ounces vinegar for each 10 pounds of material.

Storage and Use: Same as snap beans.

Turnips, Rutabagas (No acid needed)

Pretreatment: Wash, peel, slice or shred.

Brine: Same as for snap beans.

Storage and use: Same as for snap beans.

Salting and Brining Charts

Salt Required to Make One Gallon of Brine of Different Strengths

       15% brine   1 1/2 pounds salt per gallon of water
        5% brine   1/2 pound salt per gallon of water

Amount of Salt Recommended	Equivalent in Granulated Salt	Equivalent in Flake (Dairy) or Medium Salt
1 ounce	1 tablespoon + 1 teaspoon	2 tablespoons + 1 1/2 teaspoons
1/2 pound	3/4 cup	1 cup + 2 tablespoons
1 pound	1 1/2 cups	2 1/4 cups
1/2 cup	5 ounces	3 1/2 ounces
1 cup	10 ounces	7 ounces

Sauerkraut [9]

There are many methods of making sauerkraut. This one seems to be the simplest.

Ingredients:

    Cabbage . . . . 50 pounds
    Pure granulated salt . . . . 1 pound (1 1/2 cups)

Remove the outer leaves and any undesirable portions from firm, sound heads of cabbage. Wash. Cut into halves or quarters, removing cores. Use a shredder or knife to cut the cabbage into shreds about the thickness of a dime.

In a large container, thoroughly mix 3 tablespoons salt with 5 pounds of shredded cabbage. Let the salted cabbage stand for several minutes to wilt slightly. This allows packing without excessive bruising of the shreds.

Pack the salted cabbage firmly and evenly into a large, clean crock. Using a wooden spoon or your hands, press down just until the juice rises to the top. Repeat the salting, shredding and packing of cabbage until the crock is filled to within 3 or 4 inches of the top.

Cover the cabbage with a thin, clean cloth such as muslin or several layers of cheese cloth and fold the edges down against the inside of the crock. Cover with a plate or round paraffined board

[9]U.S. Department of Agriculture, *Making Pickles and Relishes at Home*, Home and Garden Bulletin G92. (Washington, D.C.: U.S. Government Printing Office).

that just fits inside the container so that the cabbage is not exposed to the air. Put a weight on top of the cover so that the brine comes up to the cover but not over it. A glass jar filled with water makes a good weight.

A newer method of covering the cabbage during fermentation consists of placing a plastic bag filled with water on top of the fermenting cabbage. The water-filled bag seals the surface from exposure to air, and prevents the growth of film yeasts or molds. It also serves as a weight. For extra protection, the bag with the water in it can be placed inside another plastic bag.

Any bag used should be of heavyweight, watertight plastic and intended for use with foods.

The amount of water in the plastic bag can be adjusted to give just enough pressure to keep the fermenting cabbage covered with brine.

Formation of gas bubbles indicates fermentation is taking place. A room temperature of 68° to 72° F. is best for fermenting cabbage. Fermentation is usually completed in 5 to 6 weeks.

To store: Heat sauerkraut to simmering (185° to 210° F.). Do not boil. Pack hot sauerkraut into clean, hot jars and cover with hot juice to 1/2 inch of top of jar. Adjust lids. Process in boiling-water bath, 15 minutes for pints and 20 minutes for quarts. Start to count processing time as soon as hot jars are placed into actively boiling water.

Remove jars and complete seals, if necessary. Set jars upright, several inches apart, to cool.

Processing Salted or Brined Vegetables

Unless otherwise specified, all brined or salted vegetables can be processed in a boiling-water bath for 5 to 10 minutes for pints, 15 to 20 minutes for quarts, hot pack. The vegetables should be heated to simmering, then packed hot and immediately placed in actively-boiling water. Start timing the processing as soon as jars are placed in the boiling water.

It is not necessary to process most brine ¹ or salted vegetables because the combination of salt and fermentation will preserve the vegetables. However, unprocessed brined vegetables must be kept in cold storage and there is sometimes a problem with molds and yeasts and enzymes that cause spoilage and changes in texture and flavor. Processing helps to minimize these problems. [10]

---

[10]U.S. Dept. of Agriculture, *Making Pickles and Relishes at Home,* Home and Garden Bulletin No. 92.

Common Causes of Spoilage in Brined or Pickled Vegetables

Soft pickles or kraut:

- insufficient salt
- too high a temperature during fermentation
- uneven distribution of salt
- air pockets caused by improper packing

Pink Kraut:

- yeast growth
- too much salt or uneven distribution of salt
- improperly covered or weighted

Rotted pickles or kraut:

This usually occurs at the top of the container. It is caused by exposure to air. Skim off the rotted portions of the product and discard. The rest of the batch should be edible.

Dark Pickles or Kraut:

- unwashed or improperly trimmed vegetables
- insufficient juice to cover during fermentation
- uneven distribution of salt
- exposure to air
- high temperature during fermentation, processing or storage
- long storage

HOME CANNING OF MEATS[11]

Canning will not improve the quality of meat. Therefore, can only fresh, sound meats.

Meat can be canned bone-in or deboned, raw or hot pack, in large or small pieces, or formed into meatballs or patties. The use to which you will put the canned product will determine the form in which it is canned.

Bones are usually removed from meats in order to save space in the canning jars. Chicken is the only meat ordinarily canned bone-in.

General Directions for Raw Pack

1. Clean surface of meat and remove bones and all surface fat. Leave skin on chicken.

---

[11]Methods and processing times mainly from Ruth Hertzberg, Beatrice Vaughan, Janet Greene *Putting Food By* (Brattleboro, Vt.: The Stephen Greene Press, 1973).

2. Cut meat into desired-sized pieces. Roasts and steaks can be left in large pieces. Stew meat should be cut into small pieces.
3. Pack loosely into straight-sided jars, leaving 1" headroom.
4. Add no liquid.
5. Put lids loosely on jars and place in boiling-water bath (170° F.) for about 75 minutes to exhaust.
6. Remove jars from boiling-water bath.
7. Add 1/2 teaspoon salt to pint jars, 1 teaspoon to quarts.
8. Wipe jar rims to remove all traces of fat. Fat can prevent a tight seal.
9. Tighten jar lids and process in pressure canner at 10 pounds pressure:

	Pints	*Quarts*
Meats	75 minutes	90 minutes
Poultry		
bone-in	65 minutes	75 minutes
deboned	75 minutes	90 minutes

General Directions for Hot Pack

1. Clean surface of meat and remove bones and all surface fat. Leave skin on chicken.
2. Cut the meat into desired-sized pieces. Roasts and steaks can be left in large pieces. Brown the meat, if desired. Cook meat until almost done (medium well). Ground beef and sausage should be shaped into patties or meatballs and cooked just until pink color is gone.
3. Pack hot meat loosely into straight-sided jars. Leave 1" headroom.
4. Add unseasoned broth or cooking liquid. Boiling water can be added if there is not enough broth. Leave 1" headroom.
5. Add salt: 1/2 teaspoon for pints, 1 teaspoon for quarts.
6. Wipe jar rims to remove all traces of fat. Fat can prevent a tight seal.
7. Tighten lids and process in pressure canner at 10 pounds pressure.

	Pints	*Quarts*
Meat	75 minutes	90 minutes
Poultry		
bone-in	65 minutes	75 minutes

	Pints	Quarts
deboned	75 minutes	90 minutes
Fish		90 minutes

A Note of Caution

Pressure canning is the only safe way to can meat and fish at home. Never attempt to can these foods any other way.

Avoid food poisoning! Process foods exactly as instructed. ALL VEGETABLES EXCEPT TOMATOES AND ALL MEATS, POULTRY AND FISH CANNED AT HOME MUST BE BOILED FOR 15 MINUTES BEFORE TASTING OR USING. (See also Detecting Spoilage in Canned Foods, p. 140).

SMOKING, BRINING AND CURING MEATS

PORK[12]

Pork is cured in three ways - with salt alone; with salt and sugar; or with salt, sugar and saltpeter. The last is the preferred "sugar cure." You can sugar-cure pork either dry or in a sweet-pickle brine. Because the dry cure is faster, it is popular in the South where warm weather makes spoilage a serious problem.

With either the dry or sweet-pickle cure, remember the main essentials:
- Chill the meat and keep it cold.
- Use the amount of salt in the recipe.
- Give the meat enough curing time to absorb the salt thoroughly.
- Smoke cured meat long enough to drive out excess moisture.

Weigh meat and curing ingredients carefully. Too little salt may cause spoilage; too much salt makes hard, dry, oversalty meat.

Keep meat cold while in cure. Hold curing meat at a temperature near 36° to 40° F. Higher temperatures increase the chance of spoilage. Lower temperatures slow salt penetration.

If curing temperatures drop below freezing for several days, add the same number of days to the curing time. Temperatures below 36° F. slow salt penetration.

Frozen meat is difficult to handle. If fresh meat freezes, thaw it in a chill room or in cold brine before putting it in cure.

Figure curing time carefully. Too few days in cure may cause spoilage. Too long a cure in heavy salt results in loss of quality.

---

[12]U.S. Department of Agriculture, *Slaughtering, Cutting and Processing Pork on the Farm*, Farmers' Bulletin No. 2138, (Washington, D.C.: U.S. Government Printing Office) pp. 25-33, 34-38.

Dry Curing

Check internal temperature of heaviest hams. (Push a thermometer to the center of the thickest part.) Be sure it is below 40° F.

Weigh the trimmed meat and the right amount of curing material. For 100 pounds of ham or shoulder use:

> Salt - 8 pounds
> Sugar - 2 pounds (brown, white or syrup)
> Saltpeter - 2 ounces

For bacon and other thin cuts, use only one-half this amount.

Mix curing ingredients thoroughly; be especially careful to mix the finely powdered saltpeter through the salt.

Divide the curing mixture into two equal parts, one part to use at once, the other to save for resalting. For bacon and other thin cuts, use the required amount at once; do not resalt.

Rub one part of curing mixture on all surfaces, poking some into shank ends. Pat about a 1/8-inch layer on lean face of hams. Pat a thin covering on shoulder. Frost the thin bacon strip with the mixture—the heavier the cut, the greater share of the mixture.

Fit salted meat in a clean barrel or crock, being careful not to shake off the curing mixture. Hold in a cold place, 36° to 40° F.

Figure time in cure (a minimum of 25 days): Bacon - 1 1/2 days to the pound; hams and shoulders - 2 days to the pound. Check curing time on the calendar.

Resalt with the other half of curing mixture 6 to 8 days after meat is put into cure. Salt hams and shoulders as before. For bacon and other thin cuts, add no more curing mixture. Keep pack cold, 36° to 40° F.

Give the salt plenty of time to penetrate to the center of the cuts and distribute itself evenly through the piece (2 or even 3 days to the pound, per piece, dry cure).

All the surface salt may be absorbed into the dry-cured meat before curing time is up. Give it more time to work down to the center of the cuts.

On the farm, meat often has to be cured at temperatures above 40° F. Under these conditions, speed up salt penetration:
- Salt lightly and spread the fresh, warm cuts. (Never pile warm meat or blanket it with salt.)
- Poke salt into the joints.
- Bone or slice the cuts into smaller, more quickly salted pieces.

All these methods help and may save the meat, but none are so satisfactory as curing at the proper temperature - 36° to 40° F.

Prevent Oversaltiness

The line between just salty enough to keep and too salty to taste good is narrow. Use care to make a sound and a palatable product.

Use 8 pounds of salt in dry-curing 100 pounds of trimmed pork to produce a cure that is on the salty side. If you are careful to get all the mixture packed on the faces of the hams and shoulders, 6 pounds is enough and will make the meat more palatable.

Sweet-pickle Curing

Fit the cold, smoothly-trimmed cuts into a clean barrel or crock. Cover with a cold pickle solution (36° to 40° F.) made by dissolving 8 pounds of salt, 2 pounds of sugar, and 2 ounces of saltpeter in 4 1/2 gallons of water. Weight the meat to keep it from floating above the pickle solution. Use enough solution to submerge the meat. Keep pack cold throughout the curing period—at 36° to 40° F. if possible.

Overhaul the pack about the seventh day after putting it in cure by removing all meat, pouring out the sweet pickle, repacking the meat and covering with the same restirred curing mixture. Overhaul two more times—about the 14th and 28th days.

Curing time for hams and shoulders is 3 1/2 to 4 days to the pound, with a minimum of 28 days for the lightweight cuts. Thus, a 6-pound shoulder needs 28 days in cure; a 15-pound ham, 60 days. However, a 10-pound bacon needs 15 days in cure; heavier bacon and loins, 21 days.

Bacon may receive a milder cure if you use 5 1/2 instead of 4 1/2 gallons of water to make the sweet pickle.

Pickled pork may be left in curing solution until used, but it is rather salty.

If the sweet-pickle solution sours or becomes ropy or syrupy, discard it. Scrub the meat in hot water, scald and rechill the barrel, repack the meat, and cover with new, cold, curing solution. Use 5 1/2 gallons water to make this second solution instead of the 4 1/2 gallons recommended above.

Preparing for Smoking

Remove pieces from the dry or brine pack when their curing time is up. Brush the lighter cuts to remove excess dry mixture or lift them from the brine and hold in a cold place until the heavier pieces are ready to smoke.

Soak fully-cured meat in cold, fresh water to remove some of the surface salt (15 to 30 minutes).

String meat for hanging in smoke: *hams and shoulders*, through shank; *bacon*, reinforce flank end with hardwood skewer or clean galvanized wire to hold it square in smoke.

Scrub strung meat clean with sharp brush and hot (110° to 125° F.) water so it will take brighter color in smoke.

If smoked flavor is not desired, hang cured meat to dry for about a week before bagging it.

Smokehouses

Smokehouses range from the temporary "one-hog" type made from a 50-gallon barrel to permanent structures suitable for both smoking and storing meat.

Smokehouses should be of reasonably-tight construction to permit easy regulation of temperature and flow of smoke and air. A rapid flow of air past the meat is needed at the beginning of the smoking operation to drive off the surplus moisture. Less rapid air movement near the end of the smoking period prevents excessive shrinkage in weight of the meat. A temperature from 90° to 120° F. normally is used; the lower temperatures are preferred.

A 50-gallon barrel, with both heads removed, or a box with tight sides, can be used for smoking small quantities of meat.

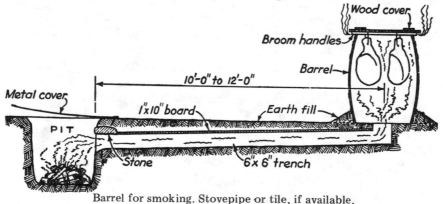

Barrel for smoking. Stovepipe or tile, if available,
could be used for the flue.

Figure 10.2

Set the barrel over the upper end of a shallow, sloping, covered trench and dig a pit at the lower end for the fire. Control the heat of the fire by covering the pit with a piece of sheet metal and mounding earth around the edges, so as to cut off most of the draft. Clean muslin or burlap hung over the top of the barrel will protect a 1-inch opening between the barrel and the cleated top, which rests on broomsticks supporting the meat.

The smoke house illustrated in Figure 10.3 is large enough for average farm needs and is easily constructed. The outside fire pit

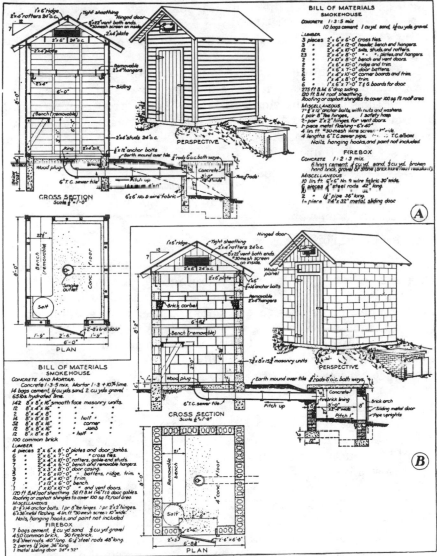

Smokehouse: Drawings and bill of materials for frame construction (A) and for cement-block construction (B).

Figure 10.3

makes temperature control easy and reduces the fire hazard. Tight construction and well-fitted ventilators provide effective regulation of the air flow past the meat.

Meat can be crowded into a smokehouse, but no piece should touch another piece or the wall. The space required varies with the weight of the cut, but 12 inches in width both ways and 2 feet in height for each piece is a fair basis for estimating the capacity of the house.

The use of movable two-by-fours across the house for hanging the meat enables the operator to adjust the hangers to the size of the hams or sides of bacon being smoked. Two or more tiers of meat can be hung in the house. A taller house, holding four or more tiers of meat, can be served by the same fire pit.

Locate the frame type of smokehouse at least 50 feet from other buildings.

A solid, frostproof foundation is essential. A concrete floor is desirable, as it can be made both ratproof and flyproof and is more easily cleaned than wood.

Smoking Cured Pork

Smoking flavors, colors and dries cured pork and slows the development of rancidity. It has slight preservative action.

Hang the cured, soaked, scrubbed meat to drip overnight to prevent streaking or smudging in smoke. A wet surface will not take a uniform smoked color. Hang so that no pieces touch.

In the smokehouse, build a fire of any hardwood—hickory, oak, apple, pecan—or even corn cobs. Hardwood sawdust is excellent. Never use pine; its smoke is sooty and strong smelling.

Heat smokehouse to 100° to 120° F., just hot enough to melt the surface grease.

Open ventilators to let out the moisture.

Close ventilators the second day, and smoke 1 or more days, or until the meat has the desired color. A thin haze of smoke is as effective as a dense cloud.

Be careful not to overheat and scorch the meat.

A fire built after the Indian fashion with the sticks radiating from the center like the spokes of a wheel, becomes lower and cooler as it burns. Building such a fire is a good precaution, for inattention to a hot fire has ruined the meat in many a smokehouse. Use green sawdust to deaden the blaze.

The use of liquid smoke, smoked salt, and like preparations intended to be applied to meat as a substitute for smoking, is prohibited in federally inspected packinghouses.

See "Testing Smoked Meat for Spoilage" on p. 142.

Wrapping and Storing Smoked Meat

If possible, plan the date for killing and curing so that the smoked meat can be bagged or put in an insect-proof place before flies appear in the spring. Keep careful watch for insect infestation throughout the storage period.

After the smoked meat has cooked, it is ready to be wrapped and stored. Wrapping protects meat from insects and partially excludes light and air, which speed development of rancidity in fat.

Unbagged smoked meat cannot be stored safely, even in well-built, flytight smokehouses. Flies or fly eggs get in, either on a piece of meat or when the door is opened. If each piece is properly cured and smoked, wrapped, bagged, and hung separately, it will be safe to store in a dry, dark, cool, well-ventilated place. Many farmers keep their hams and shoulders a year or longer until they have developed the mellow flavor characteristic of stored, smoked pork.

You can rub pepper on the meat at this time to add flavor. Ground black pepper, with or without a little red pepper, may be used.

Cover the meat with parchment paper and put into muslin bags. Use a paper wrapping that is heavy enough to keep the grease from soaking the bottom of the bag. Fold over the tops of the bags and tie them securely; make a loop in the outside tie string for hanging the meat. Do not hang wrapped meat by the string that passes through the meat because insects may enter the package along the string.

You can further protect each sack by painting it with yellow wash; for 100 pounds of hams and bacon use 3 pounds of barium sulfate, 1 1/4 ounces of yellow ocher, 1 ounce of glue (dry), and 6 ounces of flour. Half-fill a pail with water and mix in the flour—break up all lumps. Mix the ocher with a quart of water in a separate pan, add the glue, and pour into the flour-water mixture. Bring this mixture to a boil and add the barium sulfate slowly; stir constantly. Make the wash the day before it is required. Stir it frequently while using and apply with a brush. If you prefer, paint the bags with lime, clay or flour mixed with water to a rather thick consistency.

Bacon is usually more palatable when freshly cured and smoked. It does not keep as well as hams and shoulders, and most farmers prefer to use it during the spring and early summer.

Skipper Flies

If skipper fly larvae attack meat, trim off and burn the infested parts. Use the sound parts. Larvae may burrow deeply along the bone and shank. Prevent further damage by refrigerated storage.

Refrigerated Storage

Insects such as skipper flies will not multiply at temperatures below 45° F. Surface mold will grow at temperatures above 15° to 18° F.

Mild bacon is often kept in freezer storage but, to save locker space, the hams and shoulders often are held at home, unrefrigerated. Cured pork will develop some rancidity even in the freezer.

Mold Growth

Surface mold will not affect the wholesomeness of the meat, even if it adds a moldy flavor. Most mold and mold flavor can be scrubbed or trimmed off. Oiling smoked meat with edible oil, such as cottenseed oil or lard, will delay mold growth. Repeat oiling in a month or so.

Aged or Smithfield-Style Pork

The characteristic pungent flavor of aged or Smithfield-style hams and shoulders is caused, in part, by the enzymes or ferments normally in the meat. Eight to twelve months' storage at air temperatures or 50 to 70 days in heated storage (105° to 110° F.) is needed to develop this flavor fully. Cured pork ripens slowly, if at all in refrigeration.

Recipe for Smoked Sausage [13]

    2 pounds salt
    2 to 4 ounces of ground sage
    2 to 4 ounces of ground black pepper
    1/2 to 1 ounce red pepper, if desired
    1/2 to 1 ounce ground cloves, or
    1 ounce ground nutmeg, if desired
    12 ounces sugar, if the sausage is to be used quickly
    100 pounds pork trimmings

Mix the seasoning thoroughly, spread it over the trimmings and grind the whole quantity through the fine plate of the meat grinder. You may prefer to grind the unseasoned meat through a plate with 1/2-inch holes and then mix it with the spices and regrind through

---

[13]U.S. Department of Agriculture, *Slaughtering, Cutting and Processing Pork on the Farm*, Farmers' Bulletin No. 2138 (Washington, D.C.: U.S. Government Printing Office), p. 44.

the plate with 1/8-inch holes.

If you are stuffing the sausage into casings, do so immediately after grinding. The sausage should be soft enough to pack tightly in the casings without adding cold water. If it is too stiff to stuff properly, add 6 to 10 cups of cold water and knead until the mass becomes doughlike. Stuff tightly in casings and allow to cure about 24 hours in a cool place. Smoke and dry at a temperature of 70° to 90° F. for a day or two until a dark mahogany color is obtained. Do not keep this sausage until hot weather unless it is canned.

Recipe for Bologna Sausage [14]

Bologna sausage is made of ground pork and beef mixed with enough water to give the sausage the desirable fine, tenacious texture. Commercial concerns sometimes grind cracked ice with warm beef from freshly-slaughtered cattle because this method gives a finer grain to the finished product.

One standard recipe for bologna sausage is as follows:

60 pounds beef
40 pounds pork trimmings
10 quarts cold water
2 to 2 1/2 pounds salt
1 ounce saltpeter
2 to 4 ounces black pepper
1 to 1 1/2 ounces coriander
1 ounce mace
Onions, if desired

Grind the chilled beef trimmings with 19 ounces of salt. Use the coarse grinding plate, and allow the meat to cure in a cool place for about 48 hours. Add salt, in the same proportion, to the coarsely-ground pork the next evening and allow it to cure overnight. Many persons do not cure the pork.

Regrind the cured beef, using the plate with 1/8-inch holes. Then add the pork and grind the mixture again. If the pork is not cured, add the salt (13 ounces for 40 pounds of pork) before grinding. Add spices and water and mix vigorously until the mass is sticky. Thorough mixing often requires 30 minutes.

Tightly stuff the sausage into beef casings or muslin bags and allow to hang and cure in a cool place overnight. Put it in a well-ventilated smokehouse heated to 110° to 120° F. Protect the casings from the direct blaze that might cause them to scorch. The sausage

---

[14]*Ibid*, pp. 44-45.

should take on a rich mahogany brown in about 2 hours' smoking.

Immediately put the hot, freshly smoked sausage into water heated to 160° to 175° F., and cook until it squeaks when the pressure of the thumb and finger on the casings is suddenly released. The usual cooking time for sausage stuffed in beef "rounds" is 15 to 30 minutes; for larger casings, 60 to 90 minutes. Plunge the cooked sausage into cold water to chill it. Hang it in a cool place.

BEEF [15]

You can cure beef in two ways—by making it into corned beef or dried beef. Both methods use a combination of dry and brine curing in which salt, sugar, and saltpeter (potassium nitrate) are used.

Corned Beef

Corned beef is generally made from the cheaper cuts and those that have considerable fat, such as the plate, rump, and chuck.

Remove all bone from the cut and, to facilitate packing, cut pieces into uniform thickness and size. For each 100 pounds, use 8 to 10 pounds of coarse salt. Spread a layer of salt on the bottom of a clean, sterilized wooden barrel or stone crock. Next, pack a layer of meat in the container; sprinkle with salt and add the next layer of meat and salt and so on. Lightly rub each piece of meat with salt before packing. Allow the packed meat to stand for about 24 hours, at which time cover with a brine made as follows:

For each 100 pounds of meat, use 4 pounds of sugar, 4 ounces of saltpeter and 2 ounces of baking soda dissolved in 4 gallons of water. After covering with brine, weight the meat down. High-quality corned beef requires from 30 to 40 days of curing. At the end of the curing period, remove the corned beef from the cure as needed, wash, and dry or smoke.

Keep a close eye on the brine as it may become ropy, especially if the temperatures rise much above 38° F. When this happens, remove the meat, wash it thoroughly in warm water, repack in a new clean container (or in the original container, thoroughly washed and sterilized), and cover with new brine.

Dried Beef

Dried beef is made from the heavier muscled cuts, especially the round. Cut the muscles lengthwise or prepare as a whole muscle. The

---

[15]U.S. Department of Agriculture, *Slaughtering, Cutting and Processing Beef on the Farm*, Farmers' Bulletin No. 2209 (Washington, D.C.: U.S. Government Printing Office) p. 30.

curing procedure is the same as that used for corned beef except that you may add an extra pound of sugar for each 100 pounds of meat. After the meat is cured, remove it from the brine, wash, and hang up to dry for 24 hours. Smoke the cured meat in the regular manner at a temperature of 130° to 140° F. for 70 to 80 hours or until quite dry. The dried beef is ready to be used or it can be hung in a dry, dark room or wrapped and hung for storage. Dried beef is usually cut very thin for use.

Smoking Beef

The same smokehouse and procedures used for pork work well for beef.

You may store smoked dried beef in the smokehouse if it is ventilated and free from flies. A cool, dry, dark and well-ventilated basement (free of flies) is a satisfactory storage area.

HOME DRYING OF FRUITS AND VEGETABLES [16]

Vegetables

Prepare fresh, good quality vegetables. Pare and shell as you would for table use. Slice or chop thin, as desired. Peas and beans are the only vegetables normally left whole for drying. Blanch in boiling water or live steam until heated through and wilted, but not cooked. Celery, onion, and tomatoes need not be blanched.

Drying

Spread the prepared vegetables out no more than 1/2-inch deep on clean drying trays or window screens. Tacking cheesecloth to the trays before placing the vegetables on them will prevent the vegetables from falling through. Dry in a dehydrator, in the sun or in an oven. Dry at 140° F. in the dehydrator for 6 to 18 hours. Dry in the sun for not more than 2 days. If further drying is needed after 2 days, move the vegetables into the shade. Bring the trays in at night to prevent wetting with dew. Cover the vegetables with cheesecloth to keep off insects.

In the oven: Dry no more than 4 to 6 pounds of vegetables at a time. Use two to four trays spaced at least 2 1/2 inches apart. Allow at least a 3-inch space at the top and bottom of the oven. Place a thermometer on the top tray near the back. Hold the temperature inside the oven at 140° F. Leave the door open at least 4 inches if using a gas oven, less if using an electric oven. The door opening may be adjusted or the heat turned on and off to maintain the proper

---

[16]Creuss, Faust, and Mrak, *Home Drying of Vegetables and Fruits.*

temperature. Examine the food and turn the trays frequently to prevent scorching. Keep the room well-ventilated.

Packaging:

Fumigate sun-dried products. Products dried with artificial heat need not be fumigated if packaged immediately. To fumigate, see Chapter XII, Keeping Food Safe From Pests.

As soon as the product is dried, package in dry, scalded, insect and moisture-proof containers. Tighten lids to prevent entry of moisture and insects. The seal does not have to be of the vacuum type required for regular canning. Pack as tightly as possible without crushing.

Fruits

Prepare fresh, good quality fruits.

Cherries, Grapes, Plums and Prunes

These fruits must be dipped in a lye solution to crack their skins. Dip only whole, uncut fruits.

To make the Lye solution:

Place 2 tablespoons lye in a gallon of cold water. Stir with a wooden spoon to dissolve. Dip the fruits into the solution for 5 to 30 seconds according to the maturity of the fruit. The dipping should be long enough to form many small cracks in the skins. These appear after washing. Rinse the fruit very thoroughly in clear, cold water to remove the lye solution before pitting, slicing, and placing on trays.

Clingstone peaches may be peeled with a lye solution. Use a solution of 4 to 6 tablespoons lye to a gallon of cold water. CAUTION: Do not use aluminum utensils for lye solutions. If lye gets on the skin wash off with vinegar. (See soapmaking instructions for first aid for lye burns and poisoning.)

Sulfuring:

Sulfuring preserves color and decreases loss of vitamins A and C in apples, apricots, white cherries, nectarines, peaches, pears, plums and large prunes.

1. Do the sulfuring outdoors.
2. Place the fruit on slatted wooden trays, one layer deep.
3. Stack the trays 1 1/2 inches apart.
4. Use a tight wooden or cardboard box slightly larger than the trays.
5. Place the bottom tray at least 10 inches above the burning sulfur

or stack the trays beside the sulfur.

6. Cut an opening 1 inch by 6 inches at the bottom of the box for ventilation. Close the opening after the sulfur is burned up.

7. Place the sulfur in a clean metal container, such as a tin can. The container should be just deep enough to prevent overflow.

8. Use 2 teaspoons sulfur per pound of fruit if sulfuring time is less than three hours. If more than three hours, use three teaspoons sulfur per pound of fruit.

9. Set fire to the sulfur. Do not leave the match in the can. Keep the flame away from the fruit. Cover.

10. Keep covered until the sulfur is completely burned. Close the opening when the sulfur is burned and leave closed and covered for the required sulfuring time.

Sulfuring Box (cut away view)

Figure 10.4

Sulfuring Time:

Apples	60 minutes
Pears, sliced	60 minutes
quartered	120 minutes
Large stone fruits	Same as pears
White cherries	10 to 15 minutes

Hot Syrup Blanch

This process is used to sweeten the fruit and also to help preserve the color in apples, nectarines, peaches, pears, plums, and large prunes that are not sulfured. The fruit may darken somewhat if not sulfured, but the product has a good flavor. Figs are often blanched in syrup.

To prepare syrup:

Use 1 cup corn syrup or 1 cup sugar to 3 cups water. Or use corn syrup diluted with an equal amount of water. Heat to the simmering point. Add prepared fruit. Simmer for 10 minutes. Remove from heat and let stand for 10 minutes. Lift out the fruit and drain.

Steam Blanching

This is another method of preparing fruit for drying.

Fruit	Steam Blanching Time		Syrup Blanch Time
Apples			20 minutes
Pears			20 minutes
Large stone fruits	5 to 20 minutes, if desired		
Berries, except strawberries	1/2 to 1 minute		
Cherries			20 minutes
Figs	20 minutes	or	20 minutes

USE YOUR FREEZER

The freezer is often overlooked as a place for storing the emergency food supply. Power failure can interrupt the operation of the home freezer, but the majority of emergencies for which we are storing our food would not involve power failure. There are procedures to follow in case of power failure to avoid spoilage.

The Freezer

Normally the freezer compartment of the refrigerator does not maintain a cold enough temperature for long-term storage of frozen foods. A temperature of 0º F. or below is required for best results in storing foods. The freezer compartment of the refrigerator usually will not maintain that cold a temperature. And if the freezer is self-defrosting it should not be depended upon for long-term storage because the self-defrosting mechanism works by raising the temperature of the freezer compartment to just above freezing and blowing air through the freezer. Both the higher temperature needed to defrost and the circulating warmer air are undesirable because they lead to drying out and deterioration of the frozen food.

Check the temperature at several places inside your freezer and adjust the thermostat as needed. The door shelves are usually the warmest area. Store foods that will be used the soonest in the warmest areas. If your freezer does not maintain 0º F. or below, plan to use your frozen food within a few days of purchase.

Place your freezer in a cool place for most efficient operation.

Check the gasket occasionally. Keep it clean and in good condition. Have it replaced if it deteriorates. A good test is to place a piece of paper in the door and close it. If the paper can be very easily pulled out of the door, the gasket is not sealing the door tightly enough. If the gasket appears to be in good condition and the paper still slips out easily, perhaps the hinges on the door need adjustment.

Tips on Freezing

Freezing does not prevent spoilage and deterioration of the food. Frozen food will not keep indefinitely, nor will freezing improve the quality of the food stored.

Always store like foods together. Put the freshest packages on the bottom or in the back. Label and date all containers before freezing. Use the oldest first and plan your meals so that your frozen food is used within the recommended storage period. Keep a record of what you have in your freezer and consult this when planning your meals and purchases.

Unfrozen foods or foods that have a temperature above 0° F. should be brought to 0° F. as quickly as possible. Place them in contact with the refrigerated surfaces of the freezer, leaving space around the other sides of the containers for air to circulate. Once properly frozen, the packages can be rearranged for space saving.

Defrosting

Defrost the freezer frequently by scraping the frost off the shelves as soon as it forms a thin layer. Always use a flexible scraper that will not damage the inside of the freezer. If the frost reaches a depth of 1/2", defrost completely. Frost decreases the storage space, interferes with the maintenance of a proper storage temperature and can overload the freezer motor causing the freezer to stop freezing and require a costly repair. Follow the manufacturer's directions for defrosting your freezer.

If food must be removed from the freezer during the defrosting, or the door must be open for more than just a few minutes, protect your foods from thawing by wrapping in several layers of newspaper and placing in boxes. Return the food to the freezer as soon as possible. Run the freezer for 10 to 15 minutes after defrosting and before replacing the food. This will bring the temperature in the freezer down to the proper level.

To defrost the empty freezer quickly, set a large fan in front of the open freezer. The rapid circulation of the air by the fan will speed up the defrosting considerably.

Selecting and Buying Frozen Foods

Buy from a reputable dealer who will vouch for the quality of his merchandise. Note the condition of the freezer cabinet—whether it is clean and the way the food is stacked in it. There is a line on the inner side of many cabinets near the top. Food should never be stacked above this line. Select foods only from clean cabinets in which the food is stacked no higher than the proper fill line.

Select packages that are clean and firm. If food has warmed enough to soften it, you can be sure that it has already lost quality. Signs that indicate improper storage or handling are: seepage, soggy cartons, food that is normally frozen in separate pieces frozen into a block. Avoid packages that have any of these conditions.

Make sure that packaging material is not torn, crushed or stained. Frozen food that is exposed or improperly packaged dries out and develops off-flavors.

Select frozen food last when shopping. Protect it from thawing on the way home by putting it in insulated bags. Put it in the freezer as soon as you get home. Never leave frozen food sitting in the car to thaw while shopping or running errands. Quality diminishes with thawing and refreezing.

If you buy frozen food by the case or in large quantities, check the condition of the food in at least one container soon after you buy it. If the food is not bright colored and solidly frozen or shows signs of deterioration, return it or plan to use it within a short time.

Judging Quality of Frozen Foods

The food should be almost free from frost, solidly frozen, bright in color, fresh flavored and showing no undesirable changes in texture.

In Case Of Power Failure

If you have advance warning of a power failure, set your freezer thermostat at its lowest setting right away. The lower the temperature in the freezer, the longer the food will remain frozen with the power off. If power outages are frequent in your area because of storms, take this precautionary measure any time a storm is anticipated that may cause an outage.

Try to find out how long the outage will last. If you can expect normal operation within a day or two or before the food in your freezer will thaw, buy some dry ice to put in your freezer. You will need 50 pounds per 20 cubic feet of freezer space. This will keep a full freezer below freezing for two to three days. Do not set the dry ice directly on the food packages. Put cardboard or several layers of newspapers between the ice and the food. If left in one large block, the ice will last longer. Dry ice evaporates, even if kept cold.

If the fully-loaded freezer is left unopened, the food will remain frozen without dry ice for two to three days and the half-full freezer will remain below freezing for about one day. Food in an almost empty freezer will thaw rapidly. The food in the freezer compartment of your freezer will remain solidly frozen up to eight hours.

If the power will not be restored while the food will still be frozen, plan to take it to a locker plant or perhaps a neighbor will have room in his operating freezer.

If the food cannot be kept frozen, plan to can, dry, brine, or cook and eat it. Many foods can be cooked and then refrozen, if they thaw completely. Partially-thawed foods can be refrozen if their temperature does not go above 40° F. and there are still ice crystals in the food. They should be used as soon as possible after refreezing because their quality will be diminished. [17]

A Word of Caution

Check your freezer frequently to be sure it is operating. Don't lose a freezer full of food because someone pulled the plug or the motor is not operating.

To avoid motor failure and costly repairs, keep the freezer defrosted and never run the freezer at the coldest setting for more than a short time.

---

[17]U.S. Department of Agriculture, *Home Care of Purchased Frozen Foods*, Home and Garden Bulletin No. 69, (Washington D.C.: U.S. Government Printing Office, 1960).

CHAPTER XI

DETECTING SPOILAGE

General Precautions

All canned foods,[1] whether home or commercially canned, should be carefully examined when opened. Do not taste home-canned fruits or tomatoes or commercially-canned foods until they have passed the appearance and odor tests. Then taste only a small portion.

Home canned meats and low-acid vegetables MUST be boiled for at least 15 minutes before tasting or eating. Covering the pan while boiling will make any off-odor more apparent. After boiling, smell the food. If there is no apparent off-odor, taste just a bit.

When heating commercially-canned foods for serving, note the color. Any unusual color may indicate spoilage. An odor so slight as to go unnoticed when the product is cold may be quite easily detected when the product is heated.

Canned food should be discarded if:
- The ends of the can are bulged or the seal on the can or jar is broken.
- It contains gas bubbles or if the liquid squirts out of the can when opened.
- It is unusually soft or if it is mushy, slimy or moldy.
- It has any peculiar or unusual smell. (Canned smoked products will have an odor upon opening, but this dissipates quickly.
- The liquid is cloudy. (Minerals in hard water or starch from overripe vegetables may cause cloudiness. This is not spoilage. Boil and smell as a precaution.)
- The taste reveals any queer, sour or musty off-flavor.

Burn spoiled food or throw the closed jar or can away with the food. Do not give spoiled food to animals since it can poison them, too. It is advisable to discard all jars in which spoilage has occured.

Do not discard spoiled food where children or animals might find it and eat it.

Some Causes of Spoilage

---

[1] From *The All American Way of Canning and Cooking with All-American Pressure Cookers,* (Mannitowoc, Wisc.: Wisconsin Aluminum Foundry Co., Inc.).

Fermentation:

Any bulged can or any can or jar with a loose seal should be considered suspicious. The bulging is due to the production of gas due to fermentation. The gas is carbon dioxide, although some other foul-smelling gases may be mixed with it. The product is sour, usually soft, discolored, and offensive in odor.

Fermentation comes from under-cooking or from introduction of air through a leak.

Flat Sour:

With flat sour there is nothing about the outside appearance of the can to suggest spoilage. The product is often soft and mushy but it may even appear sound and firm. It smells and tastes sour. Most of the flat sour is caused by a type of organism that develops best at luke-warm temperatures. More thorough processing and speed in working so as to avoid holding the product at lukewarm temperatures are the preventatives.

Corn, peas, green beans, greens and asparagus are the principle offenders in flat sour.

To avoid flat sour watch these points:

(1) Can only fresh products. The germs may develop before the product is canned and all the cooking in the world will not remove the sour taste. Two hours from garden to can is a good motto.

(2) Don't let pre-heated or pre-cooked or scalded products stand at lukewarm temperatures. Get them into the cans or jars as quickly as possible and have them as hot as possible when they are packed.

(3) Have the water boiling (for cans) or quite hot (for jars) so it does not take too long for the temperature to come up after packing the canner. Have a good fire so that you can speed up the work.

(4) Do not try to can too much at one cooking.

(5) Do not let the cans or jars stand after packing and before processing.

(6) Do not pack the jars or cans too tightly. Heat can easily penetrate to the center of loosely-packed food.

(7) Cool quickly. Do not stack hot cans or jars.

(8) Store in a cool place.

Botulinus

This type of spoilage rarely occurs alone in canned foods, but is usually found in connection with other spoilage. In its well-developed stage, a rank, cheesy odor is typical of this type of spoilage. Discarding without tasting all canned foods which show any signs of spoilage makes rare the chances of botulinus poisoning, although appearance may not always indicate the presence of this kind of spoilage.

Botulinus spores are found in the soil. Thorough washing of all soil-contaminated products is a good precaution. Be careful not to underprocess. That is why a pressure canner adds safety to the canning of meats and vegetables. Never can meat or low-acid vegetables without a pressure canner for processing.

The Imps of Spoilage

Molds:

Molds thrive in dampness and darkness, feed upon sugar and starches, grow well in acids, and must have air. They are found in jellies, preserves, fruits and tomatoes. They are easily controlled for they are killed by short exposures to boiling or even less than boiling temperatures.

Yeasts:

Yeasts feed upon sugars and form gas causing the product to ferment and the cans to bulge or jars to lose their seal. They need air and will not grow in acids. They are easily killed by boiling or less-than-boiling temperatures.

Bacteria:

The big troublemakers are the many types and varieties of bacteria. They grow best in protein foods such as meat, beans, and peas. They do not thrive in sweets or acids. Some varieties do not need air. A few varieties produce spores that are highly resistant to heat.

The imps of spoilage are found everywhere: in the soil, on the surfaces of fruits and vegetables, and in the air. None of them is big enough to be seen by the naked eye, but the microscope plainly reveals them.

Meats, peas, corn and beans were the hard nuts to crack of canning, because they are such good foods for bacteria. Man's increasing knowledge of the kinds of bacteria and their action enables him now to can these products easily and safely.

Testing Smoked Meat for Spoilage [2]

Often you can detect sourness in smoked pork when the warm

---

[2]U.S. Department of Agriculture, *Slaughtering, Cutting and Processing Pork on the Farm*, Farmers' Bulletin No. 2138, (Washington, D.C.: U.S. Government Printing Office), p. 33, 34.

meat is removed from the smokehouse. You may notice a taint a week or two after smoking. Most of the meat that safely reaches this stage may be considered sound.

Run a sharpened length of stiff wire along the bone to the center of the ham from both the hock and loin ends. If the trier brings out a sweet odor, the meat is sound. If the trier carries an unpleasant odor, cut open the piece and examine it carefully for spoilage. If there is a definite odor of putrefaction, destroy the entire piece. Try shoulders in the shank, at the shoulder point, and under the bladebone.

Change of Color in Canned Foods [3]

1.   Darkening at the tops of jars may be caused by oxidation due to air in the jars or to underprocessing.

2.   Overprocessing may darken the contents of the entire jar.

[3]U.S. Department of Agriculture, *Home Canning of Fruits and Vegetables*, Home and Garden Bulletin No. 8, (Washington, D.C.: U.S. Government Printing Office, 1972), p. 30.

CHAPTER XII

KEEPING FOOD SAFE FROM PESTS

Control of Insects in Food

Temperature and humidity affect insects to a great degree. Most insects are inactive at low temperatures and will not reproduce unless the temperature reaches above 70 degrees. At very low temperatures, insects stop eating and, unless they are able to hibernate, the insects die. Very high temperatures also kill insects but such high temperatures may also damage the stored food.

Most insects are active and able to reproduce in a range of humidity from 11.5% to 14.5%. A moisture content of 12.5% is ideal for feeding and reproduction of the major grain pests. High humidity in grain leads to the growth of molds that kill the insects, but the molds also spoil the grain for human and animal consumption.

Rice and granary weevils cannot breed in wheat that has less than 10% moisture. The adults soon die. As temperatures rise, their ability to breed in dry grain increases. Moisture above 10% encourages weevils. These pests cannot survive in grain that has less than 9% moisture.

Under most circumstances, dry wheat with 10% moisture or less can be stored indefinitely without serious damage from insects.

Methods for Eliminating Insects

These methods of insect control have been found to be effective:

(1) *Heat:* Use this method only where other methods are not practical. Heat destroys some of the vitamins and alters the physical and chemical composition of foods. Wheat that has been treated with heat will not sprout and makes poor quality bread.

Dehydrated fruits, ground cereals, flours and oats are some of the foods that can be fumigated with heat.

Spread the food no more than 1/2 inch deep in shallow pans. Heat in a 150º F. oven for at least 20 minutes. The temperature of the food must remain at 140º F. for at least 10 minutes to kill all stages of most insects. Leave the oven door ajar to prevent overheating.

Dried fruits can be packed loosely in jars and then sealed and processed in the oven for 20 minutes at 150º F. Fruits that are sun-dried at home must be fumigated before storing.

Dried fruits can be placed in a mesh bag and dipped in boiling water for six seconds, as an alternative to oven heating. After dipping in water, the fruit must be dried in an insect-free place and then the fruit can be stored in insect-proof containers.

To control the bean weevil in beans and other legumes, heat to 145º F. for two hours to kill all stages. [1]

(2) *Dry Ice:* Place two ounces of dry ice in the bottom of a five-gallon container. Pour wheat or other whole grain in on top of the dry ice. Place the lid on the container, loosely. Allow the dry ice to evaporate, about 30 minutes, then seal. If the lid bulges, open carefully and reseal.

A word of caution: If water condenses on the inside of the container, this moisture must be removed to prevent the growth of fungus and molds in your stored grain. To help prevent condensation, treat your grain in a cool room. Wipe any condensation off the inside of the lid. A dessicant, such as silica gel, charcoal or salt, could be placed inside the container as a precaution. Put the dessicant in a cloth bag.

(3) *Dusts:* It is not usually recommended to mix dust with food products because of the difficulty in removing the dust from the food when it comes time to eat it. However, this method of insect control has been found to be effective and can be used if modern methods of storage are not available.

Small quantities of dust are not harmful to the human digestive system.

The dust is sprinkled in the beans, wheat, and whole grains at the rate of 1 part dust to 1000 parts of grain or beans.

"Dusts suitable for this purpose are finely divided silica gel, rock phosphates, precipitated chalk, magnesium oxide, aluminum oxide or other local material found to be satisfactory." [2] Diatomaceous earth is useful for this purpose. In Northern Africa ordinary road dust is used.

These dusts seem to work by scratching the delicate parts of the insect body and allowing the insect to dehydrate. As the moisture content of the grain increases, this method becomes less effective because the insects do not dehydrate as easily in a humid environment.

To remove the dust from the grain, rinse in clear water or shake thoroughly in a fine mesh bag.

---

[1]E.O. Essig, *Insects and Mites of Western North America*, (New York: Macmillan Co., 1958).

[2]J.A. Anderson and A.W. Alcock, Eds., *Storage of Cereal Grains and Their Products*, Monograph Series, Vol. II, (St. Paul, Minnesota: American Association of Cereal Chemists, 1954), p. 263.

(4) *Low Temperature:* Insects at all developmental stages can be killed by exposure to low temperatures for certain lengths of time. At temperatures of 0º to 5º F. most grain beetles and moths are killed in one day.

Storage of beans and other legumes at 32º to 34º F. prevents development of bean weevils and does not injure germination.

(5) *Insecticides:* Pyrethrins in combination with piperonyl butoxide or sulfoxide are insecticides of low toxicity to humans and they readily break down when exposed to heat and light. They can be mixed with organic dust, such as wheat dust, and dusted on wheat that is dry and free from insects, to provide good insect control. Do not use the grain within three weeks of application of the insecticide. [3] Expose the grain to light for at least 48 hours before using.

(6) *Sifting:* Sifting flour through a No. 64 wire screen will remove most of the eggs, larvae and other stages of insects.

Control of Insects in Storage Areas

Pyrethrum is an organic insecticide of short-term effectiveness and low toxicity to humans. It breaks down in light. [4] It is sprayed on plants in the garden, and it can be safely dusted on such stored foods as wheat and dried fruit. It is effective against many household pests. It can be dusted on floors and shelves. Any food that has been dusted with this insecticide should be washed, if possible, or exposed to light for a day or two in order to be sure that the toxic effects of the insecticide have dissipated. Follow the directions on the package.

Another method of fumigating shelves and floors is to paint them with an insecticide solution. A 2% solution of chlordane, 1/2% solution of dieldren in deodorized kerosene, or 2 tablespoons malathion in a gallon of water can be used. Paint shelves and baseboards. Spray under cabinets. Do not spray near open packages of food, on dishes, or on the skin. Never use kerosene near flour, milk, or wheat. Avoid spraying near pilot lights or open flame. Remove the food from the area to be treated and return it when the odor has dissipated.

5% chlordane dust or spray can be used in out-of-the-way places that contain no food and are inaccessible to children and pets.

Be cautious when using any insecticide. Insecticides are poisonous to humans and pets as well as insects.

---

[3](My local agricultural extension agent tells me that pyrethrins degrade within three weeks.)

[4]Robert L. Metcalf, *Organic Insecticides: Their Chemistry and Mode Of Action,* (New York: Interscience Publishers, Inc. 1955), p. 44, 68.

A substitute for insecticide would be to dust storage areas with diatomaceous earth. This is deadly to insects but harmless to humans.

Ants: Small bottles of Antrol may be placed in ant trails to control ants, or ant stakes may be placed around the foundation of the home. Keep these insecticides out of the reach of children. They are very toxic.

Sprays will help to control ants. Controlling aphids will also help to control ants.

Control of Rodents

Seal cracks in foundations and around doors, windows, water pipes and vents. Cover vent openings with wire screen. Keep the yard and house free of debris and trash. Piles of trash and debris provide hiding places for rodents. Garbage attracts rodents.

Place all food in metal, glass or heavy plastic containers. Mice, squirrels and other rodents can eat through paper, wood, cardboard and light plastic. They can eat through the plastic lids that are sold to seal cans of shortening and other foods.

To kill rodents, set out bait where children and pets will not get it. It is very toxic. Traps are effective against rodents. The city dog pound or animal control center often has squirrel traps. Squirrel traps are baited with nuts or peanut butter. Bait mouse traps with small bits of cheese or bacon. Pieces of fresh vegetables may also be used in mouse traps.

CHAPTER XIII

PRODUCING YOUR OWN FOOD

The ability to produce one's food, either by raising plants and animals, or by hunting and fishing, could be essential during a prolonged emergency situation.

There is a great deal of literature available on the subject of home food production which reaches beyond the scope of this book (some of which is listed in the Readiness Library on page 256). In particular, the reader may be interested in the Prentice-Hall Vocational Agriculture Series, which contains volumes on animal husbandry, crop production, and fruit growing. This chapter will be limited primarily to two important aspects for which literature is less easily obtained: sprouting and lard rendering.

Seeds for Planting and Sprouting

Among the items recommended for storage are seeds for planting and sprouting. They should be stored in a cool, dry place and protected from rodents, insects and freezing. Rotate them often enough to keep the supply fresh. The following table indicates the length of time that seeds retain their ability to germinate if properly stored.

VIABILITY OF VEGETABLE SEED [1]

Variety	No. of years of viability after harvest	Variety	No. of years of viability after harvest	Variety	No. of years of viability after harvest
Corn	2 years	Pepper	4 years	* * *	
Onions		Tomato		Beets	6 years
Parsnip		* * *		Eggplant	
Soybean		Broccoli	5 years	Melon	
Salsify		Cabbage		Squash	
* * *		Cauliflower		* * *	
Bean	3 years	Kohlrabi		Celery	8 years
Leek		Lettuce		* * *	
Parsley		Okra		Cucumber	10 years
Pea		Pumpkin		Endive	
* * *		Radish		* * *	
Carrot	4 years	Spinach			
Mustard		Turnip			

[1] Taken from *Organic Gardening and Farming*, April 1973, page 27, with permission.

Sprouting in Your Kitchen

Imagine being able to harvest a crop from two to five days after sowing the seed! It is possible right in your own kitchen using such simple equipment as a quart jar, an old nylon stocking, a few seeds and some water.

This is part of the miracle of sprouting!

Sprouted seeds are becoming more common in the American diet. They have long been a part of the Oriental diet in the form of bean sprouts.

The sprouted seed retains the nutrients contained in the dry form and gains vitamins in the process of sprouting. Those bean sprouts, besides being tasty and delightfully crunchy, are rich sources of protein and vitamin C.

There is a substance called phytate in grains. [2] It is an acid form of phosphorus which has the ability to combine with some minerals, particularly calcium, iron and zinc, to form compounds that are not readily absorbed by the human digestive system. Sprouting of grains for 72 to 120 hours neutralizes phytate. Significant reduction in phytate content occurs in shorter sprouting times. Sprouting of grains allows the body to absorb more calcium, iron and zinc. It should also be noted that phytate is neutralized by cooking and by the action of yeast. [3]

Any kind of seed can be sprouted. Peas, alfalfa, wheat, beans and lentils are the ones that are most commonly sprouted.

Sprouted seeds make wonderful additions to all dishes. They combine well with fruits, cereals, soups, stews, salads, sandwich spreads and are delicious, as well as nutritious, additions to bread. As a matter of fact, ground, raw, sprouted soybeans give bread an excellent texture and moistness.

Sprouts can be eaten raw or cooked. They should be cooked over low heat and only until tender-crisp to preserve the heat labile vitamins, especially vitamin C.

A distinct advantage of eating your beans sprouted is that they are said to cause less intestinal gas when sprouted.

How to Sprout

Sprouting is a very simple and satisfying experience. There are

---

[2] U.S. Department of Agriculture, *Food, The Yearbook of Agriculture*, (Washington, D.C.: U.S. Government Printing Office, 1959), p. 115.

[3] Robert Rodale, "Avoid Hidden Hunger", *Organic Gardening and Farming*, Vol. 20, No. 10 (October, 1973), p. 36-40.

about as many different ways to sprout as there are people and every-
one who sprouts will swear by his particular method. I have included
three simple methods here.

Method One: Pick through the seeds to remove debris and broken seeds. Seeds that are broken will rot rather than sprout, and
could spoil the entire batch. Wash the seeds and cover with warm
water. Soak for at least 12 hours at room temperature. Pour off the
soaking water and save it. Rinse well. Spread the seeds in a sprouter.
Cover with a damp cloth and let set in a dark place at room temperature. Three times a day remove the cloth and pour water over the
seeds and then pour the water off. Repeat the rinsing if desired. Save
the rinsing water. Rinse out the cloth and replace. A pinch of chlorinated lime may be added to the water once a day to help retard
mold. The sprouts are ready to use in 2 to 5 days. Keep the sprouts
in the dark until the last 24 hours of sprouting time. Then expose
them to light to develope cholorophyll, if desired.

Method Two: Place the drained, soaked seeds in a clean quart
jar. Tie a piece of nylon net or nylon stocking over the mouth of the
jar with a piece of string or a rubber band. Leave the seeds just damp.
Turn the jar neck down and set it at an angle in a cupboard or other
dark place at room temperature. Three times a day, pour water over
the seeds and then pour it off. A pinch of chlorinated lime may be
added to the rinsing water once a day, if desired. Do not let the seeds
dry out.

Method Three: Place the drained, soaked seeds in a cloth bag
and suspend it above a little water inside a large container. Cover to
keep dark and moist. Rinse three times a day, as above, to retard
mold and maintain freshness.

After sprouting, the seeds can be used immediately or stored for
future use. Drain well and place in a plastic bag in the refrigerator.
They will keep for several days this way.

They can also be blanched in boiling water for 2 to 3 minutes
and then frozen or dried for later use in cooking.

Most seeds are very easy to sprout but soybeans sour if not
handled properly. To keep soybeans fresh during sprouting, flood
with at least three changes of water each time that you rinse the
beans. Rinse more than three times a day, if possible.

There is no absolute rule about how long sprouts should be allowed to grow. Experiment and grow them to your own taste. This
table gives the usual lengths of the sprouts of various seeds:

Soybean and mungbean sprouts . . . 2 inches

Wheat sprouts . . . . the length of the seed
Alfalfa sprouts . . . . 1 to 2 inches
Lentil sprouts . . . . 1 inch long
Pea sprouts . . . . 2 inches long
Sunflower sprouts . . . . no more than 1/8 inch

Lard Rendering [4]

Any meat fat can be rendered and used for cooking and baking. To render lard, begin by cooking the leaf fat, backfat and fat trimmings. Because the caul and ruffle fats from internal organs yield a darker lard than the other fats, you will usually want to cook them separately. If you remove them carefully, these fats should be acceptable in odor and flavor.

Lard renders more rapidly and completely if you cut the fat into small pieces before putting it in the kettle. You may prefer to grind it. Start cooking slowly with a small quantity of fat that can be stored easily. When this fat has begun to melt, add the remainder. Do not completely fill the kettle, or it may boil over. To prevent sticking and scorching, stir the fat frequently and keep the fire low during the entire cooking process.

At the beginning, the temperature of rendering lard will stay at about 212° F. As the water contained in the fat tissues evaporates, the temperature will rise slowly. Do not allow it to go higher than 255°.

As rendering proceeds, the residual tissues (cracklings) brown and float. When they are more nearly completely rendered, they will gradually sink to the bottom. Take care to prevent small particles of cracklings from sticking and scorching on the bottom of the kettle. You can stop cooking when the cracklings still are floating, but complete rendering removes a greater proportion of the moisture and produces lard that is less likely to spoil.

Allow the rendered lard to settle and cool slightly before emptying the kettle. Carefully siphon or dip the liquid lard into containers. Put the rest of the lard, containing the cracklings, through a press. Strain the lard through a screen covered with 2 or 3 thicknesses of cheesecloth. Put the hot lard into 5- or 10-pound containers and store immediately at temperature near or below freezing. At this temperature, it will chill rapidly enough to produce a fine grain.

Air and light may cause a chemical change that makes stored

---

[4]U.S. Department of Agriculture, *Slaughtering, Cutting and Processing pork on the Farm*, Farmers' Bulletin No. 2138, (Washington, D.C.: U.S. Government Printing Office.)

lard rancid. For this reason, fill the containers to the top, seal with a tight cover, and store in a dark, cool place. Once lard becomes rancid, it is impossible to improve it.

If the moisture has been eliminated from the lard by thorough rendering, water souring should not develop during storage.

CHAPTER XIV

HOW TO USE STORED FOOD

The purpose of this chapter is to gather together a few hints, suggestions, basic information, and recipes that will make it easier to use many of the stored foods with which the average homemaker may not be familiar. There is no intent to replace the many good storage cooking guides and regular cookbooks that are available.

A Table of Equivalents

Equivalents

4 T. cocoa = 1 oz.
1 square chocolate = 1 oz.
5 large eggs = 1 C.
8 egg whites = 1 C.
16 egg yolks = 1 C.
2 T. granulated sugar = 1 oz.
2 C. granulated sugar = 1 lb.
2 2/3 C. brown sugar = 1 lb.
2 2/3 C. powdered sugar = 1 lb.
1 lb. potatoes = 4 medium size
1 lb. tomatoes = 3 medium size
2 T. butter = 1 oz.
4 C. grated cheese = 1 lb.

1 C. granulated sugar = 1/2 lb.
1 C. butter = 1/2 lb.
1 C. lard = 1/2 lb.
1 C. flour = 1/4 lb.
1 C. rice = 1/2 lb.
1 C. cornmeal = 5 oz.
1 C. steamed raisins = 6 ox.
1 C. currants = 6 oz.
1 C. stale bread crumbs = 2 oz.
1 C. nutmeats = about 5 oz.
1 C. water = 1/2 lb.
2 C. ground meat = 1 lb.
1 lb. fresh shelled peas = 1 C.

Yield

1 C. uncooked rice = 2 C. cooked
1 C. uncooked noodles = 1 1/4 C. cooked
1 C. uncooked macaroni = 1 C. cooked
1 C. uncooked spagetti = 1 1/4 C. cooked

Can Contents

No. 1 can = 2 C.
No. 2 can = 2 1/2 C.
No. 2 1/2 can = 3 C.

No. 3 can = 4 C.
No. 10 can = 13 C.

Equivalents of Capacity

3 t. = 1 T.
2 T. = 1/8 C.

4 T. = 1/4 C.
5 1/2 T. = 1/3 C.

Equivalents of Capacity (cont.)

1 fluid oz. - 2 T.	2 pints = 1 quart
2 C. = 1 pint	16 oz. - 1 lb.

Abbreviations

t. = teaspoon	lb. = pound
T.= tablespoon	oz. = ounce
C.= cup	qt. = quart

Substitutions

When the Recipe Calls For:	*Use:*
1 can sweetened condensed milk	6 oz. evaporated milk, 1/2 C. milk powder, 1/2 to 1 C. sugar. Combine and bring to a boil. Cool
1 C. milk	1/2 C. evaporated milk + 1/2 C. water *or* 1 C. reconstituted dry milk
1 C. sour milk	1 C. buttermilk *or* 1 C. sweet milk + 1 T. vinegar *or* lemon juice in baked goods calling for baking soda, use 1 C. sweet milk + 1 3/4 t. cream of tartar
1 C. sifted all-purpose flour	1 C. + 2 T. cake flour
2 T. flour, for thickening	1 T. cornstarch
1 C. sifted cake flour	1 C. minus 2 T. all-purpose flour *or* 3/4 C. + 2 T. all-purpose flour + 2 T. cornstarch
2 t. baking powder	1 1/8 t. cream of tartar + 1/2 t. baking soda
1 C. butter, in baked goods	1 C. shortening + 1/2 t. salt
1 t. Italian seasoning	1/4 t. each: oregano, basil, thyme, and rosemary + a dash of cayenne
1 t. marjoram	1 t. oregano
1 t. pumpkin pie spice	1/2 t. cinnamon, 1/4 t. ginger, 1/8 t. each nutmeg and ground cloves
1 t. allspice	1/2 t. cinnamon + 1/8 t. ground cloves

When the Recipe Calls For:	*Use:*
few drops red pepper seasoning	dash of cayenne
1 t. Worchestershire sauce	1 t. steak sauce
1/2 C. catsup or chili sauce	1/2 C. tomato sauce, 2 T. sugar, 1 T. vinegar, 1/8 t. ground cloves
1/2 C. tartar sauce	2 T. pickle relish, 6 T. mayonaise and 1 t. lemon juice
1 C. tomato juice	1/2 C. tomato sauce + 1/2 C. water
1 C. beef or chicken broth	1 bouillon cube or 1 envelope *or* 1 t. instant or granulated beef *or* chicken bouillon or extract dissolved in 1 C. water
1/4 C. cinnamon sugar	1/4 C. sugar + 1 t. cinnamon
1 C. molasses	1 C. dark corn syrup *or* 1 C. brown sugar + 3/4 C. water *or* 1 C. honey
1 sq. unsweetened chocolate	3 T. cocoa (not cocoa mix) + 1 1/2 teaspoons fat
1 C. raisins	1 C. cut-up prunes *or* 1 C. cut-up dates
1 package (10 oz.) frozen, sliced strawberries or raspberries	1 C. sliced fresh strawberries or raspberries + 1/3 C. sugar
12 oz. frozen sliced peaches	1 1/3 C. fresh peach slices + 1/3 C. sugar
1 lb. fresh shrimp	1 (5 oz.) can shrimp
1 lb. ground pork	1 lb. pork sausage
fresh pork sausage	canned pork sausage
bacon	bacon flavored bits (TVP)
cooked ham	canned ham or luncheon meat
1 can Chinese noodles	1 can potato sticks *or* 1/2 recipe fresh noodles, fried
1/2 lb. fresh mushrooms	3 or 4 oz. can mushrooms

What to Do When You Run Out

Shortening:

Any meat fat can be rendered and used for cooking and baking.

See pages 151 to 152 for rendering instructions. Many foods can be prepared without shortening with edible results.

Eggs:

Eggs can be omitted from baked products with satisfactory results. Increase the baking powder by 1 teaspoon for each egg omited from the recipe. Stick to recipes calling for only one egg, if possible, when baking without eggs. Too much baking powder in a recipe can give the product an unpleasant taste.

Another solution is to substitute gelatin for eggs. To replace each egg, soften 1 teaspoon unflavored gelatin in 3 tablespoons water. Then add 2 1/2 tablespoons boiling water and stir until dissolved. Refrigerate until thickened, like egg white, and beat until frothy before adding to the batter.

Meat:

Substitute vegetable sources of protein, such as beans, nuts, sprouts, or use cheese, milk, and eggs to provide protein in the diet.

Vegetables:

Sprout seeds to eat as vegetables. Substitute fruit for vegetables.

Citrus fruits and juices:

Increase amounts of other fruits and tomatoes in the diet, add sprouts to the diet or supplement with vitamin C tablets.

Flour:

Grind wheat, beans, corn or other seeds for flour.

Milk:

Soybean milk can replace part of the nutrients usually obtained from milk. To supplement the calcium, eat calcium-rich vegetables such as beet greens or broccoli. Adding a little vinegar to the water in which you boil bones for soup stock will leach out some of the calcium and make it available to your body.

Six Weeks' Suggested Food Storage Menus

Asterisks indicate that a recipe is included in this book. See the index to recipes on page 163.

WEEK ONE

Breakfast	Lunch	Dinner
Creamed chipped beef of biscuits	Spreadwiches* Carrot and raisin salad	Bean soup Whole wheat muffins

Breakfast	Lunch	Dinner
Broiled peach halves Milk	Grapefruit Tang	Asst. relishes Rhubarb-blueberry pie Milk
Scrambled eggs* w/bacon bits Toast Mandarin oranges Butter and Jelly Milk	Glorified Wheat* Salisbury steak w/mushroom sauce Mashed potatoes Rolls Milk	Chicken and noodles* Mixed vegetables Chocolate pudding Milk
Cinnamon-apple oatmeal Toast Milk Orange juice Butter and Jelly	Salmon Casserole Texas toast Milk Fruit	Chinese-style fried rice w/tofu cubes* Carrots with onions Mixed Jello cubes Almond cookies Milk
French toast* Syrup* Tomato juice Milk	Cream of asparagus soup Corn muffins* Cheese slices Fruit	Pinto bean tamales Cole slaw Applesauce Milk
Cracked Wheat cereal Date muffins Butter and honey Orange juice	Sausage pizza Buttered limas Lemon cream pie	Pepper beef* Rice Buttered carrots Milk Fruit
Eggs Foo Yung Plain muffins Milk Peaches Butter	Tomato soup Chicken-rice casserole* Milk	TVP patties parmesan* Corn Buttered spagetti Orange juice
Fried grits Bacon Milk Grapefruit segments	Veg. beef soup Open-faced cheese sandwiches Tapioca pudding	Chili* Marinated vegetables Rolls and Butter Fruit

All menus in this group can be prepared without fresh foods.

WEEK TWO

Breakfast	Lunch	Dinner
Blueberry pancakes	Hot Chicken Sandwiches	Chow mein w/fried noodles

Breakfast	Lunch	Dinner
Syrup	Fruit	Rolls
Pears	Orange tang	Hot apple pie w/cheese
Milk		
Egg nog	Vienna Sausage	Bulgar wheat meatballs
Cinnamon coffee	sandwiches	Buttered noodles*
cake	Veg. soup	Spinach
Stewed apricots	Cookies	Milk
Orange juice	Milk	
Sourdough pancakes*	Jellied seafood	Ham towers*
Maple syrup	salad	3-bean salad
Mandarin oranges	Rolls	Mashed potatoes
and pineapple	Orange cake	Milk
Milk	Milk	
Scrambled eggs	Soybean chowder*	Salmon Patties*
Fruit cocktail	Cheese sandwiches	Hominy in cheese
Oatmeal muffins	Orange juice	sauce
Grape juice		Molded veg. salad
Milk		Milk
Rice cakes*	Split pea soup	Beef cubes and gravy
Orange-pineapple	Pinto bean bread	Wheat pilaf
sauce*	Butter	Stewed tomatoes
Milk	Custard	Green beans
Banana bread	Ham spread sand-	Corned Beef
Sausage patties	wiches	Cabbage
Purple plums	Sauteed zucchini	Boiled potatoes
Milk	corn and onions	Buttered carrots
	Milk	
Canned Boysen-	Spamwiches*	Baked lasagna
berries	Fruit	Green beans w/bacon
TVP cereal	Peanut butter	bits and onion
Milk	cookies	Vanilla puddings
Orange juice	Milk	Date bars

All menus in this group can be prepared without fresh foods

WEEK THREE

Breakfast	Lunch	Dinner
Cinnamon baked	Quiche Lorraine	Spanish rice
apples	Tossed green salad	Diced buttered ruta-
		bagas

Breakfast	Lunch	Dinner
Fried luncheon meat Hash browned potatoes Grape juice	Bread and butter Milk	Orange and pear salad Cookies Milk
Mushroom omelet Orange juice Toast Butter and jam	Macaroni and cheese Mixed fruit Milk	Hot dogs w/ sauerkraut Peas Boiled potatoes Rolls Milk
Waffles Blueberry syrup Butter Milk Tang	Ham sandwiches Cherry Jello w/ fruit cocktail Milk	Italian hamburger stew* Texas toast Pound cake w/fruit sauce
Oatmeal Bing cherries TVP muffins Honey butter Milk	Baked Chicken Yams Sauteed wheat sprouts* Milk	Cold meat platter Potato salad Baked beans Rolls Butter Vanilla Ice cream
Pears Creamed tuna on toast Hot cocoa	Chicken soup* Peanut butter sandwiches Milk	Burritos* Marinated green beans Carrot sticks Pineapple upside-down cake
Fruit Compote Toasted cheese sandwiches Orange-pineapple juice	Barbecued beef sandwiches Vegetable Milk	Orange-baked ham* Baked Potatoes Turnips with butter sauce Peas
Cheese omelet Apricot Nectar Toast Butter	Spaghetti w/meat sauce French bread Fresh orange Milk	Deep dish chicken pie Harvard beets Milk Lemon pudding cake

WEEK FOUR

Breakfast	Lunch	Dinner
Cream of wheat	Corn chowder	Ravioli

Breakfast	Lunch	Dinner

Milk
Orange juice and
   yogurt*
Buttermilk donuts
	Lime gelatin salad
	  w/cottage cheese*
	   and fruit
	Bread sticks
	Milk
		Parsley buttered
		   carrots w/onions
		French bread

Spinach souffle Potato pancakes V-8 juice Milk	Cream of potato soup Yogurt* and fruit Oatmeal muffins	Chili loaf* Baked potatoes Green vegetable Pineapple cheese cake Milk
Granola w/fruit* Milk Apple cheese salad Grapefruit juice	Hot tuna sandwiches* Asst. relishes Raspberry ice	Cheese strata French onion soup Green vegetable Milk
Pigs in a blanket Grape Tang Pears	Deviled Eggs Bread and butter Grapefruit sections Cupcakes Milk	Soybean meatloaf* Green vegetable Scalloped potatoes Milk

Polenta
Apricots
Orange Tang
Milk
	Ham TVP Sandwiches
	  w/alfalfa sprouts*
	Cheese-topped
	  potato boats
	Milk
		Beef stroganoff
		Rice
		Diced beets
		Pumpkin pie

Corned beef hash Tomato juice Bread and butter	Clam chowder* Pineapple cream cheese sandwiches Milk	Beef and noodles II * Green vegetable Lemon pound cake Milk

Cornmeal mush
Fried ham
Apricots
Milk
Toast and butter
	Lima beans & ham
	Orange Jello w/
	  carrots and
	  pineapple
	Bread and butter
		Tomato juice
		Baked chicken
		Baked acorn squash
		Baked potatoes
		Chocolate cake
		Milk

WEEK FIVE

Breakfast	Lunch	Dinner
French toast* Sausage	Vegetable soup Cheese slices	Gluten Roast w/onion gravy

Breakfast	Lunch	Dinner
Tang Milk	Rolls Cake Milk	Bread and butter Green vegetable Custard Fruit Milk
Oatmeal Fruit Toast and butter Milk Juice	Limas and ham Stewed tomatoes Corn Muffins* Milk	Beef stew* Bread and margarine Jello and fruit Milk
Rolled wheat cereal* Orange juice Bacon Toast Milk	Lentils Rye bread and butter Yogurt and fruit* Milk	Roast beef Carrots Potatoes Onion Gravy Rolls and butter Milk
Cheese Rarebit Toast Honey stewed prunes Cocoa Juice	Meatless meatloaf Mashed potatoes Vegetables Milk	Cabbage casserole* Perfection salad Milk Cupcakes

Fruit cobbler
Cheese wedges
Orange juice
Milk
	Mini pizzas
	Vegetable soup
	Vanilla pudding
	Milk
		Scalloped potatoes
		   and diced luncheon
		   meat
		Vegetables
		Bread and butter
		Fruit
		Milk

Granola with fruit*
Milk
Muffins
Juice
	Cream of tomato
	   soup
	Sliced ham and
	   cheese
	Bread and butter
	Milk
		Enchilladas
		Vegetable
		Milk
		Waldorf salad
		Rolls

Yeast waffles Syrup* Milk Grapefruit sections	Chili-macaroni casserole* Vegetables Milk Fresh apple cake	Ham in casserole Carrot and apple salad Rolls Custard Milk

WEEK SIX

Breakfast	Lunch	Dinner
Whole or cracked wheat cereal Stewed fruit Toast Orange juice Milk	Tuna-green bean casserole* Cornbread* Milk Chocolate pudding	Hamburger-bean Goulash Marinated tomatoes Bread and butter Milk
Cinnamon rolls Fried luncheon meat Juice or fruit Milk	Cream of spinach soup Toasted cheese sandwiches Milk Cookies Jello	Scalloped corned beef and potatoes Vegetables Rolls Milk Fruit compote
Rice pudding Sausage patties Fruit Juice	Cheese souffle Vegetables Wheat-nut rolls Milk	Baked chicken and sweet potatoes* Green beans Bread and butter Cherry pie Milk
Scrambled eggs* Toast Hash browns Juice	Apple-bean bake Rolls Pickles Antipasto Milk	Beef and noodles I* Vegetables Oatmeal cake Milk
Breaded or hard-cooked eggs in cream sauce Bacon Fruit Toast, Milk	Beef potato medley* Wheat sprout salad* Orange juice	Salmon Patties* Spinach souffle Raisin bread pudding Milk
Chipped beef on toast Cocoa Fruit	Tuna-Soybean sandwiches Carrot sticks 24-hour salad Milk	Mexican Bulgur chili Vegetables Rolls Raisin bars Milk
Cheese blintzes* Fruit compote Milk	Soybean chowder* Stewed tomatoes Milk Golden Rice Pudding	Tamale pie* Peas Milk

INDEX TO STARRED RECIPES

Soybeans

The soybean is really an amazing vegetable. Pound-for-pound, the soybean has more protein than red meat. As a matter of fact, it contains twice the protein of lean beef. One cup of cooked soybeans will supply the equivalent of 3 ounces of lean meat in the diet. The protein in soybeans is high quality, providing adequate amounts of almost all of the essential amino acids needed by our bodies. Besides being high in protein, soybeans are also remarkably low in starch, thus, making them suitable for even the diabetic diet. The starch content of soybeans is only half that of other beans. Soybeans are a good source of phosphorus, lecithin, iron, calcium, and vitamin B. The fresh soybean has some vitamin A and sprouted soybeans are high in vitamin C. Soybeans remain somewhat chewy when cooked, although when cooked in a pressure cooker they become softer.

Fresh Green Soybeans

These are easily grown in the home garden. They are a fast growing plant that needs plenty of growing room. The pods are gathered when full and lumpy but while still green. The beans are eaten shelled.

To prepare: Wash. Cover with boiling water and let stand for 5 minutes. Rinse in cold water. Snap the pod in two and squeeze out the beans. Cover with boiling salted water and simmer for 9 to 15 minutes, or until tender.

Dried Soybeans

Always be sure to purchase edible soybeans. There are several edible varieties. The light varieties are the most common. Mung beans are an edible soybean.

To cook: Pick over and wash. Cover with water and let stand overnight. If the soaking water is bitter, discard. Otherwise, cook in the soaking water. Simmer, covered, until tender. Time will vary with the variety. Usually the beans will cook in 1 1/2 to 3 hours. If cooked in the pressure cooker, the cooking time will be 15 to 30 minutes for most varieties. Beans cooked under pressure become quite tender. Refrigerate cooked beans until ready to use them.

To mash or puree: The hot beans can be mashed with a fork or put through a sieve. They can also be whirled in a blender with a little of the cooking liquid.

To bake: Partially cook soybeans in salted water. Then combine with sauce and seasonings and bake in the oven for several hours until tender and tasty. Any recipe for baked beans may be used.

Sprouted Soybeans

These are crisp, have an interesting taste and can add variety as well as vitamin C to the diet.

To serve sprouted beans: Use fresh as greens in salads or add to cooked foods. The sprouted beans retain all of their protein value in addition to gaining an amazing amount of vitamin C. Avoid overcooking in order to preserve the vitamin C. Usually sprouts are added near the end of the cooking time or are stir-fried until tender-crisp in a small amount of oil.

To serve as a cooked vegetable: Saute in butter or simmer in a little water for 10 to 20 minutes, just until tender.

Soybean Oil

This oil is pressed from the dried beans. It is a high quality oil for cooking and frying.

Soybean Flour

This product is made by grinding the dried beans. If ground at home from the whole beans, it will have a very beanlike flavor and odor. Dishes in which full-fat or home ground flour is used require fewer eggs and less shortening because of the fat content of the flour.

Soy flour is particularly useful in low carbohydrate diets because of the low starch content. It also adds considerable nutrition to the products made from it. One pound of soy flour has the same amount of protein as 30 eggs.

Soy flour cannot be used alone in baked goods because it has no gluten to bind the ingredients together as does wheat flour. The recommended way to use this flour is to replace one or two tablespoons wheat flour with the same amount of soy flour for every cup of flour used. This would have much the same effect on the nutritional value of the product as adding extra eggs to the recipe. 1/2 cup soy flour equals approximately 2 eggs in protein content. Larger proportions of soy flour can be used, but the more soy flour used the more of a soy taste the product will have and the heavier the product will be.

Soy Bits or Unflavored TVP Granules

These resemble ready-to-eat breakfast cereals. They are quick cooking. They can be eaten as cereal or used to thicken gravies and puddings or as meat stretchers. To cook, cover with water and simmer for 3 to 5 minutes. They will triple in volume during cooking.

Soybean Milk

Cover 1 cup of soybeans with water and let soak overnight. Drain water and wash the beans. Place half of the beans in a blender with 2 cups water and whirl at high speed until the beans are chopped the consistency of cornmeal. Repeat with the remaining beans. Place the beans and liquid in a large saucepan or double boiler and add 2 more cups of water. Bring to a boil and simmer for 15 minutes (or 30 minutes in a double boiler). Line a colander or large strainer with a clean cloth. Several layers of cheesecloth will do. Set the colander over a large container. Pour the beans and liquid into the cloth and let stand until all the liquid has dripped through. Squeeze the beans in the cloth to remove any remaining liquid. The liquid is creamy white and is the soy milk. The pulp left in the cloth should be saved. Refrigerate the pulp and the milk.

To use soy milk: Add a little salt and sweetener to make a palatable drink. Use plain or sweetened in baking or cooking to replace cow's milk. This is often used as a milk substitute for the baby who is allergic to cow's milk.

Soybean Pulp

Actually there are two substances that are called soybean pulp or mash. The first is the pulp left from the making of soy milk. The second is the mashed whole bean. Soybean pulp can be used in a variety of ways. It can be used as a substitute or extender for meat in casseroles, meatloaf, croquettes, meatballs, sandwich spreads, souffles and soups. The pulp may be added to baked goods to replace up to 1/4 of the flour. It may be used in place of pumpkin to make pumpkin pie. It spoils rather quickly and should be used within a day or two.

Soy Sauce

This is a fermented soybean product. It requires an extended period of fermentation and is therefore not suited to home production. It is used to season and color sauces, gravies, soups and meats.

Soy Nuts

Soak the dried beans in water overnight. In the morning, drain and spread on a towel and pat dry. Deep-fat fry a few at a time until crisp and golden. Salt while warm. Eat like salted nuts. The beans can also be oven roasted. Spread the soaked and towel-dried beans on baking pans and bake in a 350° oven until brown and crisp. They may be sprinkled with a small amount of oil before baking, if desired.

Add soy nuts to your granola for extra nutrition.

Soy Cheese or Tofu

This is the result of souring of the soy milk, much as cottage cheese is the product of soured cow's milk. It can be made in several ways.

Method 1: Heat the soy milk to lukewarm and set in a warm place to sour and thicken. When thick, cut into cubes and place in boiling water and cook for one minute. Pour the milk and curd mixture into a cloth-lined colander set in a large container. Allow to drain completely. Season the cheese with salt.

Method 2: To 6 cups soy milk add 4 T. lemon juice or vinegar. Stir just to mix. Allow to set in a warm place until the curds have separated from the whey. Pour through a cloth-lined colander set in a large container. Allow to drain until dry. Season with salt.

Method 3: Cover 1 cup of soybeans with water and allow to soak overnight. Drain water and wash beans. Whirl in blender, adding 6 C. water, until the beans are chopped very fine. Place the mixture in a large saucepan and bring to a rolling boil. Strain through a cloth-lined colander into a large container. Allow to set until the pulp is dry. Save the pulp. Bring the milk to a boil. Remove from heat and stir in 4 T. lemon juice or vinegar. Stir until just blended. Complete as in Method 2 above.

Save the whey that drains from the soy cheese. It can be used in soup, bread or other foods in place of other liquids.

Soy cheese can be used in many ways that cottage cheese and cream cheese are used. It can be used as a meat substitute in casseroles. Or it can be served breaded and fried in place of meat.

Recipes Using Soybeans

Only a few recipes are included here. Most of them are ones that I have personally developed. For additional recipes I would recommend that the reader purchase copies of *The Soybean Cookbook* by Dorothea Van Gundy Jones and *Tasty Imitations - A Practical Guide to Meat Substitutes*, by Barbara A. Salsbury. These are very comprehensive works on the use of soybeans and the best books on the subject that I have found.

SOYBEAN MEATLOAF

Combine:

1 lb. hamburger	1 t. salt
1 1/2 C. soybean pulp	pepper, to taste
1/2 C. rolled oats	garlic powder, to taste
1/4 C. evaporated milk	2 T. minced dried onion or 1 me-
1/4 C. catsup	dium onion, chopped
1 egg	2 T. water

Form into a loaf and place in large casserole dish. Bake at 400° for 45 minutes. Baste top with barbecue sauce or catsup about 10 minutes before done, if desired.

SOYBEAN CHOWDER

Follow recipe for CLAM CHOWDER on page 170 substituting 1 cup cooked soybeans for the clams.

BUTTERMILK SOY BREAD

1 1/2 C. soy milk, lukewarm	2 t. salt
	3 T. oil
1 C. buttermilk, at room temperature	5-6 C. flour
4 t. yeast	
1/2 C. honey	

Dissolve yeast in warm soy milk. Stir in remaining ingredients with enough flour to make a stiff dough. Mix well. Knead for about 10 minutes. Let rise then form into 2 loaves. Place in greased loaf pans and let rise until doubled. Bake at 375° for 40 to 50 minutes. This bread browns easily.

OATMEAL CRACKED WHEAT SOYBREAD

4 t. yeast	3 T. oil
3/4 C. soy milk, at room temperature	2 t. salt
	1 C. oatmeal
2 1/4 C. boiling water	1/3 C. cracked wheat
4 T. molasses	1/3 to 1/2 C. milk powder
4 T. honey	about 5 C. flour

Dissolve yeast in soy milk. Stir oatmeal and cracked wheat into boiling water. Cool to lukewarm. Stir into yeast mixture. Add remaining ingredients with enough flour to make a stiff dough. Mix well. Knead on floured surface for about 10 minutes. Let rise until doubled. Form into 2 loaves and place in greased loaf pans. Let rise until doubled. Bake at 375° for about 40 to 50 minutes. This bread browns easily.

SOY WHEY BREAD

Soy whey is what I call the liquid left after making soy cheese from soy milk. Soy milk could be substituted for soy whey in this recipe.

Place 2 C. soy whey in a pan and bring to a boil. Stir in 1/4 C. instant mashed potatoes. Cool to lukewarm.

Place 3/4 C. warm soy whey in a large bowl and stir in:

4 t. yeast	3 T. oil
3 T. sugar or honey	lukewarm potato water
2 t. salt	about 5 C. flour

Mix well. Turn out onto a floured board and knead until smooth. Kneading in as much flour as needed to keep the dough from being sticky. Place in a bowl and cover. Let stand in a warm place until doubled. Turn onto floured board and shape into two loaves. Place in greased loaf pans and let rise, covered, until doubled. Bake 40 minutes at 400°. Remove from pans and cool on wire racks.

SOYBEAN BREAD

4 t. yeast	3 T. oil
1 1/2 C. warm water	1/2 C. honey
3/4 C. soy milk, at	1 1/2 t. salt
room temperature	about 6 C. flour
1 C. soy pulp or	
mashed soy beans	

Dissolve yeast in warm water. Add remaining ingredients with enough flour to make a stiff dough. Mix well. Turn out onto a floured board and knead about 10 minutes, or until smooth and elastic. Return to bowl and cover. Let rise in a warm place until doubled. Punch down and form into loaves. Place in greased baking pans and let rise in a warm place until doubled. Bake at 350° for about 1 hour. This bread browns easily. Makes 2 loaves

Recipes Using Bean Flours

Bean flours are made by grinding dry beans. They contain more protein than wheat flour or other grain flours. Soybean flour is highest in protein and contains less starch than wheat or rye flours or other bean flours. The soybean proteins are of higher nutritive quality than the proteins of other beans.

All the bean flours are good sources of vitamin B and are rich in calcium and iron.

Bean breads are made by combining one part bean flour or mashed cooked beans with four to five parts wheat flour. This combination avoids too much of a bean flavor and gives you the benefit of the gluten in the wheat flour to make a high quality bread product.

LIMA BEAN BREAD

2 C. lima bean flour	2 T. sugar
1 or 2 packages yeast	4 t. salt
8 1/2 C. flour	3 C. milk
2 T. fat	

Dissolve the yeast in the milk. Add remaining ingredients with enough flour to make a stiff dough. Mix well. Turn out onto a floured board and knead about 10 minutes, or until smooth and elastic. Return to bowl and cover. Let rise in a warm place until doubled. Punch down and form into loaves. Place in greased baking pans and let rise in a warm place until doubled. Bake at 350° F. for about 1 hour. Makes 2 loaves.

Recipes for Soups

CLAM CHOWDER

Place in a large pan and cover with water:

    2 large potatoes, diced
    1 onion, diced

Cook until tender.
Add:

1 can clams, drained	2 slices crisp bacon, crumbled
1 large can evaporated milk	salt and pepper to taste
1 milk can water	

Heat to serving temperature. Do not boil or the soup may curdle.

CHICKEN SOUP

Early in the day combine in a large kettle:

1 C. dried carrots	1/2 to 1 C. dried diced potatoes

1/4 C. dried onions	1 or 2 packets G. Washington broth
4 C. canned tomatoes	salt, pepper, and garlic to taste
1/2 C. dried celery	water to cover
2 T. dried parsley	

Simmer until vegetables are tender, about 4 to 6 hours. Or simmer for 30 minutes and then cook for 5 minutes in a pressure cooker. Add meat from one canned chicken, 1/2 C. dry rice, broth from the chicken and chicken bouillon. Simmer until rice is cooked.

Recipes Using Canned Roast Beef

BEEF AND NOODLES I

Place in kettle:

1 or 2 cans roast beef	dash of garlic powder
3 sliced carrots	1/4 C. chopped onion *or*
1 t. salt or seasoned salt	1 T. dried onion
pepper to taste	2 bouillon cubes

Cover with water and simmer until vegetables are tender. Mix with 1 recipe homemade noodles, cooked in water and drained. Or use about 1/2 to 1 lb. commercially made noodles. Serves 6.

BEEF AND NOODLES II

Mix:

1 or 2 cans roast beef	1/4 to 1/2 pkg. onion soup mix
1/4 to 1/2 pkg. mush-room soup mix	1 1/2 to 2 C. water

Simmer for 15 minutes or until onions are cooked. Mix with cooked, drained noodles. Serves 6.

BEEF-POTATO MEDLEY

Saute 1 chopped onion in small amount of oil. Drain gravy from 2 cans roast beef. Chop the meat and save the gravy.

Add meat to onion with:

2 cans tomato sauce	1/4 t. nutmeg
1 t. salt	1/4 t. pepper

Cook and slice 4 medium potatoes. Arrange half of potatoes on bottom of 2 qt. casserole. Cover with meat mixture. Top with remaining potatoes.

Beat:

2 eggs	1 1/3 C. milk

Pour over potatoes and meat. Sprinkle with 1/2 C. grated parmesan or cheddar cheese. Bake at 350° for 45 minutes. Let stand 15 minutes before serving. Serves 6.

PEPPER BEEF

Saute:

    1 medium green pepper, cut in strips or chopped
    1 medium onion, thinly sliced or chopped in small amount of oil.

Add: 2 cans roast beef. (Remove and reserve gravy)

Brown slightly.

Stir in: 1/2 can tomato soup diluted with 1/2 C. water.
Add gravy from roast beef, if desired. Simmer for about 10 minutes. Serves 4 to 6.

STEW

Combine:

1 1/2 to 2 C. dried potato slices	2 T. dried onion
	1 C. dried carrots

Cover with water and bring to a boil. Simmer 5 minutes. Let stand until vegetables are reconstituted.

Add:

    2 envelopes G. Washington broth
    2 t. beef bouillon
    salt and pepper to taste

Cook until vegetables are tender. Add 2 cans roast beef. Simmer to blend flavors. Thicken gravy, if desired. Serves 6 to 8.

Recipes Using Canned Chicken

CHICKEN AND NOODLES

Debone 1 canned chicken. Save stock. Mix chicken and stock with 1 can cream of chicken soup. Add some water, if needed. Heat. Mix with cooked noodles or rice. Serves 6.

CHICKEN RICE CASSEROLE

3/4 C. rice	1 can cream of chicken soup
1 can cream of celery soup	1 can hot water

Mix. Place in baking dish. Pour 1/2 package dry onion soup mix over it. Place chicken pieces on top. Sprinkle with remaining onion soup mix. Cover. Bake until chicken is cooked at 325⁰. Serves 4 to 6.

BAKED CHICKEN AND SWEET POTATOES

Carefully remove skin, bones and broth from 1 canned chicken. Place chicken pieces in shallow baking dish. Sprinkle with salt and pepper. Top with 1 or 2 cans sweet potatoes, drained. Spread with 1/4 C. apricot preserves and sprinkle with 1/4 C. brown sugar and 2 t. lemon juice. Dot with 2 T. margarine. Baste with a small amount of chicken broth. (Save the rest for gravy or soup). Bake 20 to 30 minutes at 350⁰. Serves 4.

Hint: To remove broth easily from the chicken, open one end of the can and set upright in a container of hot water to liquify broth.

Recipe Using Salmon

SALMON PATTIES

Combine:

1 large can salmon, deboned and flaked	1/4 t. pepper 1 t. salt
2 C. stiff mashed potatoes	1 beaten egg

Form into patties. Roll in egg and cracker or bread crumbs. Pan fry until browned. Serve with mushroom soup sauce, tartar sauce or red sauce (1/4 C. catsup, 1 t. soy or Worchestershire sauce and 1/2 to 1 t. prepared mustard.)

Recipes Using Canned Luncheon Meat

SANDWICH SPREAD

Grind together:

1/2 can luncheon meat	1 stalk celery
2 hard cooked eggs	1 T. minced onion (or 1 t. dried soaked in water for 15 minutes and drained)

Stir in:

1 t. prepared mustard	3 - 4 T. pickle relish
enough mayonaise to moisten	

Makes 2 C.

SPAMWICHES

Butter both halves of sandwich buns. Place slices of canned luncheon meat and cheese on buttered side of one half of each bun. Spread other buttered side of bun with mustard and add pickles, if desired.

Place a slice of tomato (either canned or fresh) on top. Cover with other half of bun. Wrap in foil and heat at 400° for about 10 minutes or until cheese melts. Serve warm.

SPAM AND BEANS

1 can Spam, cubed
1 can French cut
  green beans
1/2 lb. cheese, cubed or
  grated

1/2 C. fine buttered bread crumbs
4 oz. mushrooms

Place in layers in casserole. Pour on 1 1/2 C. thick white sauce (3 T. flour, 3 T. butter, 1 1/2 C. milk cooked until thick.) Add green peppers and onion to sauce, if desired. Top with bread crumbs or cornflake crumbs. Bake at 350° for 30 minutes.

Recipes Using Ground Beef and TVP

CHILI LOAF

Mix:

2 lbs. ground beef
1 1/2 C. crumbs (bread, crackers or cornbread) or 1 C. oats
1 or 2 packages chili seasoning mix (not chili powder)
1 C. milk or water
2 eggs, beaten

Form into loaf and bake at 400° for about 1 hour. Drain fat and slice. Serve hot or cold. Makes good sandwiches.

JIM DANDY CHILI

1 lb. hamburger,
  browned and drained
1 med. onion, chopped
  and sauteed
1 green pepper,
  chopped and sauteed
1 t. cumin powder

1/4 to 1/2 C. catsup
1/2 t. chili powder
1/2 t. oregano
2 cans kidney beans or 4 C. cooked
  beans
salt and pepper to taste

Combine and simmer for about 45 minutes or until peppers and onion are cooked. For hotter chili, increase chili powder to 1 t.

TAMALE PIE

1 lb. ground beef,
  browned and drained
1 qt. tomatoes

2 cans tomato sauce
2 t. chili powder
1/4 to 1/3 C. raisins

1/2 C. onion, chopped   3 - 4 T. sugar
   and sauteed   salt and pepper to taste

Combine and simmer several hours until dark and thick. Add 1 can pitted olives. Pour into baking dish. Top with cornmeal topping. Bake until bubbly and top is set and lightly browned. Serves 10 to 12.

Topping: Stir 1 C. cornmeal into 4 C. cold water and bring to a boil. Cook, stirring until quite thick.

ITALIAN HAMBURGER STEW

Brown 1 lb. hamburger. Stir in and brown 1 chopped onion.

Drain off fat.

Add:

> 3 to 4 potatoes, cut up
> 3 to 4 carrots, cut up
> 1 can tomatoes (No. 303 or No. 2)
> 1/2 to 1 t. Italian seasoning
> Salt and pepper to taste.

Stir. Cover and bake at 350° F. until vegetables are just tender.

TVP PATTIES

Combine:

> 1 C. unflavored TVP   3 C. water

Bring to a boil and simmer 3 minutes.

Stir in:

> 6 T. powdered potatoes   1/8 t. pepper
>   (or enough to make a   1/2 t. salt
>   fairly stiff mixture)   dash of garlic powder
> 1/4 C. milk powder   1 t. Worchestershire sauce
> 1 T. flour   1 egg
> 2 t. bouillon granules or
>   2 cubes

Optional:

> minced onion   G. Washington broth, 1 packet
> 2 t. cumin powder

Drop by large spoonsful into slightly greased hot frying pan. Brown on both sides. Serve hot. Gravy or catsup make good accompaniments for this dish.

TVP PATTIES PARMESAN

Bread patties with bread crumbs. Brown on both sides. Place in baking dish. Cover with spagetti sauce. Sprinkle with parmesan cheese. Bake until browned and bubbly.

TVP BURRITOS

Make TVP patties - on page 175. After browning patties well, break up the patties with a fork and stir in 2 t. cumin powder, or more if desired.

Make flour tortillas. Fill with TVP mixture, grated cheese, diced tomatoes, onions and lettuce. Top with taco sauce.

Makes 6 large burritos.

TVP SANDWICH SPREAD

3/4 C. flavored TVP	2 T. pickle relish
1/4 C. mayonaise or salad dressing	1 T. minced onion

Cover TVP with water and let soak for about 15 minutes, or until soft. Drain excess water. Stir in other ingredients. Chill. Makes about 1 1/2 cups.

Sprinkle with sprouted alfalfa or shredded lettuce, if desired.

Hint: To make unflavored TVP taste more like meat, marinate overnight in bouillon or broth before adding to cooked dishes.

CABBAGE CASSEROLE

1 lb. ground beef, browned and drained	1/4 t. pepper
	1 t. caraway seeds
1 (No. 2) can tomatoes	1 grapefruit sized head of cabbage
1 t. salt	cut into 1" pieces

Combine and simmer for 20 to 30 minutes, or until cabbage is tender. Serve over rice.

SLOPPY JOES

1 lb. ground beef, browned and drained	salt and pepper to taste
	garlic powder to taste
1/4 C. chopped onion or 2-3 T. onion soup mix	1 t. dry mustard
3 T. chopped green pepper	1 t. Worchestershire sauce
2 C. tomato sauce	1/4 C. sugar
1/2 t. chili powder	1/4 C. lemon juice

Simmer together for 1 hour. Serve over buns.

Variations:

Add 1/3 C. chopped celery

Use pizza sauce instead of tomato sauce

Recipes Using Ham

ORANGE BAKED HAM, PORK OR LUNCHEON MEAT

Sprinkle slices of meat in a baking dish with salt and pepper to taste and a small amount of flour. Top with 1 can drained mandarin oranges. Pour orange juice or syrup from mandarin oranges over the top, cover and heat thoroughly. The juice must boil and combine with the flour to glaze the meat.

HAM TOWERS

On squares of foil or in the bottom of a covered baking dish place stacks of:

> ham or luncheon meat slices or chunks
> marshmallows or brown sugar
> butter
> cooked yams
> pineapple rings, peach halves or pear halves

Wrap up or cover and bake 10 - 20 minutes at 350° or until hot.

Recipes Using Tuna

TUNA-VEGETABLE CASSEROLE

Drain:

> 2 cans vegetables (lima beans, corn, green beans, peas or mixed vegetables)
> 2 cans tuna

Place tuna in bottom of casserole dish.

Mix:

vegetables	3/4 t. celery salt
1 can cream of celery	1/2 t. salt
soup	pepper
1/2 C. evaporated milk	

Pour over tuna. Bake at 425° for 25 minutes. Spread 3 tablespoons mayonnaise or margarine over top and bake 10 minutes longer. Serves four.

HOT TUNA SANDWICHES

Mix:

1 can tuna	pickle relish
mayonaise	onion
hard cooked egg	

Spread between slices of bread or on buns. Top salad mixture with cheese. Wrap in foil or place in a tightly covered baking dish. Heat until warm and cheese melts. Serve warm.

TUNA GREEN BEAN CASSEROLE

Prepare 1 package noodles almondine, as directed, stirring in 1 can tuna, drained, and 1 can French style green beans, drained. Top with cheese and almonds. Bake at 350° until bubbly.

Scratch recipe:

Cook 1 lb. noodles and drain.
Stir in:

1 can cream of mush-
    room soup
  1 can French style
    green beans, drained
	1 can tuna, drained
	1/2 C. milk

Top with cheese and sliced almonds. Bake at 350° until bubbly.

Making Beef Jerky

BEEF JERKY — AIR DRYING METHOD

Use lean meat. Cut the meat with the grain of the muscle into strips about 12" long and 1/2" thick. Drape over a rope or clean clothes line in a semi-shaded location. Wrap with cheese cloth to protect from flies. Let dry until hard and dark. Bring in the house if it rains or there is dew at night. Meat may be marinated before drying (see below). Be sure to dry the surface of the marinated meat before placing it on the line to dry. Do not dry jerky in direct sunlight or when the humidity is high. The meat may spoil before it dries. Store in tightly closed clean jars.

BEEF JERKY—OVEN DRYING METHOD

Prepare meat as above. Make a marinade of 1/4 C. soy sauce or Worchestershire sauce, garlic, salt and pepper to taste. Smoked salt or liquid smoke may be added to the marinade, if desired. Marinate the meat for several hours in the refrigerator. Dry the surface of the meat and place on racks in the oven at 150°. Prop the oven door open about 4" to help control the heat and to allow moisture to escape. Allow to dry to desired hardness. For long storage the meat should be very hard and dry. Thoroughly dry meat can be stored in jars on the shelf. Partially dried meat must be refrigerated.

BEEF JERKY—DRY CURED AND SMOKED

Prepare meat as above for air drying. Make a curing powder or 3 lbs.

salt, 4 T. allspice, 5 T. black pepper. Rub this generously over the surfaces of the meat. Allow to cure in a cold place, such as the refrigerator, for several days. Smoke in a cold smoker until desired amount of smoking has been reached. Hang to air dry or oven dry. (The meat may be soaked in clear water for several hours after curing to remove some of the salt. Hang to air dry for 24 hours after soaking before smoking.)

Recipes Using Pasta

NOODLES

Beat 2 eggs. Add 1/2 t. salt and about 1 C. flour. Mix well. Knead on a lightly floured board until smooth and elastic. Cover and let stand for about 20 minutes. Roll out very thin into a large rectangle. Roll up jelly roll style and slice into pieces the desired width. Unroll immediately. Use at once or allow to dry and store for future use.

To cook: Drop into boiling water and cook until done, about 5 minutes.

These noodles can be used in all recipes calling for noodles or macaroni. Dried eggs can be used in the recipe.

For ravioli noodles: Add 2 T. milk to dough.

CHILI—MACARONI CASSEROLE

Cook 2 C. dry macaroni until tender. Heat a one pound can of chili with beans with one can undiluted tomato or mushroom soup. Mix with cooked, drained macaroni. Serve.

Sourdough Recipes

The following sourdough recipes are from *Make a New Start With Sourdough*, by Edythe K. Watson, *Relief Society Magazine*, Vol. 57, February 1970, No. 2, page 106.

HOTCAKES OR WAFFLES

The night before, set the starter.

In the morning, combine:

2 C. starter	1 t. soda
1 t. salt	1 or 2 eggs
1 T. sugar	3 T. oil (6 T. for waffles)

Mix well. Cook immediately on a hot griddle or hot waffle iron.

MUFFINS

The night before, set the starter.

In the morning set aside 1/2 C. starter for the next time and combine:

starter	1 t. soda
1 1/2 C. whole wheat	1 C. plumped raisins
flour	1/2 C. oil
1/2 C. sugar	1 or 2 eggs
1 t. salt	

Mix just to blend ingredients. Fill greased muffin tins 3/4 full. Bake at 350° for 30 to 35 minutes.

CHOCOLATE CAKE

Mixture No. 1

2 1/2 C. sourdough starter   1/2 C. flour
1/3 C. dry powdered milk

Mixture No. 2

1/2 C. sourdough starter   1 1/2 C. flour
1 C. milk

If using mixture No. 1, add other ingredients and immediately pour batter into greased 9" x 9" pan and bake at 350° for 25 minutes.

If using mixture No. 2, prepare mixture at night and let stand overnight at room temperature. Then add remaining ingredients and proceed as above.

Remaining ingredients:

1 C. sugar	1 t. cinnamon
1/2 C. shortening	1 1/2 t. soda
1/2 t. salt	2 eggs
1 t. vanilla	3 squares melted unsweetened chocolate

Cereal Recipes

PEANUT BUTTER AND HONEY GRANOLA

Combine in a saucepan and heat slightly:

2 T. oil
1/3 C. peanut butter
1/4 to 1/2 C. honey

Mix together:

2 C. rolled wheat or wheat germ
3 1/2 C. rolled oats

Stir in honey mixture. Mix well. Spread on baking sheets, thinly. Bake at 350° for about 20 minutes, stirring occasionally, until lightly toasted. Remove from oven and stir in 1/2 C. raisins or other chopped dried fruit. Serve with hot or cold milk. This can also be cooked like oatmeal.

GRANOLA

Mix together:

1-20 oz. jar wheat germm (5 C.)	10 C. oatmeal
2 C. slivered almonds	2 C. coconut

Add either:

1/2 C. + 2 T. brown sugar mixed with 1/2 C. salad oil and 2 t. vanilla

or

1/2 C. + 2 T. honey mixed with 1/2 C. salad oil and 2 t. vanilla
Stir well. Spread no more than 1/2" deep in shallow baking dishes. Bake at 350°, stirring every 15 minutes, until toasted lightly. Do not burn. Stir the corners well. Remove from oven and stir in raisins or cut up dried fruit. Store in tightly closed containers. Serve with hot or cold milk. No added sugar is needed. Keeps best when refrigerated or frozen.

ROLLED WHEAT

Bring to a boil:

2 C. water	1/2 t. salt

Stir in and simmer until done (10 to 20 minutes for regular rolled wheat, 1 to 5 minutes for quick cooking):

1 C. rolled wheat

Recipes Using Powdered Milk

TO RECONSTITUTE DRY MILK:

Use 3/4 C. non-instant or 1 1/3 C. instant milk powder plus enough water to make 1 quart, for most brands.

To mix: Sprinkle milk powder on top of water and stir or beat or blend in the blender or shake in a jar. Have water at room temperature or slightly warmer. Lumps will dissolve, if not too large, if the milk is allowed to sit in the refrigerator overnight. Stir in the morning. Chilling improves flavor.

BUTTERMILK

Mix non-fat dry milk according to directions above. Add 1/2 C. buttermilk to 1 pint reconstituted dry milk and leave, covered, on sink counter overnight or until well clabbered. Refrigerate. Use as for regular buttermilk, saving 1/2 C. each time to renew. If buttermilk develops a yeasty smell after being stored several days or after using your homemade buttermilk for starter in this buttermilk recipe several times, use the rest of the homemade buttermilk up and use 1/2 C. commercial buttermilk as a starter for your next batch. The yeasty smell develops from growth of yeast plants that fall into the buttermilk from the air. It is not spoiled. As a matter of fact this makes an excellent sourdough starter.

COTTAGE CHEESE

> 1 1/3 C. instant or 3/4 C. non-instant powdered milk
> 1 C. cold water
> 2 C. very hot water
> 1/2 C. buttermilk, at room temperature

Dissolve milk in cold water. Add remaining ingredients and mix well. Pour into glass or crockery container. Put in quite a warm place. When curd has formed and separated from the whey (18 - 24 hours, usually), cut the curd into 2" squares and gently heat for a few minutes to firm the curd. The more you stir, the smaller the curd. The more you cook it the tougher the curd. Place a cloth in a colander and pour the cheese and whey into it. Collect the whey in a bowl and use to make bread. It has proteins and other ingredients that help to condition bread dough and make it more nutritious. After the curd is dry, add cream and salt. Dry cheese may be used in recipes that call for farmer's cheese or ricotta cheese.

WHIPPED TOPPING

> 1/2 C. ice water
> 1/2 C. powdered milk
> 1/4 to 1/2 C. sugar
> 2 T. lemon juice

Place water in bowl. Sprinkle milk powder over water and beat until thick. Add sugar and lemon juice and beat until as stiff as possible. Chill. Use as soon as possible as this topping loses volume as it sits. May be rewhipped if necessary. Makes 2 1/2 C. topping.

This may be used as is or mixed with whipped cream in salad dressings, frozen desserts or bavarians and fruit whips.

YOGURT

Combine:

> 1 1/2 C. instant or 1 C. non-instant milk powder

3 1/2 C. warm water

Bring to a boil. Cool, covered, until lukewarm. Stir in 3 T. yogurt or 1 package yogurt culture. Make sure yogurt is at room temperature. Pour into warm jars, place in a pan of warm water and cover. Let stand in a warm place until set, about 4 hours. Keep the yogurt warm as it is setting. Another method is to pour the lukewarm milk mixture into a jar, cover and place inside a large insulated picnic jug. Pour warm water into the jug about halfway up the jar. Close the lid and allow to sit until the yogurt is set.

If the yogurt fails to set in 4 hours, you probably have not kept it warm enough. If the yogurt separates, you may have had the mixture too warm or allowed it to sit too long before refrigerating. If the mixture fails to set, rewarm it and allow to sit longer. If it separates, strain it through a cloth, saving the whey to use in bread and use the curd as cottage cheese or cream cheese.

ORANGE JUICE AND YOGURT

Stir 1 C. or more yogurt into 1 quart orange juice. Sweeten to taste with honey.

Recipes Using Powdered Eggs

Powdered eggs can be used in place of fresh eggs in any recipe. When cooked alone the taste is quite different from fresh eggs. However, there is no noticeable difference in the taste of most dishes in which powdered eggs are used.

RECONSTITUTING: Just before using, sprinkle 2 1/2 T. egg powder over 2 1/2 T. water and beat vigorously. This is the equivalent of one whole egg. For use in recipes calling for dry ingredients such as flour or sugar, the egg powder can be combined with the dry ingredients and the water added with the liquids.

FRENCH TOAST

Reconstitute powdered eggs as indicated above. For each egg used, stir in 2 1/2 to 5 T. milk. Dip bread slices in the egg mixture and bake on hot griddle until browned on both sides. Serve with syrup or jam.

SCRAMBLED EGGS

Reconstitute powdered eggs. Add 1 to 2 T. milk for each egg. Fry as you would fresh eggs but cook until dry and crumbly. If the eggs that you are using are pasteurized or labeled salmonella-free, the eggs may be left moist.

Recipes Using Quick Mixes

WHITE SAUCE MIX [1]

    1 C. flour
    1 C. margarine
    4 t. salt
    3 1/3 C. instant dry milk solids

Mix with a pastry blender or fork until crumbly like cornmeal. Store in a covered jar in the refrigerator. Vary the amount of mix to obtain the desired thickness of sauce.

    With one cup liquid use:
    Thin sauce -   1/3 C. mix
    Medium sauce -   2/3 C. mix
    Thick sauce -   1 C. mix

Place in a heavy saucepan. Add water slowly, stirring constantly. Cook until smooth and thickened. Season to taste.

Chopped or grated cheese added after cooking makes a quick cheese sauce.

HOT CHOCOLATE MIX [1]

    1 lb. instant cocoa or chocolate mix
    10 C. instant dry milk
    6 oz. dried instant cream or coffee creamer
    1 to 1 1/2 C. powdered sugar, to taste

Mix well and store in air tight container. Label to read:
    Add 1/3 C. mix to 1 C. boiling water

Variation: Substitute granulated sugar for powdered.
            6 C. non-instant milk may replace instant milk

COCOA MIX [1]

    7 C. instant non-fat dry milk or 4 C. regular dry milk
    1 C. cocoa
    1 C. sugar
    1 t. salt

Blend all ingredients and store in a covered container. Label to read:
    Add 1/3 C. to 1 C. water

PANCAKE QUICK MIX (Makes 10 recipes of batter)

Combine in a large container:

    1 2/3 C. powdered eggs   4 T. + 1/2 t. baking powder

---

[1]From Emily Griffith Opportunity School, Denver, Colo.

3 C. + 2 T. powdered milk   5 t. salt
12 1/2 C. flour   3 T. + 1 t. sugar

Store in an airtight container. Refrigerate if possible.

To prepare:

Combine 1 3/4 C. mix with about 1 1/2 to 1 3/4 C. water and add 3 T. oil for hotcakes or 6 T. oil for waffles. Bake on hot griddle or waffle iron. Makes about 12 four-inch pancakes or 3 large waffles.

Variations:

1. Omit powdered eggs and use 1 fresh egg for each recipe of batter that you mix.
2. Substitute 4 1/2 C. powdered buttermilk for the milk powder. Reduce baking powder to 3 T. + 1 t. Add 5 t. soda.
3. Reduce baking powder to 3 T. + 1 t. and add 5 t. soda. When preparing batter mix in 1 T. lemon juice or vinegar for each cup water used.

BISCUIT MIX

In a large container mix:
2 C. shortening   1 T. salt
9 C. sifted flour   1/4 C. baking powder

Mix until crumbly like cornmeal. Store in an airtight container. Use like Bisquick.

QUICK MIX SCONES

2 C. biscuit mix   1/4 C. milk
2 T. sugar   1 egg, beaten

Mix well. Roll into a circle 1/2" thick. Brush with melted margarine. Sprinkle with cinnamon sugar or plain sugar. Cut into wedges. Bake at 425° for 12 to 15 minutes.

QUICK MIX BISCUITS

Combine:
2 C. biscuit mix   2 T. sugar
1/4 C. milk

Pat out to 1/2" thickness. Cut and place on baking pan. Bake in 425° oven for 12 to 15 minutes.

PASTRY MIX[2]

4 C. shortening   12 C. sifted flour
2 T. salt

---

[2]From Emily Griffith Opportunity School, Denver, Colo.

Mix flour and salt in large container. Cut in shortening until the mixture resembles coarse cornmeal. Store in a tightly covered container in a cool place.

How to Make the Pie Crust:

	Size of pie	Amount of Pastry Mix	Amount of Cold Water
One crust	7 or 8 inch	1 1/4 C.	1 to 2 T.
Two crust	7 or 8 inch	2 C.	2 to 3 T.
One crust	9 inch	1 1/2 C.	2 to 3 T.
Two crust	9 inch	2 1/2 C.	3 to 4 T.

Sprinkle cold water, 1 T. at a time, over the mix, tossing lightly and stirring with a fork. It should not be sticky.

Hint: Use ice water. Put the water in a salt shaker. Add only enough water to make the dough stick together.

Recipes for Syrups, Sauces, and Spreads

MAPLE-FLAVORED SYRUP

Boil:
    1 C. water
Stir in:
    1 C. brown sugar
    1 C. granulated sugar

Boil until syrup is free from sugar granules. Remove from heat. Stir in:
    1/2 t. vanilla
    1/2 t. maple flavoring

For a thicker syrup add 2 C. Karo syrup and double the amount of flavorings or use 3 C. sugar to 1 C. water and the same amount of flavorings.

Karo syrup can be flavored with maple flavoring (1/2 t. per 2 cups of syrup) if no sugar is available or if Karo is preferred.

FRUIT SYRUPS

1.　Add: 1/2 to 1 C. water to 1 C. jam. Stir to mix well. Heat to melt jam and warm syrup. Strain out seeds, if any.
2.　Melt jelly over low heat. Stir in water to desired consistency. Whirl in blender to remove lumps, if desired.
3.　Add sugar to desired sweetness to fruit juice (about 1 C. sugar to 1 C. juice). Dilute juice with water, if desired,

before adding sugar. Taste until desired strength of juice flavor is reached. Gently heat juice and sugar until sugar is dissolved.

4.   Substitute syrup drained from canned fruit for juice in recipe No. 3.

FRUIT SAUCE FOR HOTCAKES, WAFFLES, SHORTCAKE, ETC.

Mix:

2 C. canned or frozen fruit, chopped if desired, and the syrup
1 T. flour or 1/2 T. cornstarch
cinnamon or nutmeg, if desired

Cook until thickened. Serve warm.

PEANUT BUTTER

Place shelled roasted peanuts in blender. Add a small amount of vegetable oil. Whirl to a paste. Add salt and enough oil to thin to desired consistency.

Variation: Other roasted nuts can be used instead of peanuts.

Basic Directions for Making Yeast Breads

STRAIGHT DOUGH METHOD:

1. Place yeast in a large bowl. Add warm liquid ingredients and fat, preferably melted or very soft. Stir to dissolve yeast. The liquids must be no hotter than 120º F. Excess heat will kill the yeast.

2. Stir in the dry ingredients, mixing in flour last. Add only enough flour to make a soft dough that is not sticky. (Some doughs are supposed to be sticky, but the recipe will usually indicate this). You may use more or less flour than the recipe calls for. Moisture content in flour varies and this will affect the amount of flour used.

3. Dump the dough out onto a floured surface and knead until it is smooth and very elastic. You will notice as you knead the dough that it changes from a soft blob that keeps any shape that you give it to a firmer, stretchier ball or mass that springs back to its original shape when you press on it. This happens because the gluten in the flour is being broken down by the kneading process and becoming elastic. The longer you knead, the more developed the gluten becomes and the better the texture of the finished bread. Bread that has not been kneaded long enough will be coarse in texture and crumbly. Most dough should be kneaded for 5 to 10 minutes.

How to Knead

Place the dough on a floured surface. Push the heel of your right hand down hard into the middle of the dough. Lift your hand and turn the dough 1/4 turn and fold over one corner with your right hand, pushing down firmly with the heel of your hand as you fold. Continue turning and folding and pressing (kneading) until the dough is smooth and elastic.

4.   Place the dough back into the mixing bowl. Cover with a plate, cloth or plastic wrap. Let stand in a warm place (try the top of the refrigerator or a warm window sill) until doubled in bulk. When you plunge your finger into the dough, the indentation will remain. Be careful not to expose the dough to too much heat. 80 to 85 degrees is best. You do not want to cook the dough while it is rising.

5.   Turn the dough out onto a lightly-floured surface. Divide into portions for loaves and shape into loaves. To shape loaves: Flatten the dough into a rectangle about as wide as the pan is long. Roll up the dough tightly, like a jelly roll, pressing it tightly together to press out all air bubbles. Seal the edge and ends. Place seam side down in a greased loaf pan. Be careful not to get too much flour on the dough while shaping the loaves. Flour can cause streaks in the dough and air holes in the bread.

6.   Cover the pans with a cloth and set in a warm place to rise. When almost doubled in bulk, place the loaves in a preheated oven and bake for the specified time.

Be careful not to let the bread rise too much. If it rises too much, the air holes become too large and the bread may be crumbly, dry and uneven in texture. The bread may even fall during baking. If the loaves rise too much it is best to reshape them and let them rise again.

Always bake the bread in a preheated oven.

7.   The loaves are usually ready to remove from the oven when well browned on the top and lightly browned on the bottom. When tapped, the loaf is firm and has a hollow sound. Overcooking makes the crust thick and the bread dry. Bread baked in glass pans must be baked at 25º lower than the temperature specified in the recipe. Otherwise the crust will be thick.

8.   Remove the bread from the pans immediately after baking to prevent the bottom crust from becoming soggy. Some people prefer to butter the tops of the loaves either before or after baking.

9.   When the bread is cool the crust will be somewhat hard. To soften, place the bread in a plastic bag and seal. In a few hours the crust will be soft and tender. Always wait until the bread is completely cool before doing this.

SPONGE METHOD:

1.   Place yeast or starter in large bowl. Add warm liquids and soft or melted shortening. Stir. (Do not add egg!)

2.   Stir in dry ingredients and half of the flour. Mix well, stirring about 2 minutes.

3.   Cover and set in a warm place until it is bubbly and light and doubled in volume. This is called a sponge.

4.   Stir in eggs, if the recipe calls for them. Add remaining flour and beat hard. Turn out onto a floured board and knead. The loaves can be shaped now or the dough can be allowed to rise again before shaping.

Sometimes it is easier to add the second half of the flour by kneading. Place the flour in a pile on a clean surface. Make a well in the middle of the flour and pour out the sponge onto it. Sprinkle flour on top of the sponge to keep it from sticking to your hands and mix and knead until the dough will take up no more flour and it is smooth and elastic.

5.   Follow steps 5 - 9 of the straight dough method to complete preparation.

OATMEAL BREAD

Bring to a boil:
    1 1/2 C. water
Stir in:
    1 C. oatmeal
Cool to lukewarm.
Combine:
    1/2 C. lukewarm water
    3 T. sugar
    2 t. salt
    3 T. shortening or oil
    1 pkg. yeast

Stir to dissolve yeast. Stir in oatmeal and about 4 C. flour to make a soft dough. Knead on a floured board until smooth and elastic, about 10 minutes. Place in a bowl, cover and let rise in a warm place until doubled. Shape into two loaves and place in greased loaf pans. Cover and let rise until doubled. Bake in preheated 400° F. oven for about 40 minutes, or until done.

POTATO BREAD

Stir 1/4 C. instant potato granules or powder into 1 C. boiling water. Cool to lukewarm. Or use 1 small potato mashed fine in 1 C. water. Dissolve 1 pkg. yeast in 1 3/4 C. warm water.
Add:

        3 T. sugar
        2 t. salt
        3 T. shortening or oil
Stir in about 5 1/2 C. flour to make a soft dough.

Mix well. Knead for about 10 minutes on a floured board, working in
enough flour to keep dough from being sticky. The dough should be
soft. Knead until smooth and elastic. Place in bowl and cover. Let rise
in a warm place (80 to 85 degrees), until doubled in bulk. Punch down
and shape into two loaves. Place in greased loaf pans. Cover and let
rise in a warm place until doubled. Bake in preheated oven at 400° F.
for about 40 minutes or until done.

I'M OUT OF YEAST. HELP!!!

        I hope that we can all avoid that cry by, first, storing a sufficient
amount of yeast for several months' baking and, second, taking one
of the following steps to insure an unlimited supply of yeast, should
our stored supply begin to run low.

YEAST PATTIES

Combine:
        1 or 2 teaspoons dry yeast or 1 cake
        2 C. warm water
        2 T. sugar
        1/2 t. salt
        1 C. flour

Stir well. Cover and let stand in a warm place overnight. In the
morning, stir in a pinch of ginger and enough cornmeal to make a
stiff dough.

Save 1/2 cup for current baking needs. Make patties of the rest. Drop
large spoonsful onto waxed paper or foil or lightly greased baking
sheets. Flatten to 1/4" thick. Allow to dry overnight. In the morning,
turn the patties over to allow the bottoms to dry. When thoroughly
dry, store in a tightly covered container in a cool place.

To use: Crumble one or more patties into about 2 cups warm water
and allow to sit for about 1 hour to soften. Stir in about 1 cup flour
and 1 tablespoon sugar and allow to sit, covered, in a warm place for
several hours until bubbly and yeasty. This is a sourdough starter. Use
in place of yeast in baking. Be sure to allow for the flour and water as
you mix your recipe.

To make a new batch: Substitute one or more yeast patties for the
yeast in the master recipe above.

SOURDOUGH STARTER

Combine:

2 C. warm water	1 pkg. yeast
2 1/4 C. flour	1 T. sugar

Mix well. Cover and let sit in a warm place overnight. Reserve at least 1/2 cup for the next batch (in place of yeast.) Store the reserved portion in the refrigerator in a covered jar. If used daily, the starter can be stored on the kitchen counter.

TIPS ON MAKING AND USING SOURDOUGH STARTER

1. All starters can be made without yeast. To do so, mix all the ingredients except the yeast. Then allow to sit uncovered in a warm place for several hours. Wild yeasts from the air will become active in the batter. Cover and leave in a warm place until bubbly and yeasty smelling. This may take several days.

These starters are usually not as satisfactory as those made with yeast because there is a tendency for undesirable yeasts and molds to get into the batter and cause it to spoil.

2. Potato or potato water in sourdough hastens the fermentation.

3. Milk hastens the fermentation in sourdough and gives the baked products a good taste.

4. Sourdough starters can be used in any recipe in place of yeast. They can also be used in place of baking powder or soda in certain recipes.

5. Estimate the amount of flour and water contained in your starter. Make appropriate adjustments in your recipe to compensate for this. For the starter recipe given above, 1 cup of starter contains about 3/4 cup flour and 2/3 cup of water.

6. To renew starters: Substitute a small amount of starter, usually 1/2 cup, for the yeast in the basic recipe.

I'M OUT OF BAKING POWDER AND SODA. NOW WHAT?

1. Mix hardwood ashes with boiling water. Do not use ashes from pine or other softwoods. Let ash settle and use liquid as baking soda. You'll have to experiment to determine the amounts to use.

2. Mix as needed: 1 1/8 teaspoons cream of tartar and 1/2 teaspoon soda for each teaspoon baking powder.

Quick Breads

CORN MUFFINS

Mix:

1 1/2 C. cornmeal	3/4 C. liquid from corn

1/2 C. flour	1 t. salt
3/4 C. buttermilk	1/4 C. oil
2 t. baking powder	1 egg
1/4 C. sugar	1/2 t. soda

1 can (No. 303) corn, drained and liquid reserved
2 T. finely chopped onion and green pepper, optional

Grease muffin tins. Fill tins half full. Bake at 450° for about 15 minutes, or until done.

CORN BREAD

Mix:

1 C. cornmeal	1 t. salt
1 C. flour	1 egg, beaten
3 t. baking powder	1 C. milk
2 T. sugar	1/4 C. melted shortening or oil

Bake at 425° for 30 minutes for cornbread or 20 minutes for muffins.

INDIAN OR FLOUR TORTILLAS

Mix well:

4 C. flour	2 T. lard or shortening
1/2 t. baking powder, if desired	2 C. water
2 t. salt	

Knead dough well, about 10 minutes. Roll or pat out tortillas from balls the size of walnuts. Roll very thin. Bake until browned slightly on both sides.

CHEESE BLINTZES

Soften 1 jar pineapple cheese spread.
Beat 2 eggs until light.
Add:

    1/2 t. salt
    1 C. water
    1 C. flour

Beat to make a smooth batter. Heat and grease lightly a heavy frying pan. Pour 2 T. batter into pan and spread thin. Fry over very low heat on one side only until set. Fill with cheese spread. Roll and top with sour cream. Dust with powdered sugar. Serve warm.

Variations: Use cream cheese instead of pineapple cheese spread. Serve topped with fruit or fruit toppings.

RICE CAKES

Prepare pancake batter as usual. Add about 1/2 C. cooked rice to each 2 C. batter. Bake as usual. Serve with fruit topping or fruit syrup.

Cooking With Honey

Honey is included in most food storage plans because of its pleasant taste and because it is somewhat higher in nutritional value than sugar.

Honey can be used, cup for cup, to replace sugar in most recipes calling for sugar. Because honey absorbs moisture from the air, cakes and bread will stay fresh longer when made with honey, but crisp cookies made with honey will lose their crispness after a day or so.

Combine the honey well with either the shortening or the liquid ingredients and then blend well with the remaining ingredients to prevent a soggy layer from forming on top of the baked product.

If honey is measured in the same cup as the shortening, it will all pour out of the cup.

Fruit Leather

Fruit leather is a confection made from pureed fruit. Fresh, canned or dried fruit can be used. The leather can be sweetened with honey or sugar, as desired.

Preparing the Fruit:

Fresh Fruit: Peel, core and chop fresh fruit into a large kettle. Add just enough fruit juice or water to keep the fruit from scorching. Cook until soft. Drain off excess juice. Run through a food mill or puree in a blender.

Dried Fruit: Reconstitute dried fruit with water or fruit juice. Then proceed as with fresh fruit.

Canned Fruit: Drain syrup from the fruit and puree.

Making the Leather:

Combine in a large kettle:
    Fruit puree
    Sugar or honey to taste

Cook over low heat, stirring frequently to prevent scorching. When very thick, remove from heat and spread thinly on a greased baking sheet. Dry in a 150° F. oven until no longer sticky on top. Air dry until leathery. Peel from cookie sheet and dust both sides with cornstarch. Roll up in plastic wrap or foil to keep fresh.

Miscellaneous Recipes

GLORIFIED WHEAT

Combine:

2 C. wheat sprouts	1 C. crushed pineapple
1/2 C. chopped nuts	1 C. marshmallow bits
1/2 C. coconut	1 package prepared whipped topping

Stir gently until mixed. Serve at once.

SAUTEED WHEAT SPROUTS

Saute wheat sprouts over a low flame, in a little butter. Cook only enough to warm through.

HOW TO USE DRIED CHILIES

Wash in cold water or scald to remove skins. Remove veins, stems and seeds. Soak in hot water, 1 cup for every 6 chilies, for 1 hour. Whirl in blender in soaking water. Strain or use with liquid.

DRIED ZUCCHINI

Zucchini is very easy to dry. Slice the squashes thin, crosswise. Lay them out on a clean sheet in a warm, dry place to dry. The attic is a good place for this. Cover them with cheesecloth to keep off insects and to help keep out dust. When dry and leathery, store in paper sacks until ready to use.

To use, soak in warm water until reconstituted. Then use in any recipe calling for zucchini.

DRIED SWEET CORN

Remove husks and silk from sweet corn. Place in a pan with one inch water on bottom. Cover and steam until cooked. Lay out to dry being sure to not let the ears touch one another. Turn occasionally to let the entire ear dry. Protect from flies. When dry, corn may be removed from ears by rubbing two ears together over a container or large cloth. Store in a cool, dry place and protect from insects and rodents.

To cook: Soak for 1 1/2 to 2 hours. Cook 20 minutes or more until tender. Will about double in volume.

POPCORN

Store popcorn in quart jars. When ready to use, sprinkle a few drops of water over the amount you want to use, in another jar. Replace the lid tightly and shake to distribute the water evenly. Let sit for several hours so that the corn can absorb the water. This helps the corn to pop better. One tablespoon of water per quart of corn is enough.

CHEESE POPCORN

Pop 2 quarts of popcorn. Toss with 2 T. melted butter and 2 T. powdered cheese. Salt to taste.

PART THREE

STORING NON-FOOD ITEMS

CHAPTER XV

WHAT AND HOW TO STORE

Suggested List of Non-Food Storage Items

FOR KEEPING CLEAN (* indicates essential items for flood clean-up)

   *Soap: 20 lbs. laundry soap per person
         15 to 18 bars hand soap per person
         Tincture of green soap (for injuries)
   Sal Soda (to extend soap supply)
   Dishwashing detergent
   Bath towels, wash cloths, dish towels, clean rags*
   Paper supplies: towels, napkins, facial tissues, toilet tissue
   Shampoo
   *Cleansers
   Shoe Polish
   Ammonia, lye, borax (for soapmaking)
   *Liquid bleach
   Toothpaste and brushes
   Combs and brushes
   Hair care supplies
   Shaving supplies
   Deodorant
   *Scrub brush and bucket
   *Extra broom
   *Mop & extra mop head
   Washboard and 2 large wash tubs
   *Disinfectants

FIRST AID

   First aid dressings, sterile gauze, adhesive tape, compresses
   Clinical thermometer
   Rubbing alcohol
   Hot water bottle
   Ice Bag

Sterile castor oil or mineral
Apple cider vinegar
Ear syringe
Eye dropper
Dry mustard (emetic)
Oil of cloves
Petrolatum
Baking soda
Kaopectate or other diarrhea remedy
Antibiotic ointment
Pain relieving spray
First Aid Manual
Boric acid

FOR COMFORT AND HEALTH

Calamine Lotion
Sunburn lotion
Cornstarch
Hand lotion
Cold remedies
Cough syrup
Cotton swabs
Foot remedies
Epsom salts
Antacids
Sanitary napkins and extra belt
Vitamins
Aspirin
Ointment for diaper rash

WASTE DISPOSAL

Two 50-gallon drums, with lids (for disposal of human waste)
Lime
Fly spray
Deodorizers
Newspapers

CLOTHING

Walking shoes and boots
Sweaters
Dresses
Patterns for slippers, moccasins, gloves and mittens
Silk kerchiefs
Disposable diapers
Men's work clothes
Socks
Underwear
Shoe laces

BEDDING

Sheets, pillowcases   Pillows

Baby blankets   Blankets, quilts, mattress pads
Sleeping bags   Rubber sheeting

SEWING SUPPLIES

Yardage: bolt of muslin
              flannel, gingham, denim, wool, etc.
Scissors, needles, pins, machine needles, buttons, safety pins,
Hooks and eyes, snaps, elastic, zippers, trims, hem bindings
Thread - all colors
Leather for moccasins, belts, gloves, etc.
Yarn for sweaters, mittens and slippers

FUEL AND COOKING SUPPLIES AND HEATING SUPPLIES

Matches   Newspaper logs
Coal   Old tires
Briquets   Wood or coal cooking and heating
Black walnuts   stove
Wood   Camp stove and fuel

LIGHTS

365 large candles (4 1/2 to 5 hours burning time)
Kerosene, white gasoline or lamp oil
Lamps or lanterns
Wicks or mantles
Light bulbs
Flashlights, batteries and extra bulbs

WATER AND WATER PURIFICATION TABLETS

SEEDS, SPROUTER AND GARDENING SUPPLIES

Untreated seeds, for sprouting
Treated seeds, for planting
Sprouter
Garden tools: Shovel, rake, hoe, hose, watering can, sprinkler,
      fertilizer, etc.

MISCELLANEOUS

Can and bottle openers
Pencils and paper
Plastic wrap, plastic bags, foil, waxed paper
Wheat grinder
Small food grinder for preparing baby food
Saw, nails, screws, hammer, faucet washers, fuses
Pipe wrench

Axe, hone, hunting knife
Fishing gear
Rifle and ammunition
Portable radio and batteries
Paper plates and cups
Disposable knives, forks and spoons
Ice chest and reusable ice packs
Rope
Tent
Lumber
Burlap bags
Pry bar
Storage information and emergency information

CANNING SUPPLIES (even if you don't can)

Jars, rings, lids   Salt
Parafin   Ascorbic acid
Vinegar   Pectin
Sugar   Sulfur for drying fruits
Spices

FIRE FIGHTING SUPPLIES

Buckets
Sand
Water
Hoses
Extinguishers
Ladder

How to Store Non-Food Items

Canning Jars and Lids

Always store jars clean and, if possible, keep them full of something. Either have them full of food or fill them with water and store.

If you do not want to store your water this way, put lids loosely on the jars and store them upside down and in boxes to keep them as clean as possible. Having clean jars that need only a rinse before scalding will cut down on the work on canning day.

Rotate lids every other year. They should be kept cool and dry. The rubber gaskets will deteriorate with age.

Rotate rubber rings every other year also.

Store enough lids for two years' worth of canning and enough jars for at least one year, even if you do not plan to do any canning.

Chlorine Bleach

Store in a cool place and keep containers tightly capped. Bleach will lose its potency with age. Most bleach will remain potent for at least two years.

Fuels

Store all petroleum-based fuels in a cool place, away from heat. Keep out of the reach of children and away from foods, especially wheat, milk and flour. Keep liquid and paste-type fuels tightly capped.

Keep wood, coal and charcoal dry. They will not burn well if wet.

Store all fuels where they are readily accessible in an emergency.

Check with your local fire department about regulations regarding fuel storage.

Parafin and Candles

Parafin is used for sealing jams and jellies, as a fire starter, or to make fuel tablets for use in a tin can stove. It can be used to seal the lids of storage containers or to coat cheese to prevent drying.

Store parafin and candles in a cool place to prevent melting.

To melt parafin, place it in a jar or can in a pan of boiling water. Never melt parafin over direct heat.

Flashlight Batteries

Heat robs batteries of their power. For longest life store them in a cool place. The refrigerator is an excellent place to store batteries. Leave them in their cardboard sleeves or put tape over the terminals. This will help to prevent accidental discharge.

Detergent and Other Cleaning Supplies

Keep these products out of the reach of children. Do not store with food, as many of these products have perfumes in them that might permeate foods, especially milk, wheat and flour. Foods contaminated with any of these products, should they become accidentally mixed, would be unfit to eat.

Keep these products dry.

Unwrap bars of soap and store them in an open box or paper bag. They will last longer when used if allowed to dry out before using.

Most of these products will store indefinitely. Changes of color should not affect their performance.

Keep liquid products tightly capped to prevent evaporation.

First Aid Supplies

Remember to keep all medicines out of the reach of children.

Store these supplies in a cool, dry place. A waterproof container is recommended.

Rotate regularly. Many first aid supplies will deteriorate with age. The adhesive on tape and bandages will soften with heat and age. Many ointments will go stale or lose their strength with age. They will separate if subjected to heat. Cough syrups and other liquids will evaporate and may become stronger. Always discard products that show any changes, especially if they are meant to be taken internally. Alcohol will evaporate even from a tightly-closed container. It is still usable. As hydrogen peroxide ages, it turns to water. Exposure to air and light will also cause peroxide to break down. If it still bubbles on a cut or turns the skin white when applied and allowed to dry, it is still good.

Always clean out your medicine cabinet and first aid kit at least once a year and discard anything that looks old. Always discard prescriptions that are over a year old unless your doctor or pharmacist has told you that you can keep them longer. Consult your doctor or pharmacist about how long to store any products that have no expiration dates printed on the label.

To Safely Discard Drugs:

Pills and non-volatile liquids should be flushed down the toilet. Then rinse out the containers, replace the caps and throw into the trash.

Volatile liquids should never be poured into the sewage system because of the danger of explosion. Pour volatile liquids out on an unused spot of earth in the yard or hand them directly to the trash collector when he comes to collect your trash.

Children are real scavengers and will often eat or drink things that they find in the trash can. Prevent accidental poisoning by never placing anything in the trash can that can be harmful to children or pets.

First Aid Manual, Food Storage Manuals, and Emergency Information

Store these books where you can find them quickly in an emergency. Read them and become familiar with their contents before the need arises to use that information.

Bandages

Sterile bandages can be made from old sheets, towels, table linens, etc., packed in clean 1 lb. coffee or 3 lb. shortening cans, sterilized in the cans and then sealed with plastic tape. The bandages can be wrapped in brown paper or foil, also.

Procedure for making the bandages is as follows: Tear clean material into 1 1/2 to 2 1/2 inch strips and roll or fold. Pack tightly into cans or wrap in brown paper or foil. Bake for 1 hour 15 minutes in 375º F. oven. (Smaller packages may be ready in about 20 minutes). A pan of water on the bottom of the oven prevents bandages from turning yellow. Leave in the oven until cold. Remove and seal immediately. The cans can be covered before baking if metal lids are available. If not, seal with plastic lids that have been washed in hot soapy water. Plastic tape is suitable for sealing the lids or packages.

Sterility can only be assured if the bandages are baked in the cans with the lid on for the full hour and 15 minutes. Bandages prepared any other way would be suitable for most uses, however. Bandages can be sterilized just before use, if necessary.

Store the bandages in a cool, dry place. Replace every one or two years. Deterioration will take place in the material with prolonged storage.

Matches

Keep dry and store away from heat. It is recommended that you store wooden stick matches and not paper or wooden safety matches.

Keep out of the reach of children.

Paper Products

These products will keep a very long time if kept cool and dry.

Vitamins

The length of time vitamins can be stored will depend upon several factors. Cool, dry, dark storage conditions are essential for vitamins. Gelatin encapsulated or sugar-coated vitamins will retain their potency longer than tablets. Tablets will store longer than liquids. Some brands remain fresh longer than others. Many brands now have an expiration date printed on the label. If none is given, plan to store them no more than 3 - 4 years. Ask your pharmacist about which brands to store. Plan to rotate your vitamin supply.

Aspirin

Aspirin begins to break down soon after manufacture. Cool, dry conditions will prolong its potency. A vinegar odor and crumbly texture will tell you that the aspirin is decomposing.

PART FOUR

OTHER ASPECTS OF EMERGENCY PREPARATION

CHAPTER XVI

EMERGENCY COOKING, HEATING AND LIGHTING

Emergency Cooking and Heating Facilities

Perhaps one of the hardest adjustments for a homemaker to make is an adjustment to unfamiliar cooking facilities. Therefore, I would strongly advise that the homemaker make advance preparations for any emergency that would require a substitute method of cooking.

Portable Stoves

As many of us know from our experiences in outdoor living, a gas or butane-powered portable stove can be almost as convenient to use as a kitchen range. Their principal drawbacks would be smaller size than the kitchen range, no oven, and the problem of fuel storage. This type of stove would be best reserved for short-term emergencies of no more than a month.

To operate the stove, consult the manufacturers instructions. There are too many types of stoves to attempt to give operational details here.

Additional equipment that you might need:

Fuel (see Fuel Consumption and Burning Time Chart page 213).
Funnel for filling fuel tank on liquid fuel stoves
Oven that sits on the stove burners
Matches
Toaster device that sits over a burner

Wood or Coal-Burning Stoves

Heaters:

Heaters are generally small stoves, such as the pot belly stove or Franklin stove, meant for heating one room. They usually burn coal or short lengths of wood. Many have flat tops with room for cooking. The tops are usually small, however, limiting the number of pots that will fit at one time.

Laundry Stoves:

These small stoves were originally meant for heating water for laundry. Some have small ovens, built-in water reservoirs and cooking lids. Their small size makes them excellent for emergency cooking and heating.

Cook Stoves and Ranges:

These large stoves usually have an oven and a large cook top with several lids and a griddle area. Many have warming ovens and a water reservoir for heating water. These are the most versatile stoves for cooking and heating the kitchen. Their large size could be a disadvantage for the individual with a small home.

Durability

Cast iron stoves with grates in the firebox are more durable than stoves made out of sheet metal and without grates.

Installation

The floors and walls near the stove must be protected from heat. Any wall or ceiling through which the stovepipe passes must also be protected from heat.

The stove should be set on a fireproof base. A permanent base of brick or cement is best. Sheets of an asbestos-cement compound can also be used and are especially convenient to use to protect the walls.

Extend the base 18 inches beyond the stove on all sides to protect the floor from cinders and sparks that sometimes fall out of the stove.

Even though the wall or floor might be covered with a fireproof covering, overheating can ignite combustible materials behind the covering. Therefore, dense materials such as brick, that transfer heat slowly, are better protection than those, such as metal, that transfer heat easily.

Set the stove at least 18 inches from all walls and combustible surfaces for maximum safety.

The stove must be connected to a proper stovepipe and chimney. These allow the smoke and soot to be discharged outside of the house and provide a supply of fresh air for the fire.

Buy the size of stovepipe that fits tightly onto the smoke collar. Be sure all joints are tight.

There should be a damper in the section of pipe closest to the stove for convenient control of the draft.

The pipe is joined to an insulated chimney of metal or brick to pass through the wall or ceiling and roof to the outside. The chimney must extend a certain distance above the roof for fire safety. The top of the chimney should be equipped with a spark arrester.

Check with local fire and building authorities for local regulations concerning installation of stoves and chimneys.

How to Use Your Stove:

Two basic principles of fire building are (1) that small, easily-ignited materials are used to ignite larger, longer burning materials, and (2) that fire needs air to burn. Wood or coal should be stacked in the firebox in such a way as to allow air to reach all pieces while burning. Follow these general steps in preparing the fire in your stove:

1. Open the grates and shake as needed. Remove ashes. Close grates.

Basic Fire
Figure 16.1

2. Lay a basic fire with paper at base.
3. Open the damper and drafts wide.
4. Light the paper with a match.
5. When the fire is burning well, add larger kindling.
6. Let the fire burn rapidly for a minute to burn out the cinders and soot in the stove and pipe.
7. Adjust damper to admit just enough air to keep the fire burning steadily. This is just short of the point where the fire starts to smoke.
8. Adjust drafts as needed. A hot fire can take more damping than a slow one. To speed up a slow fire, open the drafts or damper as needed.
9. Add coal or cord wood after the fire is hot. Break coal into pieces just small enough to fit into the fire box for a slow fire. For a hotter fire, use smaller pieces of coal. The larger the piece of coal or wood, the longer and slower the fire will burn.
10. Do not put too much fuel into the stove at one time. When adding more fuel to a wood fire, stir up the embers to help ignite the new fuel. Never stir a coal fire.

The Oven

The oven is beside the firebox and is heated by the hot air that circulates over the top, down the far side and across the bottom.

Soot and ashes accumulate in the spaces around the oven. These must be cleaned out for proper oven heating.

The oven of a wood or coal stove will not bake like the modern gas or electric oven. There will be hot and cool spots.

The only way to learn the peculiarities of your oven is to experiment. Place an oven thermometer inside the hot oven. Move it to various areas and familiarize yourself with the way the oven heats.

If one part of the oven bakes faster than another, you may have to turn or rotate baking pans during the baking period.

Always preheat the oven with a hot fire. Then let the fire die down a bit before baking. A steady fire is necessary for constant temperature in the oven.

Baking times as given in modern recipes are useless when baking in a wood or coal oven. Careful watching is needed to determine when the baking is done.

Increase oven temperature by adding more fuel to the fire and opening the drafts a little. To cool a hot fire, open a lid or open the oven door a crack and starve the fire for fuel.

Baking Tips

1. Flour test: The oven will be at the proper temperature for baking bread and pies (about 400º F.) if a bit of flour sprinkled on the bottom of the oven browns slowly.

2. Bread can be baked directly on the bottom of the oven without pans. Sprinkle a little cornmeal in the oven before putting the bread in. This helps to prevent sticking.

3. When baking several things at once, give each pan a turn in the hottest part of the oven for more even baking.

4. If crust browns too rapidly, cover with foil or brown paper or put the item, pan and all, in a brown paper bag.

5. Cast iron pans will bake more evenly than lighter-weight pans.

The Cook Top

You can cook directly on the surface of the griddle area of the cook top or in pans placed on the cook top.

The temperature varies in different parts of the cook top. The hottest area is to the side and rear of the firebox.

To regulate the cooking temperature, move the pan to a hotter or cooler area of the cook top. For extra-fast cooking, place the pan over an open lid hole. This will cause the bottom of the pot to blacken, however.

Wooden or plastic pot handles will burn. Use pots with metal handles.

Long-handled wooden spoons and long-handled forks are a must for stirring. The long handles keep your arms away from the hot stove top and the wooden handles transfer heat more slowly than metal ones.

If you have a stove without an oven, you can bake on the top of the stove by putting the item to be baked in a covered Dutch oven.

Cleaning

Daily:
1. Shake the grates and remove ashes.
2. Wipe outside of stove with a cloth or soft paper.
3. Wash off grease with soap and water.

Weekly:
1. Clean soot and ashes from top, bottom and sides of oven.
2. Brush soot from bottom of lids.
3. Clean flues and draft openings.
4. Rub cold stove with soft thick cloth moistened with a few drops of kerosene or light lubricating oil.
5. If desired, polish with black stove polish. Never polish the stove when hot.

Safety

1. NEVER use oil or gasoline to help start the fire. There is danger of explosion.

2. Keep flues and pipes clean of soot, cinders and ashes. A heavy accumulation of these substances could result in a fire if you don't get smoked out first.

3. Always assume that there are live embers in the ashes that you clean out of the stove. Dump them on an open spot of ground and drown them with water or place them in a covered fireproof container and store them well away from any combustible material. Never set them next to the house or other structure.

4. Check occasionally to make sure that there is no combustible material around the top of the chimney. Birds' nests and leaves are the biggest problems.

5. Control the heat of your fire. Overheating the stove can overheat the walls, floors, ceilings or roof and result in a tragic house fire. For room heating, a slow, steady fire is best. Do not expect to heat every corner of the room like you do with modern heating equipment.

6. Because modern homes are so air-tight, it is necessary to leave a door or window slightly ajar. Combustion uses oxygen. It sometimes produces carbon monoxide gas. This gas is odorless and toxic. If you notice drowsiness or disorientation, you may be the victim of carbon monoxide poisoning. Children and pets will usually be affected first

because of their small size. Seek fresh air immediately to counteract carbon monoxide poisoning. Always vent a stove or fireplace to the outside. Do not burn a large, unvented fire indoors.

Tools To Use With Your Stove

Oven cleaning tool: You will need a long rod with a flat, blade-like piece of metal attached to the end. The blade is about 1 " wide and 3 inches long. This tool fits through small openings near the oven and is used to scrape the ashes and soot from around the oven.

Poker: This tool is used to stir up the fire when adding new fuel.

Lid Lifter: For lifting the lids on top of the stove.

Stiff Brush: For cleaning soot off bottoms of lids and inside pipes and flues.

Ash pan: For collecting the ashes that you shake from the grate.

Shovel: A small shovel would be useful for scooping up ashes from the firebox.

Fuel

Anything that will burn can be used as emergency fuel but one must weigh the advantages against the disadvantages of each in deciding which fuel to store and use.

Paper:

Paper has the advantage of being plentiful. Newspaper logs can be made from rolled newspapers and individual pieces can be used for kindling.

The major disadvantage of using paper as fuel is that it leaves large accumulations of soot in the stove and pipes.

Wood:

Wood for storage should be as dry as possible and cut into convenient lengths and split.

It has the advantage of being plentiful in most areas of the country and relatively inexpensive. It is easy to store.

The major disadvantage, as with paper, is that it leaves large accumulations of soot in the stove and pipes.

Wood combustion gives off gases that are volatilized at 1100° F. Incomplete burning of these gases is a source of accumulation of creosote, tarry substances and acetic acid in the stove and pipes. These products cause some loss of heating efficiency and corrode the stove and pipes.

For complete combustion to prevent these problems, there must be sufficient air around and over the fuel bed and the air must mix with the gases while they are hotter than 1100° F.

There is good combustion in small, hot fires. Never let a fire smoulder.

A short stovepipe will prevent the gases from cooling in the pipe and allowing the acetic acid and creosote to condense out.

Soft and light woods burn quickly and produce a hot fire. They also produce the most soot. They are usually best for small, quick, cooking fires and kindling.

Hard and heavy woods burn slowly and steadily and leave behind the least amount of soot. They are usually used for long-burning fires for heating and baking.

The heat-producing efficiency of wood is one third that of oil and one-half that of coal.

Woods Ranked by Heat Value of Oven-dried Wood [1]
(highest to lowest)

I.	Hickory	VI. Paper Birch
II.	White Oak	Red Maple
III.	Beech	VII. Norway Red Pine
		Southern Pine
IV.	Sugar Maple	VIII. Elm
	Red Oak	
	Yellow Birch	IX. White Pine
V.	Ash	X. Aspen

Burning Characteristics of Various Kinds of Woods: [2]

Acacia - good heat, smoky
Alder - poor firewood
Almond - long burning, fair amount of heat
Ash - fast burning, good kindling, lots of heat
Beech - one of the best firewoods
Birch - when mature burns freely, good heat
Cherry - difficult to ignite, long lasting fire, fierce heat, best when partially seasoned
Elm - steady, slow fire, hard to start
Hawthorne - long lasting, good heat, sparks, one of the best firewoods
Hazel - good firewood

---

[1] Kalman Steiner, *Fuels and Fuel Burners* (New York: McGraw - Hill Book Co., 1946).

[2] A.D. Webster, *Firewoods: Their Production and Fuel Values* (London: T. Fisher Unwin, Ltd., 1919).

Lime - smoulders, poor firewood
Maple - good firewood
Oak - long lasting, good heat
Pear, apple - good heat, long lasting
Pine - burns easily, good kindling, sparks, hot fire
Pine cones - good kindling
Poplar - poor firewood, little heat, smoulders, best mixed with coal
Spruce - smoulders, sparks
Sycamore - good heat, should be dried
Walnut - long burning, too valuable for furniture to be used for fire-
    wood
Willow - little heat, smoulders, mix with coal

Store wood in a dry place and cover to keep dry. The drier the wood, the more efficiently it burns.

Coal:

There are two types of coal: bituminous and anthracitic coals. Generally, the anthracitic coals are more satisfactory to use.

Anthracite is a smokeless coal. It is long-burning and large quantities can go into the stove at one time.

For most small stoves and kitchen ranges, chestnut-sized coal is the best. The larger the coal, the larger and deeper the fire pit should be.

To start a fire with anthracite:

(1)   Leave 1 to 2 inches of ash on the grate.
(2)   Ignite kindling on the grate.
(3)   Add a light layer of coal.
(4)   Build up the depth of the coal bed as the fire gets going good. A deep fuel bed is desirable.
(5)   When adding new fuel, slope fuel bed upward toward the back of the fire pit, leaving exposed a spot of glowing coal at the front to ignite the new fuel.
(6)   Never stir up the fire when adding new fuel.

To bank the fire for the night:

(1)   Shake the grate just until glowing ash starts to fall through into the ash pit.
(2)   Add fresh coal.
(3)   Close the ash pit damper and open the check damper.

Clean the ash pit regularly.

Bituminous coal:

There are two kinds of bituminous coal: low volatile and high volatile. Both are smoky coals. They must be treated differently than anthracite to reduce the smoking.

Low Volatile Bituminous:

(1)   To fire the coal, pile it in a cone-shaped pile. Pile the kindling next to the coal and ignite.

(2)   When adding new fuel, break up the center of the burning pile with a poker but do not stir up the fire.

High Volatile Bituminous:

(1)   When igniting a new fire or adding new fuel to a fire, in order to reduce the amount of smoking, pile the burning or burnt coal to one side of the firebox and clear away the other side down to the ashes.

(2)   Leave a 3 or 4 inch layer of ashes on the grate.

(3)   Pile fresh coal in the cleared area.

(4)   If the old coal is not burning hotly, ignite it with kindling piled against the side of the old coal. The burning coal will ignite the fresh coal and volatilize the gases as it burns, thus reducing smoking.

(5)   Put a layer of fine slack coal on top of the part of the fresh coal that is farthest from the burning coal. This helps the fire to burn better. Use one-fifth as much slack coal as the total amount of coal in the firepit.

(6)   Never put fresh high volatile coal on top of the burning coal. It will smoke and can cause an explosion.

(7)   Never mix the ashes with the coal. Mixing causes klinker formation.

Always leave a layer of ash under the coal fire to protect the grate. Poke holes through it to allow good air circulation.

Makeshift Stoves

Oildrum Stove

Several types of stoves can be constructed from oil drums. (Figure 16.2). Their operation would be similar to that of the coal or wood-burning stoves described above.

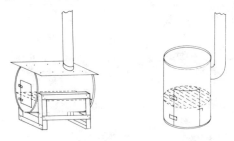

Figure 16.2

Tin Can Stoves

These are made from No. 10 cans. They are heated with tuna can fuel blocks or with Sterno. These should be used only outdoors or in very well-ventilated rooms. (Figure 16.3)

Figure 16.3
Tin can stove made from No. 10 can

Tuna Can Fuel Blocks

Cut strips of corrugated paper about 1 1/2 inches wide. Coil tightly to fill a tuna can. Insert a wick in the center, if desired. Pour melted parafin or wax over the paper until the paper coil is completely filled to the top. Let sit to harden. (Figure 16.4)

Figure 16.4

To use:

Protect the surface on which the can will sit, if needed. It will get quite hot and some of the parafin may spill. Light the wick or cardboard coil with a match. Set the tin can stove over the fuel block and either cook directly on the end of the No. 10 can or place your pan on the stove.

To extinguish:

Place a metal lid tightly over the tuna can to exclude any air. The fire will soon die.

Barbecue

This is strictly an outdoor method of cooking. A commercial type of barbecue cooker can be used or a grill can be placed over an open fire of wood, coal or charcoal.

Parafin Fire Starter Tablets

Grease the cups of a muffin tin or line them with cupcake papers or foil. Or, grease the insides of small cans to use as molds. Fill each mold 1/2 inch deep with dry sawdust. Insert a wick or small piece of candle in the center of the sawdust. Pour melted parafin or wax over the sawdust. Let

OUT-OF-DOORS COOKING

Trench fire

Trapper blaze

Charcoal grill

Figure 16.5

harden. Unmold.

To use:

Build your fire. Set one or more of these starter blocks under the wood or charcoal and ignite them.

Kerosene Lamps [3]

Kerosene lamps must be kept clean and filled if they are to burn with a good light and without odor. The reservoir should be filled to within an inch of the top. The charred portion of the wick should be rubbed off, the char removed from the wick tube and the burner. Turn the wick down just below the top of the tube. The chimney should be cleaned either by rubbing with tissue paper or by washing in hot soapy water, rinsing in clear water and wiping perfectly dry. If there is any moisture on the chimney when the lamp is lit, the glass is likely to crack. The outside of the lamp and the shade should be dusted. It saves trouble to keep the materials used in cleaning lamps together in a tray, basket or box.

FUEL CONSUMPTION AND BURNING TIME [4]

Gas lantern (Coleman, two-mantle)
    5/12 quart will burn 5 hours.
    To burn at the rate of 5 hours per day, you would need 38 gallons
        for one year.

Kerosene lantern (1-inch wick)
    1 quart kerosene burns 45 hours.
    To burn 5 hours per day, you would need 10 gallons for a year.

Flashlight Batteries
    6 to 7 hours continuous burning.

Candles
    3/4" by 4" lasts 2 hours 20 minutes.
    7/8" by 4" lasts 5 hours.
    2" square candle 9" tall will burn at the rate of 1" per 7 hours
        or will last 63 hours.

---

[3] U.S. Department of Agriculture, *Housecleaning Made Easier*, Farmers' Bulletin No. 1180, (Washington, D.C.: U.S. Government Printing Office).

[4] Adapted from "Family Storage Plan", compiled by Bob R. Zabriskie (Salt Lake City, Utah: Bookcraft, Inc., 1966). Used with permission.

CHAPTER XVII

CLOTHING AND BEDDING

Making Do

During prolonged emergencies, the ability to make do is essential. The homemaker who can make over clothing, make quilts and comforters from scraps, old clothing and old blankets and sew clothing without patterns will find herself well prepared.

Quilting is the original "make do" art. Not only can the homemaker produce warm bedding, home decorations and clothing for her family by quilting, but her creations can be beautiful works of art. The quilting book recommended in the Readiness Library in Appendix I, *The Standard Book of Quiltmaking and Collecting*, contains the basics of quilting as well as many lovely patterns.

The used clothing store can be a gold mine for the homemaker who can make over clothing. A garment purchased for only a few cents or a few dollars can become a favorite item of clothing for any member of the family, often with little reworking. Or the fabric in the garment can be recut from a different pattern. This is especially true when making clothing for children. One used robe, purchased for $ .50 can become a child's sleeper with the only added expense being a zipper and perhaps a pattern. To make over clothing the homemaker uses the same skills that she uses in sewing on new fabric. Any good sewing book can be used as a guide. I like the *McCall's Step-by-Step Sewing Book* because it is simply written, well-illustrated and inexpensive.

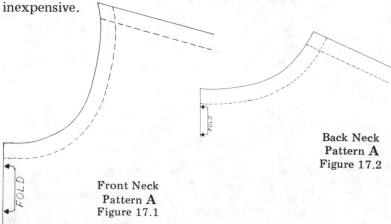

Back Neck
Pattern **A**
Figure 17.2

Front Neck
Pattern **A**
Figure 17.1

During an emergency, if the homemaker finds herself unable to purchase printed patterns and she cannot borrow what she needs, she will have to improvise.

One way to make clothing without patterns is to take apart a used garment that you know fits and use it as a pattern to cut a new garment.

Numerous styles of garments can be made from simple patterns that the homemaker can draft with the aid of a few simple measurements. Instructions for two basic styles are included in this chapter.

Knowing how to cut and sew garments such as these can help to reduce clothing expenses during normal times as well as during an emergency.

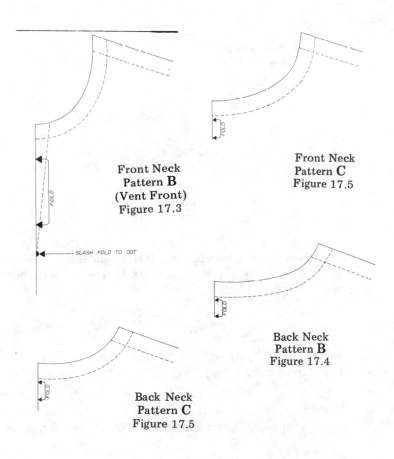

Front Neck
Pattern **B**
(Vent Front)
Figure 17.3

Front Neck
Pattern **C**
Figure 17.5

SLASH FOLD TO DOT

Back Neck
Pattern **B**
Figure 17.4

Back Neck
Pattern **C**
Figure 17.5

Note: Add seam allowance to either center front or center back for opening!

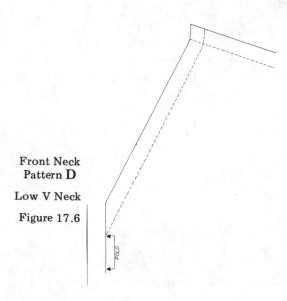

Front Neck
Pattern **D**

Low V Neck

Figure 17.6

Introductory note: Make each of these garments from an old sheet or very inexpensive fabric. Make adjustment to fit. Then transfer the adjustments to the pattern before cutting expensive fabric.

PATTERN NO. 1 - HOSTESS GOWN, DRESS OR BLOUSE
      (suitable for maternity wear)

1.   Measure from your shoulder to the desired length of your garment. Add 2 to 3 inches for hems. Double this figure and add 12 inches for facings and ties. This is the amount of fabric that you will need:

Long Dress - about 3 1/2 yards fabric.

Short Dress - about 2 3/4 yards fabric
Tunic - about 2 yards fabric.

2. Measure the hips and bust. To the larger measurement add 4 to 6 inches for seams and ease. Divide this figure by 4. Example:

Bust 34" 36" + 6" = 42"
Hips 36" 42" + 4" = 10½" (figure A)

Divide the width of the fabric by 2, then subtract the figure (A) that you have just obtained.

For 45" fabric: 45" ÷ 2" = 22 1/2"
22 1/2" - 10 1/2"
(figure B)

3. Cut 12 inches from one end of the fabric and make sure that the ends of the fabric are straight.

Finished View
Pattern No. 1

Figure 17.7

4. Fold the large piece of fabric in half crosswise. This fold is the shoulder line.

5. With the fabric folded, mark the neckline using the neck facing pattern as a guide. Cut the neck out.

6. Measure down from the shoulder fold 11 inches or more depending on the desired width of the sleeves. Mark this point (A) on the selvedges of the fabric and also about 10" in from the selvedges. (B) Mark a straight line with tailors' chalk between points A and B.

7. Slash from the selvedges toward the center, along the line you just marked, for a distance equal to figure B in step 2. In our example that distance was 12".

8. Cut facings for the neck. Cut two ties each 3" x 22 1/2".

To sew:

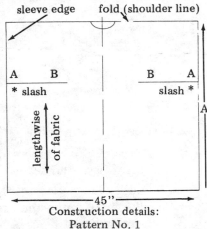

Construction details:
Pattern No. 1
Figure 17.8

1. Using 1/2 - inch seams, sew along the edges of the slash with right sides together. (Figure 17.9)

2. Fold the ties in half lengthwise and sew along one long edge and across one end. Turn and press.

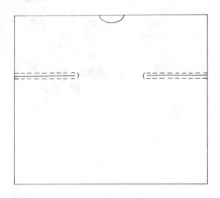

Construction details:
Pattern No. 1

Figure 17.9

3.   Sew front and back neck facings together at the shoulder.

4.   Sew the neck facings to neck edge. Trim seam. Understitch, turn and press. Tack facing to shoulder seams and center front and back.

5.   Insert the raw end of the tie into the corner at *. (Figure 17.8) Sew the side seams, reinforcing the corners where the ties are attached. The ties can be attached to tie either on the inside or the outside of the dress. A slim woman may need to trim some fabric off of each side seam. The flaps should just meet at the center front or back when the ties are tied.

PATTERN NO. 2 - GOWN, DRESS, ROBE, TUNIC OR SHIRT

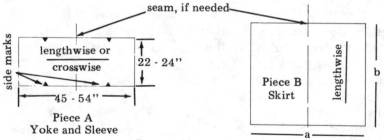

Pattern details: Pattern No. 2
Figure 17.10

Use 1/2" seams throughout.

a = hip or bust measurement (whichever is larger + 4 to 6 inches or more for ease and seams. For gathered skirt, add 10 inches or more.)

b = length of garment from shoulder (close to neck) to hem minus 1/2 the width of piece A + 2 1/2 to 3 1/2 inches for hems and seams.

c = distance from wrist to wrist across back or back width plus desired length of two sleeves + 2" for hems. (Add 1" for seam in center front and back, if needed.)

For long sleeves: c = 45" to 50"
For short sleeves: c = 1/2 of measurement a + 12"

Instructions for sewing Pattern No. 2

1.   Sew seams in piece B. (All seams are 1/2"). Press open. If the center back or front zipper is to be used, leave the seam in piece B open the distance required for the zipper. This seam is to be either the center front or center back.

Divide the top edge into fourths placing the first mark at one of the seams that you have just sewn. The points marked will be the center front, center back and the sides.

Run two lines of gathering stitches around the top of the skirt.

2.   If a center front or back seam is needed in the yoke, fold the fabric, piece A, in half, matching the short sides. Cut along the fold. Fold in half matching the c sides and mark and cut neck opening. The fold is the shoulder line.

Sew center front and back seams in yoke.

3.   Determine the placement of the side marks on the yoke. To do this, take your bust measurement, and add ease of 1" to 2". Divide this figure by four and the result is the distance either side of the

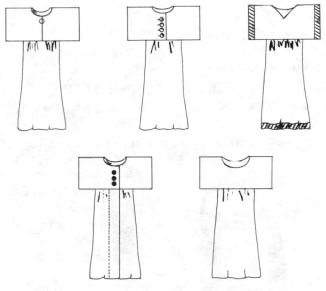

Finished Views: Pattern No. 2

Figure 17.11

center to place the side marks.

4.   Match centers of yoke and side marks on yoke with corresponding points on the skirt. Gather skirt to fit yoke and distribute fullness evenly. Sew skirt to yoke.

5.   Seam sleeves.

6.   Insert zipper or placket or button loops, if needed.

7.   Finish neck with self-fabric facings or bias bindings. Hem sleeves and skirt.

PATTERN NO. 3 - ROBE, GOWN, DRESS OR COAT

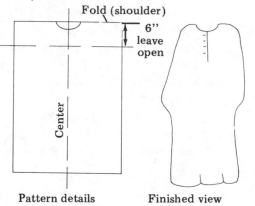

Pattern details   Finished view

Figure 17.12

1.   Measure fabric as instructed in pattern No. 1. Cut off 12" from one end of fabric for facings. Be sure that ends of fabric are straight.

2.   Fold large piece of fabric in half crosswise, matching short sides. This is the shoulder fold. Mark and cut neckline.

3.   Mark a point on each side edge 6" down from the fold. Sew side seam below this point.

4.   Finish neck edge with facings or bindings. If a high neckline is desired, insert zipper, placket or button loops into a center front or back opening.

5.   Turn in seam allowance around opening left at top of side and stitch a hem. This will finish off the hand opening. Hem skirt. (Elastic in a casing may be used to finish the hand opening.)

6.   For less fullness at the bottom of the skirt, taper sides in either of the two ways illustrated in Figure 17.13.

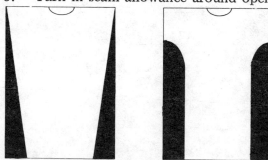

Pattern variations: Pattern No. 3

Figure 17.13

PATTERN NO. 4 - JUMPER OR DRESS WITH YOKE

_____back width of shoulders, tip to tip.

_____bust measurement

_____distance from shoulder seam at tip of shoulder to point of bust.

To draw pattern:

1.   Determine the neckline desired. If the neck is large enough to go over the head, and waist is not fitted, make the front and back pattern pieces identical. If the neck opening is small or the waist fitted, a front or back opening will be needed. Make either the front or back pattern piece 1" wider at the center to allow for a seam in which to insert a zipper or placket.

a   b   c   d

Finished Views: Pattern No. 4

Figure 17.14

2.   Draw a rectangle using 1/2 the bust measurement + 1 1/2" as the width. Mark the center with a vertical line (A). (Figure 17.15)

3.   Mark a line three inches down from the top of the rectangle (B).

4.   Draw neckline.

5.   Mark points a and b 3" on either side of the center line at the top of the rectangle.

6.   Connect points a and b with the side lines at line B. These are the shoulder seam lines (D).

7.   Divide the width of your shoulders in half. Mark a vertical line (E) that distance on each side of the center line. The point where line D crosses each line E is the tip of the shoulder and the top of the arm- hole. For a jumper, the armhole edge can be moved toward the center 1/2" or more.

8.   Measure on your pattern from the shoulder tip down the same distance as your shoulder tip to bust point measurement.

Mark a line (F) across the pattern at this point. This is the bust-line.

9. Mark a line across the pattern 1" above line F. (C).

10. Draw a curved line to connect the tip of the shoulder with the point where line C crossed the side of the rectangle. This will be the armhole seam.

11. Add 1/2" seam allowances on the arm-hole, shoulder, side seam and neck edges. Add 1/2" below line F for the yoke seam.

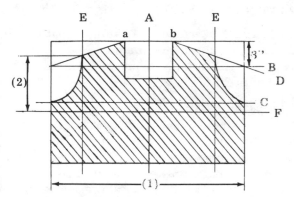

(1)   1/2 bust measurement + 1 1/2"
(2)   distance from shoulder tip to bust point

Pattern details of bodice: Pattern No. 4

Figure 17.15

This is the basic yoke pattern. Make it first out of muslin and adjust as needed. The yoke can be shortened to end higher than mid-bust. In that case, the lower part of the armhole curve is cut in the top of the skirt portion of the garment.

The yoke can also be lengthened as much as desired. Darts will have to be added under the bust in front and on both sides of the center back. To determine the placement of the bust darts, measure the distance between the points of your bust. Divide this distance in half. Measure this distance on either side of the center front and mark the centers of the darts. The darts should be 1/2" to 1" wide and should end 1" below the point of the bust. The back darts are placed about 3" either side of the center back and extend above the waist to 1" below the fullest part of the back below the armhole.

For a long yoke, taper the underarm seam slightly toward the center to make the waist fit more snugly. Always allow about 1" ease at the bottom of the yoke for comfort and ease of movement.

The yoke will need to be lined or the neck and armholes faced.

The Skirt

The skirt can be cut to fit the bottom edge of the yoke or made larger to allow for gathering or pleats. The A-line skirt fits the bottom edge of the yoke.

Gathered Skirt (Figure 17.14 a)

1. Cut fabric 1 1/2 to 2 times the hip measurement. Add seam allowances. The length of the skirt piece is the desired finished length of the skirt + 2 to 3 inches for hem + 1/2 inch for top seam.

2. Gather across the top edge of the skirt. Pin to yoke, distributing gathers evenly. Stitch yoke to skirt.

3. Variation: (Figure 17.16) Leave top of skirt ungathered for about 3 inches either side of the side seams. Also leave ungathered about 5 inches at center front and back. Less fullness is needed for this variation than for the skirt gathered all around.

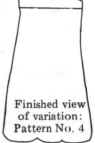

Finished view
of variation:
Pattern No. 4

Figure 17.16

A-line Skirt (Figure 17.14 b)

1. Make a rectangle as wide as the lower edge of the bodice front and desired finished length. Measure down from the top and mark where the widest part of the hips will be. Working from the center to the outside, mark the rectangle into 2 - inch vertical strips. Leaving 1/8 inch uncut at the top, cut through the pattern from the bottom toward the top along the lines you marked. (Figure 17.17)

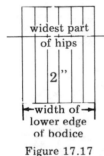

widest part
of hips

2"

←width of→
lower edge
of bodice

Figure 17.17

2. Lay the rectangle on top of a larger piece of paper. Spread the bottom of the rectangle, keeping the gaps even between the strips. Spread enough so that the skirt at the fullest part of the hips will measure at least 1/2 the hip measurement + 1" for ease. Tape the spread rectangle to the paper underneath. This method of pattern construction makes the upper seam and hem curve. Add seam allowances and hem allowance. (Figure 17.18)

A-line Skirt with Center Pleats (Figure 17.14c)

1. Draw the A-line pattern. Cut the pattern in two down the center line.

2. To the center of the pattern, add a piece of paper 8 inches wide and the length of the skirt. This will make a 4-inch wide box pleat. (Figure 17.19)

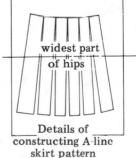

widest part
of hips

Details of
constructing A-line
skirt pattern

Figure 17.18

Pleated Skirt (Figure 17.14d)

1. Cut as for gathered skirt. Pleat as desired. Make all pleats even in width.

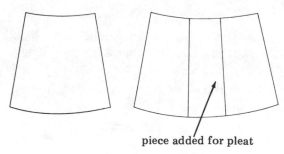

piece added for pleat

Pattern details pleated skirt:
single center pleat

Figure 17.19

Pleated A-line Skirt - box pleats (not suitable for plaids or stripes)

1.   Decide how many pleats you want and where they are to be placed.

2.   Make an A-line skirt pattern.

3.   Mark the placement of the pleats on the pattern.

4.   Cut the pattern into sections along the lines you have marked.

5.   Insert a 6 - inch to 8 - inch wide piece of paper the length of the skirt into the space for each pleat.

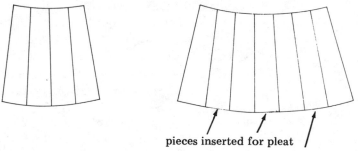

pieces inserted for pleat

Pattern details pleated skirt: multiple pleats

Figure 17.20

6.   Since this makes a large pattern, it may be necessary to divide the pattern into sections along the inside fold of one or more pleats to make the skirt pattern fit onto your fabric and to keep the skirt properly aligned with the grain of the fabric. Be sure to add seam allowances on the sides of the pattern and wherever the pattern is divided.

Pleated A-line Skirt - knife pleats
    (not suitable for plaids of stripes)

Follow directions for box-pleated skirt above, making strips for pleats 2 to 4 inches wide.

Ruffles

Tapered Ruffles

Decide on the finished length and the widest width of the ruffle. Draw a straight line twice as long as the desired finished length. Mark the center of this line. Draw a line perpendicular to the first line through the center point that you marked. On this second line, measure both sides of the first line the distance equal to the wid-

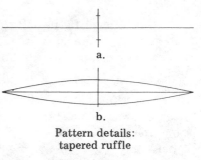

Pattern details: tapered ruffle

Figure 17.21

est width of the finished ruffle. Mark this point. Connect the ends of the first line together with a curved line that passes through the points marked on the second line. Add seam allowances all around.

Finished views of variations: Pattern No. 4

Figure 17.22

To sew:

Fold the ruffle in half, lengthwise. Make two rows of gathering stitches along the curved edge, through both thicknesses. Pin the ruffle to the garment, distribute the gathers evenly, and stitch.

Straight Ruffles

Cut a piece of fabric as wide as the desired width of the ruffle + seam allowance and hem allowance. The ruffle should be 1 1/2 to 2 times the length of the seam it is to join. Hem one edge and gather the other.

Alternate method: For a folded ruffle having no hem, cut the ruffle twice as wide as the desired finished width of the ruffle + 1 inch for seams. Fold the ruffle in half lengthwise, right sides out. Gather through both thicknesses of fabric.

PATTERN NO. 5 - BUNTING

Use pattern No. 2 for bunting with sleeves or use pattern No. 3 for bunting without sleeves. When using pattern No. 3, do not leave openings for the hands.

Width

Make the width of the pattern for the body of the garment equal to twice the chest measurement of the child. For a child with a 20" chest, the finished garment will be 20" wide at the hem. This allows plenty of wiggle room.

Tucks at the shoulders will make the garment fit better through the shoulders.

Length

Allow 2 or 3 inches of wiggle room in the finished length. One or two 2" tucks near the hem would allow for growth.

Yoke Depth (pattern No. 2)

4 1/2 to 5 inches will be more than sufficient for a young baby.

Finishing the opening

Use a center front zipper at least 14" long. A lapped placket can be used and the opening closed with buttons or snaps.

Mitts (pattern No. 2)

Mitts may be added to cover the hands. This requires a shoulder seam. Cut a piece of fabric the width of the sleeve plus seam allowances and 6" long. Fold in half crosswise, (Figure 17.23) with the right side out.

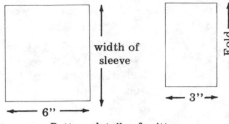

Pattern details of mitt
Pattern No. 5

Figure 17.23

Lay sleeve front piece right side down on top of these, matching edges. Seam shoulder and underarm seams. Bind or hem sleeve edge.

PATTERN NO. 6 - MITTENS

To construct the pattern:

Lay the hand you wish to fit on a piece of paper, fingers slightly spread and the thumb at a comfortable angle. With a pencil, trace around the hand, keeping the pencil about 1/2" away from the hand. Add seam allowances. This pattern can be made with or without a thumb. (Figure 17.25)

Cutting and sewing:

For each mitten you will need to cut two identical pieces of fabric. This pattern is suitable for stretchable knit fabric only.

With right sides together, leaving open at the wrist. Turn and press.

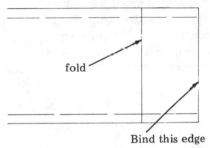

Pattern details of mitt:
Pattern No. 5

Figure 17.24

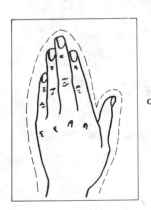

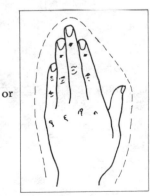

Making pattern No. 6

Figure 17.25

The Cuff:

The cuff should be a little smaller than the wrist edge of the mitten so that it will hug the wrist.

Cut the cuff from a stretchable knit fabric with the stretch going around the wrist. (Figure 17.26)

Match the short edges and seam with a 1/4" seam. Fold lengthwise along the center with the seam inside and the raw edges matching. Pin cuff to mitten, stretching the cuff edge to fit the raw edge of the mitten. Stitch the cuff to the mitten using a stretch stitch or a

zigzag stitch. Stretch as you sew. Two rows of straight stitching can be used if you have no zigzag machine. Use a 1/4" seam.

Pattern details of mitten: Pattern No. 5

Figure 17.26

PATTERN NO. 7 - HAT

1.   Measure distance from the angle of the jaw just below one ear, across the top of the head to the same place on the other side of the head. (Measurement A).

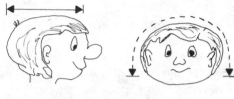

Measuring for hat pattern

Figure 17.27

2.   Measure from just behind the hairline at the front of the head to the crown. (Measurement B). (Figure 17.27)

Unlined Hat

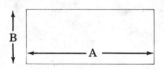

Figure 17.28
Hat pattern

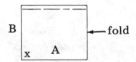

Figure 17.29
Hat construction

1.   Cut one piece of fabric as above, (Figure 17.28) adding seam allowances.

2.   Fold in half crosswise, matching B edges. Sew along one A edge from the fold to the B edge.

3.   Hem the other raw edges and add ties to the corners at x's.

4. ·   Add trimmings as desired.

Self-lined Hat

1.   Cut one piece of fabric using measurement A for the length and making it twice as wide as measurement B. (Figure 17.30)

2.   Fold in half, right sides together, matching B edges. Stitch along line C.

3.   Refold so that the outside comes over lining, right sides out.

4.   Bind or hem edges. Add trimmings and ties.

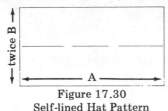

Figure 17.30
Self-lined Hat Pattern

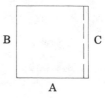

Figure 17.31
Hat construction

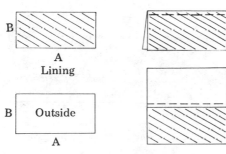

Constructing the lined hat

Figure 17.32

Hat with Separate Lining

1.   Cut two pieces using pattern for unlined hat. Sew right sides together, along one A edge. Press seam toward lining. (Figure 17.32)

2.   Fold so that B edges meet. Match the seam. Pin or baste.

Constructing the lined hat

Figure 17.33   Figure 17.34

3.   Stitch again along original seam line, sewing through all thicknesses. (Figure 17.33)

4.   Turn outside of hat over lining, hiding seam.

5.   Continue as with self-lined hat.

Alternate Pattern: (Figure 17.35)

1.   Cut off shaded areas

2.   Add seam allowances

3.   Ties go at x's

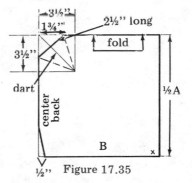

Figure 17.35

PATTERN NO. 8 - PANTS

The easiest way to make a pair of pants without a pattern is to take apart an old pair that you know will fit and use them for a pattern. If you desire to draft a pattern, take the following measurements:

++Use larger number for pull-on style pants if the hips are 11" or more larger than the waist.

*More ease is needed with woven fabrics than with knits.

**Stand against a wall holding one ruler flat against your abdomen about 9" below your waist. With another ruler, measure the distance from the wall to the first ruler.

**Sit on a hard, flat surface.

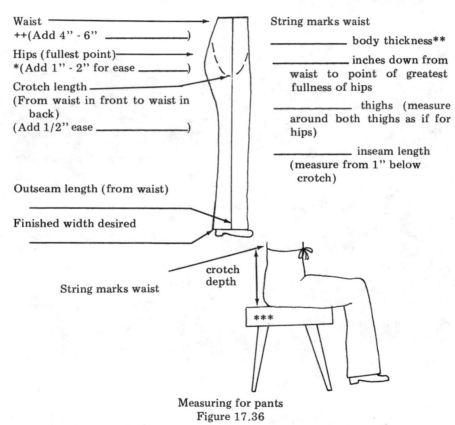

Waist ————————————————→
++(Add 4" - 6" ——————————)

Hips (fullest point)————————→
*(Add 1" - 2" for ease ————)

Crotch length ——————————
(From waist in front to waist in back)
(Add 1/2" ease ——————————)

Outseam length (from waist)

Finished width desired

String marks waist   crotch depth

String marks waist

——————————— body thickness**

——————————— inches down from waist to point of greatest fullness of hips

——————————— thighs (measure around both thighs as if for hips)

——————————— inseam length (measure from 1" below crotch)

***

Measuring for pants
Figure 17.36

Do not expect to make professional looking pants from these simple instructions. Entire books have been written on the subject of sewing pants. The pants made from these instructions are meant to be utilitarian only! These are instructions for women's pants. They should be adaptable to children's and men's pants, but do not expect them to look like the ones that you buy at the store. With considerable fitting and adjustment these pants can be made to look more professional.

CONSTRUCTING THE PANTS PATTERN

A = 1/2 hip measurement including ease + thickness of body*

B = Body thickness

C = 1/2 back hip measurement including ease

D = 1/2 front hip measurement including ease

E = 2 times desired finished width of leg

F = 1/2" to 1"

G = 1/2 back waist measurement + 1" to 2" (++ see note page 229)

H = 1/2 front waist measurement + 1" to 2" (++ see note)

I = finished length of pants (outseam)

J = crotch depth including ease

* Use 1/2 thigh measurement if larger than hips

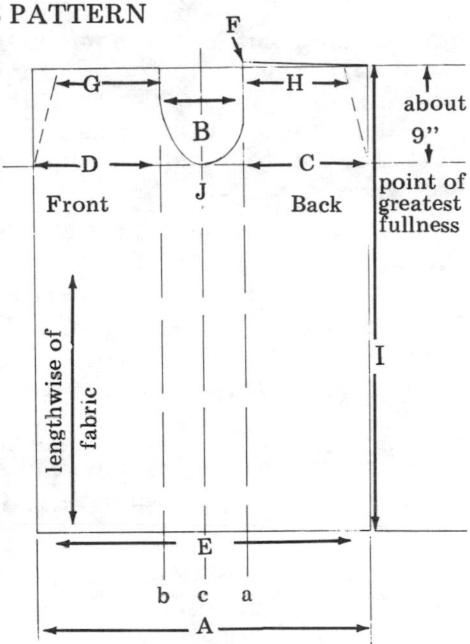

Constructing the pants pattern
Figure 17.37

1.   Start with a rectangle using measurement A as the width and I as the length. Draw a line lengthwise down the middle of the rectangle dividing it into two rectangles (line c). Mark one rectangle FRONT and the other one BACK.

2.   Determine placement of crotch seam by measuring distances C and D from the sides of the rectangle. Mark these points. Mark vertical lines parallel to line c through these points (lines a and b).

3.   Determine front and back crotch seam lengths using the formula below:

crotch depth + 1/3 of the extension = length of front crotch seam*
       *round off to the nearest 1/4"

crotch length including ease — 2 times crotch depth including ease = extension

total crotch length including ease - front crotch seam length = back crotch seam length

   Cut two pieces of string the lengths of the front and back crotch seams. Cut off 1/2 inch from the back string.

4.   Add distance F to top of waist at back crotch seam. Taper waistline from there to the original waistline at the side.

5.   Lay the string representing the back crotch length on the pattern,

along line a. Tape one end of the string at the waistline and the other at the point on line c representing the crotch depth including ease (measurement J). Try to approximate the curve shown in the illustration (Figure 17.37). Mark this curve on the pattern. Repeat with the front using the string representing the front crotch length. Note that the front crotch seam curve is shorter and steeper than the back curve.

6.   Measure from the crotch seam at the waist toward the sides. Mark distances G and H. Curve side seams above hips to pass through these marks.

7.   If measurement A is larger than E, taper side seams no more than 1/2" on each side from below hips to the bottom. Always take the same amount off each side. This pattern is not suitable for tightly fitted or belled legs.

8.   Compare inseam measurement with the length of line c below the crotch seam. Adjust if necessary. Bottom of pants should be nearly straight.

9.   Mark placement of darts or pleats, if used. Front darts should be about 4" from the center front and extend about 3" to 4" below waistline. Back darts should be about 3" to 4" from the center back and extend 4" to 5" below the waistline. Darts should always point to the areas of greatest fullness of the body and stop 1/2" to 1" short of the point of greatest fullness. If your hips are large compared to your waist (11" or more difference), use 2 darts on each side of center front and back. Make each dart about 1/2" to 3/4" wide at the waist.

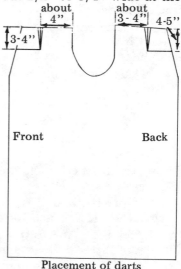

10.   Add extra length to the top of the pattern as follows:

a.   For pull-on style with casing, add 3 1/4".

b.   For pull-on style with elasticized waist, without casing, add 2 1/4".

c.   Closed band with elastic, add 1 1/2".

d.   Open band with zipper or placket, add 1 1/2".

These amounts allow 1" extra for fitting purposes. (See No. 5 in instructions for constructing pants).

11.   Add 1/2" seam allowances on

Placement of darts
Figure 17.38

crotch seam and side seams. Add 1 1/2" to 2" for hem at bottom.

The pattern is now ready for you to cut out of an old sheet or inexpensive fabric to use for fitting purposes. Sew together this trial pair and make adjustments. Transfer the adjustments to the pattern. Then you are ready to make a pair of pants to wear.

When cutting the pants, place the pattern lengthwise along the straight grain of the folded fabric. Cut two.

Remember: Pants made of woven fabric will need more ease than pants made of knit fabric.

To Construct the Pants

1.   If a placket or zipper is to be used, insert it either in the front, back, or left side seam.

2.   Sew the two pieces together along the crotch seam, right sides together. Reinforce the curved part of the seam. Clip curve or trim seam to 1/4" at curve.

3.   With right sides together, sew the side seams.

4.   Sew the darts or pleats, if included.

5.   Put pants on. Tie a string around your waist over the pants. Adjust the pants so they hang evenly and the crotch hangs correctly. Do not fit the crotch too snugly to the body. There should be about 1" ease. Mark a line of pins around the waist just under the string. Trim fabric above this line to the width indicated for the waistline finish that you desire (see No. 10 on previous page). Subtract 1" from the figures given.

WAIST FINISHES

Pull-on Style with Elasticized Casing

For this style there should be at least 4 to 6 inches ease in the waistline of the pants. Allow 2 1/4" above the waistline for the casing. Cut a piece of 1" non-roll elastic the length of your waist measurement + 1/4". Overlap the two ends of the elastic 1/4" and sew together. securely. Divide the elastic and the waist of the pants into fourths and mark with pins. Pin the elastic to the inside of the pants extending the fabric 1/4" beyond the edge of the elastic and matching the marks in the elastic and waistline. Using a narrow zigzag stitch, sew along the lower edge of the elastic joining the elastic to the fabric. Stretch the elastic and the fabric as you sew. Turn the elastic down to the inside to enclose

Pinning
the elastic
Figure 17.39

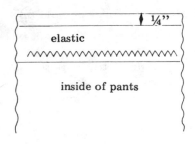

the elastic in the casing. (Figure 17.40) Sew close to the upper and lower edges of the casing, through all thicknesses, using a narrow zigzag stitch or straight stretch stitch, stretching as you sew.

Pull-on Style with Elastic Waist

For this style the waist of the pants must measure 4 to 6 inches larger than your waist measurement. Allow 1 1/4" above the waistline for the waist finish. Make a circle of elastic as described above. Divide the elastic and the waist of the pants into fourths. Pin the elastic to the outside of the pants matching the marks. As you pin, lap the elastic 1/4" over the fabric. (Figure 17.41) Join the elastic to the pants by

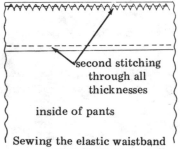

Sewing the elastic waistband
Figure 17.40

stitching close to the edge of the elastic. Use a narrow zigzag stitch and stretch as you sew.

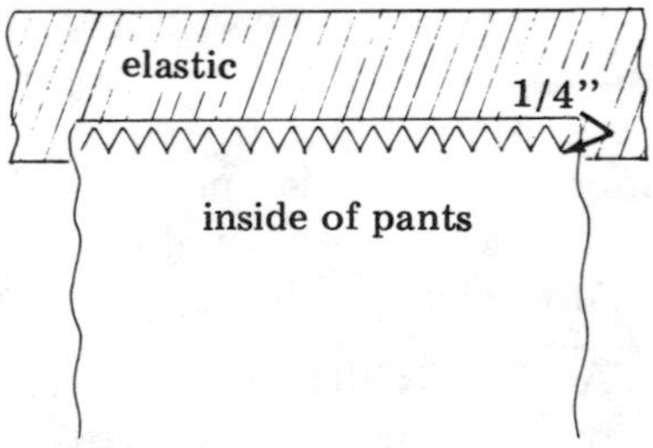

Turn the elastic to the inside of the garment. Stitch again in the lower edge of the elastic. Use either a zigzag or straight stitch, stretching as you sew. (Figure 17.42)

If desired, another line of stitching may be made at the top of the elastic through all thicknesses.

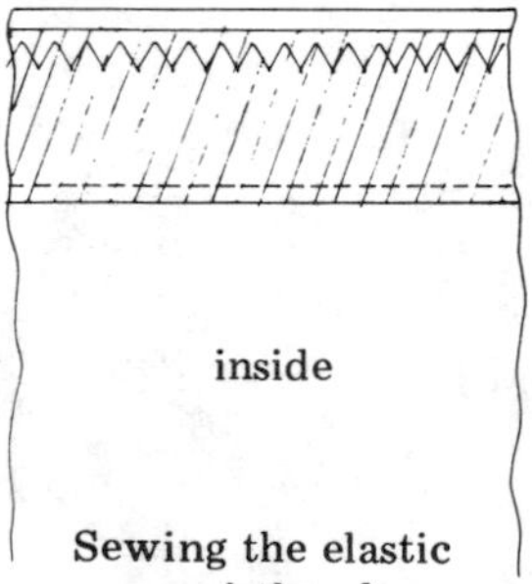

Sewing the elastic waistband
Figure 17.41

Pull-on Style with Elasticized Closed Waistband

The waist of the pants should measure 4 to 6 inches larger than your waist. Before the elastic is put into the band, the waistband should measure 1 to 2 inches larger than your waist. This style is suitable only for stretchable knit fabrics. Always check the band after joining the ends to make sure that it will stretch enough to go over your hips. Some knits do not have enough stretch to pull over the hips with the waistband being only 1 to 2 inches

Sewing the elastic
waistband
Figure 17.42

larger than your waist. If the waistband were any larger than that, the pants would appear to be gathered around the waist.

Cut the waistband 3" wide and the length of your waist plus 1 to 2 inches for ease and 1" for seams.

Sew the ends of the waistband together to form a circle. Check to see that the band will easily stretch to go over your hips. Using a 1/2" seam sew one side of the waistband to the outside of the pants, stretching the band to fit the pants. Use a narrow zigzag stitch or two rows of straight stitching. Cut and sew a circle of elastic as described in the directions for the elasticized casing. Fit the elastic around the waist of the pants on the inside of the waistband, fold the waistline seam up over the elastic. Then turn down the waistband evenly all around to the inside. The waistband will be about 1 3/8" wide on the inside.

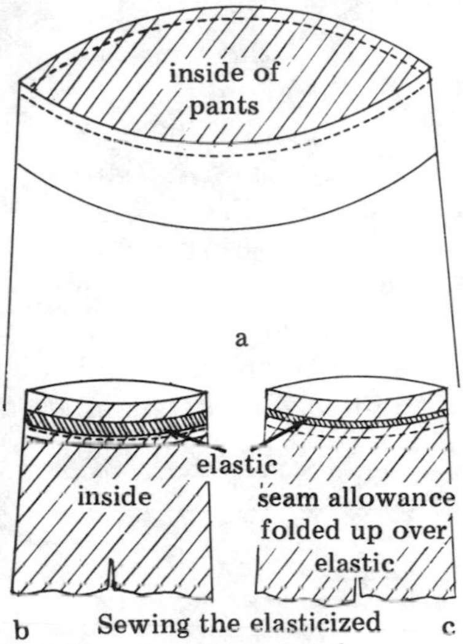

Sewing the elasticized closed waistband

Figure 17.43

Baste close to the waistline stitching. On the outside of the pants, sew in the ditch created by the waistline seam, using a straight stitch or a straight stretch stitch, and stretching as you sew. The stitching should be just barely visible.

Sewing the elasticized closed waistband

Figure 17.44

On most knit fabrics it is not necessary to turn under or finish the inside edge of the waistband. If you desire a more finished edge, bind it with bias binding or turn the edge under 1/4" and top stitch, as you would a facing edge.

Open Waistband with Zipper or Placket

For knit pants:

Cut the band 3" wide and the length of your waist plus 2" for lap and 1" for seams. After inserting the zipper or placket, lay the waistband on the pants, right sides together. Extend the end of the waistband 1/2" beyond the left side of the pants for the back or front opening or 1/2" beyond the front edge of the pants for the side opening. (Figure 17.45) Pin the waistband to the pants, leaving 2 1/2" extending beyond the other end of the waist opening, for the lap. Sew the waistline seam. Fold the waistline lengthwise along the center of the band, right sides together. (Figure 17.46) Pin the ends. Sew a 1/2" seam in the short end of the band. Finish the lap end of the band by sewing a 1/2" seam along the bottom edge and the end

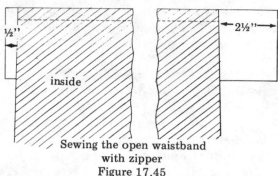

Sewing the open waistband
with zipper
Figure 17.45

of the band to form a tab. Trim seams and turn. Pin the band evenly

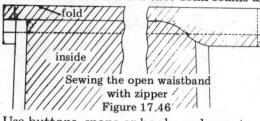

Sewing the open waistband
with zipper
Figure 17.46

along the inside of the pants. (Figure 17.47)

Stitch from the right side of the pants in the ditch formed by the waistline seam, stretching as you sew. (Figure 17.48)

Use buttons, snaps or hooks and eyes to close the band.

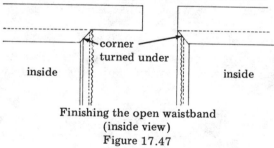

Finishing the open waistband
(inside view)
Figure 17.47

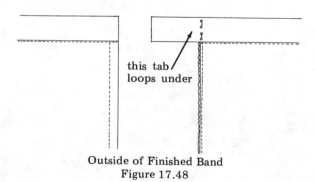

Outside of Finished Band
Figure 17.48

For pants of woven fabric:

Follow the instructions given for knit pants with these changes:

1.   Add 1/2" to 1" to the length of the waistband piece, for ease.

2.   Finish the lower edge of the waistband with bias binding or turn under 1/4" and top stitch.

LEATHER WORK

Tools and Equipment Needed for Leather Work

Should there be a need to make leather garments such as moccasins, gloves, jackets, belts and other items, proper equipment and materials will be needed for doing this. Here is a list of some of the items that one might need.

Scissors large enough and strong enough to cut leather. Tin snips are good for cutting heavy leather.

Mallet made of rawhide, wood, or hard rubber. Metal may damage leather.

Tracing Wheel for tracing patterns onto the leather.

Dressmaker's Carbon

Chalk Pencils

Thread

Awl and Needles

Punch

Lacing of different widths.

Hand Sewing Needles especially made for leatherwork.

Thimble

Rubber Cement

Small Pair of Pliers

Screw Driver

Pocket Knife

Bees Wax for waxing thread

Patterns, leather and hardware for moccasins, belts, purses, sandals, hats, tool pouches, etc. If you are well acquainted with the craft of leather work, you might want to have additional supplies for making shoes.

Instruction Books (see the Readiness Library, Appendix I).

Moccasins

1.   Cut moccasin pieces from heavy or medium weight leather. The leather must be pliable.

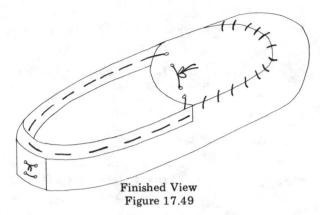

Finished View
Figure 17.49

2.   Mark and punch holes 1/4 inch from the edge and about 1/4 inch apart evenly spaced around the toe edge of the plug between points b. The first and last holes should be at points b. (Figure 17.51)

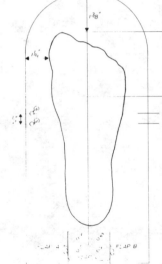

Moccasin sole and sides
Figure 17.50

3.   On the toe of the mocassin, mark and punch the same number of holes as on the plug. The holes should be 1/4 inch from the edge and evenly spaced around the toe between points b. The first and last holes should be at points b. (Figure 17.50)

4.   Punch 4 holes in the plug as shown on pattern. These holes are for the tie. (Figure 17.51)

5.   Punch an even number of holes (ie. 18, 20, 22, etc.) about 1/4 inch from the edge and about 1/2 inch apart, evenly spaced, around the heel of the moccasin between points a. The first and last holes should be at points a. (Figure 17.50)

6.   Using heavy thread especially designed for leatherwork or a heavy cord or shoe lace, lace the plug to the toe between points b, pulling lacing tight. Lace thread through moccasin from the outside then up from the inside through the plug, leaving about a 3/4 - inch end. Catch this end under the lacing as you make 2 more stitches in the same holes. Catch the end under the lacing in the next two holes. Whip stitch (in through the moccasin, out through the plug,

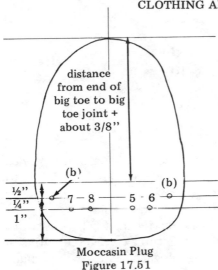

distance
from end of
big toe to big
toe joint +
about 3/8"

(b)   (b)
½"
¼"   7 – 8   5 · 6
1"

Moccasin Plug
Figure 17.51

over the edge and back in through the moccasin, etc.) all around the toe ending at point b. Take three stitches through the last hole at point b. Run the end of the lace under the stitches in the last three holes. Cut off.

7.   To form heel: Lap flap A over flap B matching cuff holes. Fold up flap C and mark and punch holes through all three flaps as marked on flap C. With a short piece of lacing, lace as follows: In through hole 1, out through hole 2, in through hole 3 and back out through hole 4. Be sure to lace through all three flaps. Tie ends securely and cut off, leaving 1/2 - inch ends. (Figure 17.49)

8.   Cuff and plug tie: Using rawhide lacing or shoe lace, insert lace from outside down through hole 5 and back up through hole 6. (Figure 17.51) Leave a 5 to 6 - inch end sticking out of hole 5. Match the first hole in the cuff with hole a. Insert the lace from the outside to the inside through hole

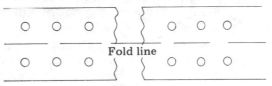

Fold line

1.   1½" wide
2.   Length - distance around heel between points (a) + ½"
3.   Holes ½" apart

Moccasin cuff
Figure 17.52

a. Lace in and out tightly around heel to hole a on the other side. Then lace through hole 7 and back out through hole 8. Cut off leaving a 5 to 6 - inch end. Tie a bow or knot.

CHAPTER XVIII

EMERGENCY SANITATION

Emergency Sewage Disposal

"Water flush toilets cannot be used, of course, when water service is interrupted. The water remaining in the fixtures is not sufficient to flush the wastes down the sewer. Clogging may result, and your living conditions become just that much more uncomfortable.

Even if water is available, local authorities may ask you not to use flush toilets, wash basins, and other fixtures connected with soil pipes. The sewer mains may be broken or clogged, which would make it impossible to carry off such wastes. Or water may be needed for fire fighting. It is necessary for every family to know emergency methods of waste disposal, in case such conditions arise.

Failure to properly dispose of human wastes can lead to epidemics of such diseases as typhoid, dysentery, and diarrhea. At the same time, sewage must be disposed of in ways that will prevent contamination of water supplies used for drinking, cooking, bathing, laundering and other domestic purposes. Here are simple steps that any family can take to prevent such dangers and discomforts:

(a) Right after a disaster, or during one, you will probably not have the time or tools to prepare a complex emergency sanitation system. If there is a delay of several days in restoring sewerage service to your neighborhood, you may find that disposal is a big problem. Your first task, however, is to make some temporary toilet provision for the members of your family, especially the children. Almost any covered metal container will do. You can use a covered pail. A small kitchen garbage container with a foot operated cover can be put to toilet use in emergencies. Anything that has a cover and will hold the contents until you can dispose of them will serve for sanitary purposes, at first."[1]

Now on the market are several types of portable toilets. Some of them are merely a toilet seat with a plastic bag attached beneath. Some have water and waste reservoirs and flushing mechanisms. Chemicals added to the flushing water help to prevent odor and the growth of disease organisms.

"(b) Keep on the premises at least one extra 10-gallon garbage

[1]Emergency Sanitation at Home, Office of Civil Defense, Department of Defense, May 1963.

can or other waterproof container with a tightly fitted cover. This should be lined with paper, and the cover should be fastened to the can to prevent its loss. Such a can may be used for the emergency storage of body wastes until the public sewerage system can be put back into action, or until other arrangements can be made. Empty your smaller vessel into it as often as necessary. A small amount of household disinfectant should be added after each use. If you live in an apartment, you may not have a large garbage can or room to keep one. In that case, two smaller covered pails or other containers will do just as well.

(c) Keep a shovel on the premises, if there are unpaved yard areas nearby. Burying human waste matter under 12 to 24 inches of earth is a satisfactory method of emergency disposal. Never deposit wastes, liquid or solid, on the surface of the ground. Insects and rodents may carry infections to other humans.

(d) A temporary pit privy may be constructed in a yard area for use by several families. This offers a good method of waste disposal over extended periods of time. The structure need not be elaborate, so long as it provides reasonable privacy and shelter. The pit should be made flyproof by means of a tight-fitting riser, seat and cover. A low mound of earth should be tamped around the base of the privy to divert surface drainage and help keep the pit dry. Accumulated waste should be covered with not less than 12 inches of earth when the privy is moved or abandoned. Outdoor

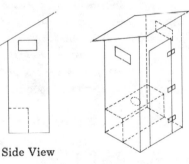

Side View

Privy

Figure 18.1

toilets should not be located in areas that are subject to flooding, and should be built at least 50 feet from any well, spring or other source of water supply. Otherwise the wastes may contaminate the water. Or they might be washed out of the pit and deposited on the ground surface where they would be exposed to flies, rodents and other animals that might serve as disease carriers.

(e) Persons in city apartments, office buildings or homes without yards should keep a supply of waterproof paper containers on hand for emergency waste disposal. Before collection, the containers may be stored in tightly covered garbage cans or other waterproof utensils fitted with lids. Homemade soil bags for this purpose may be prepared very easily by putting one large grocery bag inside another, with a layer of shredded newspaper or other absorbant material between. Apartment dwellers should have sufficient grocery bags on hand now for possible emergencies. A supply of old newspapers will come in handy for other sanitary uses, too, such as wrapping garbage and lining larger containers.

(f) Insecticides and deodorants should be used when necessary to control odors and insect breeding in containers that cannot be emptied immediately. At least 2 pints of household bleach solution should be kept on hand for disinfecting purposes."[2]

Disposal of Garbage and Rubbish

"Garbage, or any mixed refuse containing garbage, must be carefully stored and handled if odor and insect nuisances are to be prevented. Garbage should be kept separate [from rubbish].

(a) Garbage should be drained before being stored for a longer period of time without developing an unpleasant odor. After straining, wrap the garbage in several thicknesses of old newspaper before putting it into your container. That will absorb any remaining moisture. A tight-fitting lid is important to keep out flies and other insects.

(b) You should keep one or more 20 gallon garbage cans on hand for emergency use, if possible. If you live in an apartment building, get the largest kitchen garbage container for which you have space.

Final disposal of all stored garbage and refuse can be accomplished in the following manner:

(a) All stored garbage should be buried if collection service is not restored. If unpaved yard areas are available, keep a shovel handy for this purpose. Do not dump garbage on the ground, because that attracts rats and other scavengers. Dig a hole deep enough to cover it with at least 12 to 24 inches of dirt, which will prevent insect breeding and discourage animals from digging it up."[3]

"(c) Other rubbish may be burned in open yard areas or left at dumps established by the local authorities. Cans should be flattened to reduce their bulk. Do not deposit ashes or rubbish in the streets or alley ways without permission. Such material may interfere with the movement and operation of fire-fighting and other emergency equipment."[4]

---

[2] *Ibid.*
[3] *Ibid.*
[4] *Ibid.*

Sanitation and Disease Prevention

It is essential to follow the basic rules of sanitation and disease prevention during times of disaster.

Cleanliness is the most important rule. Keep the body and the environment clean.

Good handwashing is important. Wash the hands with plenty of soap and water every time they come into contact with contaminated objects or water that might be contaminated. Always wash after using the toilet, after handling persons ill with contagious disease or anything that they might have touched. Wash the hands before prepareing food and eating.

All fresh fruits and vegetables should be washed before preparing and eating them.

Wash the tops of cans before opening them.

Any food contaminated by sewage or flood water must be discarded. Contaminated containers can be washed with a strong disinfectant solution.

Disinfect all surfaces and objects contaminated by flood water or sewage. Hang clothing out in the air and sunshine after it is disinfected to allow the disinfectant odor to dissipate.

Carefully avoid contact with disease-causing organisms. Avoid all unnecessary contact with flood water or sewage. Wash with plenty of soap if you do come into contact with these.

Stay away from persons who are ill with serious contagious diseases. Isolate any member of the family that is ill. Have only one person see to the needs of the one who is ill.

Clothing can harbor disease organisms. When caring for someone ill with a serious contagious disease, cover your clothing with a gown. Before leaving the sickroom, take the gown off and leave it in the sickroom.

Avoid contact with clothing, tissues, wound dressings, bedding and other items that might be contaminated with disease-causing organisms. Launder clothing and bedding from ill persons in a disinfectant solution. Carefully wash the sickroom walls, bed, and other equipment used by the ill person. Follow the advice of local health authorities. Become immunized if advised to do so. Remain at home if so instructed.

Making Soap

The basic soap recipes given here make a very versatile soap that can be used for almost any cleaning job. However, most people will find this soap a little harsh for bathing and perhaps even for dish washing. The hand soap would probably be more suitable for those purposes.

BASIC LYE SOAP NO. 1

1 can lye	1 T. powdered borax dissolved in
2 qts. melted fat	1/2 C. hot water
1 C. ammonia	

Dissolve the lye in 1 quart of cold water. When lukewarm, combine lye, ammonia, borax and grease and stir 10 minutes. Pour into pan or boxes. Let set at least overnight. Cut into bars when cold. Cure before using.

BASIC LYE SOAP NO. 2

10 lbs. clean, washed grease, melted (11 1/2 lbs. at sea level)	2 qts. cold water
	5 T. borax
	2 T. ammonia
1/2 oz. citronella	

Mix lye and cold water and let stand until lukewarm. Heat grease until lukewarm. Add borax and ammonia and stir well. Add grease to lye, stirring constantly. Add citronella and stir until thick and the color of honey. Pour into a cardboard box lined with a wet cloth. Let set until solid enough to cut. Cut into bars. Cure before using.

GRANULATED SOAP

Made basic lye soap. After combining fat and lye solutions, stir for 5 minutes. Leave in the mixing container. Stir well every 10 to 15 minutes for a few hours, then as needed until completely dry. The soap granulates as it is stirred while drying.

The soap can also be allowed to dry in bars and grated with a vegetable grater, as needed.

HAND SOAP

1 can lye	3 T. finely ground oatmeal, optional
1/2 C. ammonia	11 C. melted and strained fat
1/2 C. powdered borax	5 C. rain or soft water
2 oz. lanolin	1/3 C. sugar
4 t. aromatic oil of lavender, rose or pine	3 oz. glycerine

Measure the water into a crock or enamel pan. Add to it, one at a time while stirring; lye, ammonia, borax and sugar. Continue stirring until cool. Slowly stir in fat, stirring constantly as you pour. Add fragrance and continue stirring for another 15 minutes. While doing so add lanolin, glycerine and oatmeal. By this time the mixture should be thick and creamy. Pour into molds the size of the bars you want or into one large mold. Let stand until firm. Cut into bars. Wrap in waxed paper, if desired. Let stand for a week, or until cured, before using.

DISH SOAP

Shave cured basic lye soap or hand soap into water. Let stand until it becomes jelly-like. Use as needed.

Tips on Soapmaking

The Fat:

Any unsalted fat will be suitable for soapmaking. Small amounts of vegetable oil may be included but mineral oil will not work in soap. The fat should be clean and fresh.

To prepare the fat, place it in a kettle and melt it until the cracklings become crisp and brown. Strain through a strainer or a piece of cloth to remove the large particles. Then place a facial tissue in the bottom of a large strainer and pour the fat through it to remove any tiny particles remaining in the fat. Return the fat to the kettle and add about 2 quarts of water for every 5 quarts of fat. Bring to a boil. Set aside and let fat solidify. Poke a hole through the fat and pour off the water. Bring to a boil again. Boil until the fat stops popping and the water is all cooked out. Repeat the washing process if there are still impurities remaining in the fat. Strain again if necessary.

Have the fat lukewarm when combining with the lye.

The Lye:

Use only pure lye. Do not use drain cleaners that contain lye. These products also contain aluminum shavings and other ingredients that would not be desirable in soap.

Handle the lye with great care. It is very caustic and can cause severe burns. Always keep lye and lye soap out of the reach of children. Take precautions when making soap to prevent anyone accidentally swallowing or handling any of the soap making ingredients. Always make soap outside. When lye is combined with water it lets off very noxious fumes. Place the water in a large container made of glass, crockery, or enameled metal. Never mix soap in tin or aluminum. Protect hands with rubber gloves, if available. Do not touch the lye or lye solution with the hands. Pour the lye into the water carefully and stir carefully to avoid splashing. When the lye solution is lukewarm, stir the fat carefully into the lye. Avoid breathing the fumes.

To discard the lye cans, cap them then place them in tightly closed container, out of the reach of children.

First Aid:[5]

Should any of the lye or lye solution get onto the skin, it is essential to wash it away immediately. Apply vinegar to the affected part, then flush immediately with plenty of water for 15 minutes. Have the vinegar out and open, ready to use, before you start making the soap.

If lye should get in the eyes, wash immediately with plenty of cool water, for at least 15 minutes. Follow with a 5% Boric Acid solution.[6] Call a physician.

If lye or lye solution or lye soap should be taken internally, give a glass of water then quickly follow with vinegar, lemon, orange or grapefruit juice freely. Follow with olive oil, butter or other cooking oil, milk or egg white. *Do not induce vomiting!* Call a physician immediately!

What Did I Do Wrong?

Soap is hard and flinty and crumbles when shaved: too much lye or not enough fat.

Soap is greasy: Not enough lye or too much fat.

Soap separates: Soap stirred too vigorously.

Curing Soap

Soap must stand for several weeks before it is ready to use. Aging helps to complete the combining of the lye and fat. It also permits the soap to dry.

Test for neutral soap: touch the tip of the tongue to the soap. If it bites, the lye is not yet completely combined with the fat. The soap should be allowed to cure longer. Cured soap is usually white.

Making Cleaning Products

HOMEMADE TOOTH CLEANER

Mix 4 parts baking soda and one part salt. Place a small amount in the palm of the hand and dip the tooth brush into it.

WINDOW WASHING SOLUTION

1. Mix one cup rubbing alcohol and one cup vinegar. Use as a

[5]The American National Red Cross, *First Aid Textbook*, 4th ed. (New York: Doubleday and Co., 1957).

[6]Antidote instructions on a can of Lewis Lye Drain Cleaner.

    spray or apply with sponge or rag.

2. 2 tablespoons vinegar in a quart of water.
3. 3 tablespoons cornstarch to a quart of water.

CARPET CLEANER

Mix:
1 C. detergent   1 gallon water
1/2 C. ammonia

Mix well. For *wool* rugs, 1 T. turpentine may be added. *Do not* use the solution with turpentine to clean man-made fibers!

WALL CLEANER (for painted walls only! Do not use on varnish!)

Mix in large container:
1 gallon hot water   1/2 C. white vinegar
1 C. ammonia   1/4 C. baking soda

OTHER INEXPENSIVE WALL CLEANERS

Bathroom: To clean water and soap spots use water softener dissolved in water.

Smoke and grease: Use 1 T. trisodium phosphate dissolved in 1 gallon water.

Lighter dirt: 1 T. washing soda dissolved in one gallon of water.

WOOD FURNITURE CLEANER

Mix:
1 pint hot water   1 1/2 T. boiled linseed oil
1 1/2 T. turpentine

Keep solution hot over hot water. (Place solution in a can and set the can in a pan of hot water. Do not put the solution on the stove or near open flame!) Apply with a clean cloth wrung out in the hot solution. Wipe dry with a dry cloth.

UPHOLSTERY CLEANER

Mix:
1 t. white detergent   1 t. white vinegar
1 pint warm water

Whip and use only the suds. Rinse well.

DUSTLESS DUSTCLOTH

Mix in a quart jar:
1 T. kerosene   1 T. raw or boiled linseed oil or reg-
1 pint warm water   ular furniture oil

Shake well. Dip a clean thin, soft, lintless piece of cloth about 18" square in the liquid. (A new piece of cheesecloth makes a good dustcloth.) Wring the cloth out well and hang it outside to dry. Store the dust cloth in a tightly covered jar or coffee can. Tightly cap the remaining solution and store it in a cool place as you would any paint or paint thinner.

SILVER POLISH

Place a piece of aluminum foil in the sink. Place your silver on top of the foil. Cover with salt water. The tarnish will disappear. Wash and dry. Or the silver can be covered with salt water in an aluminum pan.

TO CLEAN LEATHER

Smooth leather garments made from deerhide, buckskin, or elk can be cleaned in the washing machine with *lukewarm water* and *milk soap.* Do not use detergent. Turn off the washer before it reaches the spin cycle. Remove the garment from the washer and hang on a wooden coat hanger and allow to drip dry. Do not wring or squeeze. Hand wash small items. Be sure the linings, interfacings, buttons and other trims are washable.

TO REMOVE WRINKLES FROM LEATHER

Iron with the iron set at the lowest setting. Use a pressing cloth or a piece of brown paper between the iron and the leather. Keep the iron moving to prevent scorching. Never use steam.

TO RESTORE THE FINISH AND LUSTRE ON LEATHER

After cleaning, use a commercial leather finish. Follow directions on the container.

CHAPTER XIX

PREPARATION FOR THE CARE OF THE SICK

Extensive instructions in first aid and nursing techniques are beyond the scope of this book.

A list of specific medical supplies to have on hand has previously been given (see pages 196-197).

Have Nursing Manual and First Aid Manuals

A good home nursing manual would be valuable to have in one's storehouse should there be illness during an emergency and medical aid is unavailable. Become familiar with it ahead of time. Take a Red Cross Home Nursing Course, if possible. Discuss emergency medical care with your doctor so that you are familiar with what he would advise in an emergency.

Have Needed Medications on Hand

Make advance provision for anyone who is cronically ill or regularly requires medical attention or medication. Know what to do for that person should an emergency prevent you from obtaining the usual medical care. Keep on hand a good supply of any medication regularly taken by any member of your family. If the doctor regularly prescribes one month's supply of a drug, ask him if you could have a one time prescription for a two months' supply. Use the one month's supply and store the other. When the amount in use is exhausted, refill the prescription, store the refill, and use the supply that you have in storage already. This way you can keep a fresh supply always on hand. Keep at least two to four weeks' supply of any drug required by a member of your family. That amount should see you through almost any emergency. If the drug is one that will store for long periods of time and the doctor considers it safe to let you have more than a small supply, store as much as the doctor will allow, within reason.

Learn Basic First Aid Skills

Know how to administer first aid. Learn especially how to give mouth-to-mouth resucitation, treat the victim of electrical shock, bleeding, burns, poisoning, cuts and bruises and broken bones. Know what to do if an individual is unconscious. These can be frightening situations even when proper medical attention is readily available.

But when you are on your own, you need to be sure that what you
are doing will help and not further injure the person you are assisting.

CHAPTER XX

EMERGENCY BABY CARE

Feeding

Formula

If your baby is breastfed, there will be no need to store formula for him. If there is an adequate supply of well-balanced foods and adequate liquids available for mother, baby will have his needs satisfied.

The baby who is bottle fed will need to have a supply of formula available. Store the kind of formula that the baby is accustomed to drinking. An emergency is no time to try a new diet on baby. Most formulas come in powdered and liquid forms. The powdered is the most convenient to store if you also store an adequate supply of pure drinking water. Always sterilize stored water when preparing formula for baby. He will not be able to tolerate the amounts of bacteria in water that an adult can, without getting sick. If you prefer the convenience of a premixed formula, be sure to care for it properly to avoid waste. (See canned milk) Be sure to also store a supply of bottles and nipples.

Suppose that you are in your childbearing years and your family does not now include a baby? How do you prepare for the possibility that there will be a baby in the family at the time an emergency should arise? I would suggest that you plan to breastfeed. The breastfed baby will not have his system upset by sudden changes in formula or water. If you were forced to flee your home in the middle of the night because of flood, fire or earthquake, or other emergency, and had no time to prepare for the flight, your baby would be sure to be able to continue the diet to which he is accustomed. A time of tension and anxiety is hard enough on baby without the additional strain of adjusting to a new diet.

Some Advantages of Breastfeeding Over Formula in an Emergency:

1. When planning an emergency preparedness program there is no way of knowing if or when a baby or babies might have to be provided for. One would not want to store formula that might never be needed.

2. There is no preparation needed other than learning how to

breastfeed.

3.   No sterilization is required.
4.   An adequate supply is always readily available. Even triplets have been successfully nursed by their mother.
5.   There is no worry about nutritional content. Stored foods tend to lose some of their food value and palatability with age.
6.   There is no need to heat the baby's food.
7.   There is no way of knowing in advance what formulas baby will or will not be able to tolerate. No baby is allergic to his mother's milk.
8.   During a time of tension, the extra personal contact afforded by breastfeeding can help to relieve a baby's fears and anxieties caused by the tension that he senses around him.
9.   Following emergency childbirth without the aid of hospital or physician, the bodily functions triggered by the stimulation of the nursing baby could mean the difference between normal recovery and deadly hemorrage.

Although breastfeeding is the method of infant feeding intended by nature for us to use, the art of breastfeeding has become almost lost in our modern society. Some preparation before the birth of the baby will help the new mother to be successful. Contact with others who have successfully breastfed will help to make the new mother more confident of her chances of success and will help her to overcome any problems that she may encounter on the way.

The La Leche League was formed to assist mothers to successfully breastfeed their babies. Contact your local chapter for assistance. Each chapter regularly holds a series of discussions about breastfeeding that are helpful and informative.

To find the address of the nearest chapter of La Leche League write: LA LECHE LEAGUE INTERNATIONAL
          Franklin Park, Illinois 60131

For further information on breastfeeding consult the La Leche League publication: *The Womanly Art of Breastfeeding.*

Solid Food

Contrary to the popular notion today, most babies do not need solid food in their early months. Most babies will grow and develop completely normally without solid food for the first 5 to 6 months of life. Therefore, it is not necessary to store baby food on the chance that one will have a baby to feed during an emergency. If you already have a baby that is eating solid food, do store at least 2 weeks' worth of the foods that he is accustomed to eating.

Baby food is expensive and unnecessary to the storage program. If the baby is already eating commercial baby food, it may take a couple of weeks to accustom him to eating home prepared baby food. Thus the suggestion to store two weeks' worth of commercial baby foods for such a baby.

Baby food is quite easy to prepare at home. Canned fruits can be drained and run through a baby food mill or pureed in the blender. Vegetables can be prepared the same way. Ordinary applesauce is a favorite of most babies and requires no additional preparation. Cooked meats can be combined with a small amount of broth or water in the blender and reduced to a consistency that will please baby, or they can be ground in the baby food mill and then blended with a small amount of liquid to give them a consistency more palatable to baby. Avoid highly-spiced or sweetened foods, especially for the very young baby. These may cause digestive problems and will generally be refused by the baby. Most cooked cereals will be acceptable to baby's choosy palate if they are well-cooked and run through the food mill or blender. Mixing fruit with the cereal may make them more appealing.

But whatever you do, do not spring a new diet on a baby suddenly in an emergency. Babies sense any deviation from the normal and often react by becoming fussy and picky. A new diet at this time will only cause headaches for all concerned. Why not prepare your own baby food from the start, save some money, and avoid the necessity of switching baby to home prepared foods, should an emergency arise?

Clothing and Bedding

Diapers

The paper diapers that are available to the modern mother are especially handy to have in an emergency. They eliminate a lot of laundry and save water. They are easy to store and can be used for emergency bandages, bed pads for the sick bed and other uses besides keeping junior's backside dry. If they are not used they can always be passed on to some other young mother.

If paper diapers are not available and no provision has been made to provide cloth diapers, many substitutes can be found. Bed sheets, cotton yardage, especially flannel or muslin, bath towels, kitchen towels, table cloths or other flat articles of clothing and linens can be used, if necessary. Keep on hand a good supply of safety pins for diapering and other uses.

Clothing

The tiny infant really needs no more clothing than a diaper. He can be kept warm wrapped in a blanket or even a towel, old robe or anything else soft, clean and warm. However, it would be much more convenient to have on hand a few articles of clothing or at least some cotton flannel yardage for making baby clothes, should the need arise. The yardage can be used for making nightwear or other clothing for other members of the family, if not used for baby.

Bedding

Bedding for baby can be easily made from the good parts of worn twin or larger sized bed sheets and blankets. Cotton flannel yardage can be used to construct sheets and blankets for baby. Muslin yardage makes good sheets.

Bed

The newborn infant will fit very nicely into a large box or even a bureau drawer, if no crib is available. Place the makeshift bed securely on the floor to avoid accidental spills. For the older child, a floor palette will serve his needs adequately. Insulate him from the cold floor with several layers of quilts or blankets, if available. Layers of newspapers have a surprising insulating property and could be used also. Most babies will stay warm and cozy if they are put to sleep in a blanket sleeper, either with feet or of the bunting type. And these would certainly be easier to keep on the baby than would blankets in a makeshift bed. (See Sewing Without Patterns for a simple bunting pattern, page 226.)

CHAPTER XXI

ENTERTAINMENT AND RECREATION

The hours, or days, spent in a shelter before, during, and after a disaster, are usually tense. The fear, apprehension and tension will be communicated to any children in the group, making them irritable and difficult.

Much of this can be avoided with a little planning and fore-thought. Prepare a recreation kit as part of your disaster preparations. Concentrate on a few items that will be suitable for a wide range of ages and can be used for a number of activities.

A few items to include:

> Playing cards
> Chess, checkers, dominoes
> Paper, paste, glue
> Construction paper
> Scissors
> Rubber bands, string
> Pencils, pencil sharpener
> Crayons, watercolor paint sets

Also include a good book on childrens games and activities.

I would suggest: *What to do When There's Nothing to Do*, included in the Readiness Library on page 257.

Also include in the kit a few favorite games and hobby supplies for the adults.

One of the activities during the sheltering period could be the keeping of a daily journal. Record in it memorable events as well as reactions to the situation and experiences with storage and your disaster plan. Let the whole family participate in the writing. Use the journal later as a means of evaluating your planning and preparation as well as a record of the event.

APPENDIX I

A READINESS LIBRARY

Books marked with an asterisk (*) constitute a basic library.

*American National Red Cross, *First Aid Textbook*, prepared by the American National Red Cross for the Instruction of First Aid classes, 4th Rev. Ed. (New York: Doubleday and Co., Inc., 1957).

*American National Red Cross, *Home Nursing Textbook*, prepared under the supervision of Nursing Services, The American National Red Cross, 6th Revision (Philadelphia: Blackiston, 1950).

Angier, Bradford, *Feasting Free on Wild Edibles* (Harrisburg, Pa.: Stackpole Books, 1966).

Angier, Bradford, *Free For The Eating* (Harrisburg, Pa.: Stackpole Books, 1960).

Angier, Bradford, *How to Live in the Woods on Pennies a Day* (Harrisburg, Pa.: Stackpole Books, 1971).

Angier, Bradford, *How to Stay Alive in the Woods* (New York: Collier Books, 1972).

Angier, Bradford, *Living Off The Country* (Harrisburg, Pa.: Stackpole Books, 1956).

Angier, Bradford, *Survival With Style* (Harrisburg, Pa.: Stackpole Books, 1972).

Angier, Bradford, *Wilderness Cookery* (Harrisburg, Pa.: Stackpole Books, 1961).

*Bills, Jay and Shirley, *Home Food Dehydrating - Economical "Do-It-Yourself" Methods for Preserving, Storing and Cooking* (Bountiful, Utah: Horizon Publishers, 1974).

Boulton, William, M.D., *What To Do Until the Doctor Comes* (Chicago: Reilly Lee Co.).

Bowers, Warner and Lucile, *Common Sense Organic Gardening* (Harrisburg, Pa.: Stackpole Books, 1971).

Boy Scouts of America, *Field Book for Boys and Men* (North Brunswick, N. J.: 1967).

Braue, John Rahn, *Uncle John's Original Bread Book* (New York: Pyramid, 1965).

Briscoe, Alan K., *Soybean Granule Recipes* (Bountiful, Utah: Horizon Publishers, 1974).

Briscoe, Alan K., *Your Guide to Home Storage* (Bountiful, Utah:

Horizon Publishers, 1974).

*Chamber of Commerce, *Pinto Bean Cookbook* (Cortez, Colorado: Chamber of Commerce).

Churchill, James E., *The Homesteader's Handbook* (Harrisburg, Pa.: Stackpole Books, 1974).

Davis, Gary, *Kitchen Garden Sprout and Recipe Book* (Bountiful, Utah: Horizon Publishers, 1973).

*Dickey, Esther, *Passport to Survival* (Salt Lake City, Utah: Bookcraft Publishers, 1969).

*Flack, Dora D., *Fun With Fruit Preservation - Leather, Drying and Other Methods* (Bountiful, Utah: Horizon Publishers, 1973).

Gregg, Elizabeth and the Boston Childrens Medical Center Staff, *What To Do When There's Nothing To Do* (New York: Delacorte Press, 1968).

Hemard, Larry, *Leathercraft: Creative Technique and Design* (New York: Doubleday and Co., 1972).

*Hertzberg, Ruth, Beatrice Vaughan, Janet Greene, *Putting Food By* (Brattleboro, Vt.: The Stephen Greene Press, 1973).

Holley, Beverly B., *Pantry Partner - A Simple Food Storage Organizer* (Bountiful, Utah: Horizon Publishers, 1974).

Ickis, Marguerite, *The Standard Book of Quiltmaking and Collecting* (New York: Dover Publications, Inc., 1949).

Jones, Dorothea Van Gundy, *The Soybean Cookbook* (New York: Arco Publishing Co., Inc., 1963).

Kennedy, Robert H., M.D., ed., *Emergency Care*, by the Committee on Trauma, American College of Surgeons (Philadelphia: W. B. Saunders Company, 1966).

McCall Corp., *McCall's Step-by-Step Sewing Book* (New York: McCall Corp., 1966).

Nelson, Louise E., *Project Readiness: A Guide to Family Emergency Preparation* (Bountiful, Utah: Horizon Publishers, 1974).

Ogden, Samuel, *Step-by-Step to Organic Vegetable Growing* (Emmaus, Pa.: Rodale Press, Inc., 1971).

Olsen, Larry Dean, *Outdoor Survival Skills* (Provo, Utah: Brigham Young University Press, 1973).

*Page, Roland, *How To Be Prepared* (Salt Lake City, Utah: Hawkes Publications, 1973).

Perma-Pak, Inc., *Culinary Capers* (Salt Lake City, Utah: Perma-Pak Inc., 1972).

Rasmussen, Dean L., *How to Live Through a Famine* (Salt Lake City, Utah, by the author, 1970).

Reynolds, Brumford Scott, *How to Survive With Sprouting* (Salt Lake City, Utah: Hawkes Publications, 1973).

*Rodale, Robert, ed., *The Basic Book of Organic Gardening* (New York: Balantine Books, 1971).

Rosenvall, Vernice G., Mabel H. Miller, Dora D. Flack, *Wheat For Man* (Salt Lake City, Utah: Bookcraft, 1966).

Salsbury, Barbara, *Just Add Water - How to Use Dehydrated Foods and TVP* (Bountiful, Utah: Horizon Publishers, 1972).

Salsbury, Barbara, *Tasty Imitations - A Practical Guide to Meat Substitutes* (Bountiful, Utah: Horizon Publishers, 1973).

Sleight, Jack and Raymond Hull, *Home Book of Smoke-cooking Meat, Fish & Game* (Harrisburg, Pa.: Stackpole Books, 1971).

Sleight, Jack, *The Smoked-Foods Recipe Book* (Harrisburg, Pa.: Stackpole Books, 1973).

Stout, Ruth, *Gardening Without Work* (Devin: 1961).

Thomas, Dian, *Roughing It Easy - A Unique Ideabook for Camping and Cooking* (Provo, Utah: Brigham Young University Press, 1974).

U.S. Department of Agriculture, *Slaughtering, Cutting and Processing Beef on the Farm*, Farmers' Bulletin No. 2209 (Washington, D.C.: U.S. Government Printing Office).

U.S. Department of Agriculture, *Slaughtering, Cutting and Processing Lamb and Mutton on the Farm*, Farmers' Bulletin No. 2152, (Washington, D.C.: U.S. Government Printing Office).

U.S. Department of Agriculture, *Slaughtering, Cutting and Processing Pork on the Farm*, Farmers' Bulletin No. 2138, (Washington, D.C.: U.S. Government Printing Office).

U.S. Department of Agriculture, *Storing Vegetables and Fruits in Basements, Cellars, Outbuildings and Pits*, Home and Garden Bulletin No. 119 (Washington, D.C.: U.S. Government Printing Office).

White, Gregory J., *Emergency Childbirth* (Franklin Park, Ill.: Police Training Foundation, 1958).

Wiggington, Eliot, ed., *The Foxfire Book* (New York: Anchor Press, 1972).

Wiggington, Eliot, ed., *Foxfire 2* (New York: Anchor Press, 1973).

259

INDEX